Linkages in the Landscape

IUCN'S FOREST CONSERVATION PROGRAMME

IUCN's Forest Conservation Programme coordinates and supports the activities of the IUCN Secretariat and members working with forest ecosystems. The goal of forest conservation is achieved through promoting protection, restoration and sustainable use of forest resources, so that forests provide the full potential range of goods and services.

The programme makes contributions to policy at various levels and uses field projects to derive lessons to feed into the policy debate. The principles of *Caring for the Earth*, published jointly by IUCN, WWF and UNEP in 1991, are applied to these projects, which combine the needs of conservation and those of local communities. One major activity is to develop coherent and informed policies on forest conservation in order to advocate the translation of policies into effective actions. IUCN frequently advises major development institutions on forest issues, to ensure that conservation priorities are adequately addressed in their projects and programmes. The Forest Conservation Programme receives generous financial support from the Government of the Netherlands.

The IUCN Forest Conservation Programme

Linkages in the Landscape

The Role of Corridors and Connectivity in Wildlife Conservation

Andrew F. Bennett

School of Ecology and Environment
Deakin University – Melbourne Campus,
Burwood, Victoria 3125, Australia

IUCN – The World Conservation Union
2003

This publication has been made possible in part by funding from Environment Australia.

Published by: IUCN, Gland, Switzerland and Cambridge, UK

Citation: Bennett, A.F. (1998, 2003). *Linkages in the Landscape: The Role of Corridors and Connectivity in Wildlife Conservation*. IUCN, Gland, Switzerland and Cambridge, UK. xiv + 254 pp.

ISBN: 2-8317-0744-7

Cover design by: Patricia Halladay and IUCN Publications Services Unit, from an original design by McHale Ward Associates, Hertfordshire

Cover photo: Tony Stone Images, London

Layout by: Bookcraft Ltd, Stroud, UK

Produced by: IUCN Publications Services Unit, UK

Printed by: Thanet Press Ltd, Margate, UK

Available from: IUCN Publications Services Unit
                   219c Huntingdon Road, Cambridge CB3 0DL, UK
                   Tel: +44 1223 277894, Fax: +44 1223 277175
                   E-mail: info@books.iucn.org
                   www.iucn.org/bookstore

                   A catalogue of IUCN publications is also available

The text of this book is printed on 90gsm Fineblade Extra made from low-chlorine pulp

CONTENTS

LIST OF BOXES

FOREWORD

Produced on the occasion of the Vth World Parks Congress
Durban, South Africa, September 2003.

When this volume was produced four years ago the title was prescient indeed – as the Vth World Parks Congress has selected more or less the same title for its first workshop stream ("more or less" because the workshop title is "Linkages in the landscape/seascape)". In fact, we are better thinking of the term "earthscape", which can be defined as a group of interconnected ecological systems. Earthscape also avoids the linguistic complications of trying to translate landscape into the common parlance of European, let alone global languages.

The Secretariat of the linkages stream for the Vth World Parks Congress, together with the IUCN Commission on Ecosystem Management, and with the full agreement of the IUCN Forest Conservation Programme, decided that the information in this volume was still very relevant and deserved to be released to the protected area community on the occasion of the Parks Congress.

Achieving global sustainable human development will depend on how well Earth's ecosystems are managed and maintained. Ecosystems are complex open systems, inter-weaving biological diversity with ecological processes to produce a host of services for the planetary biosphere and human society. Yet few of the Earth's ecosystems are being effective-ly managed or maintained. Global fisheries are depleted, forests undervalued and clear-cut, soils eroded, biodiversity threatened and vital ecosystem processes disrupted. Protected areas have an important role to play in countering these processes. Although they are the corner-stone of biodiversity conservation efforts, they are insufficient in scale and number – either on the land or in the sea – to significantly address this gap in human management of landscapes and the processes and life they contain. Linkages are the vehicle for benefits to be provided beyond park boundaries.

Formerly, each protected area was seen as a unique investment in conservation, but now the focus is on the development of networks and systems of protected areas, so that the conservation of biodiversity and ecosystem functions can be secured at the bioregional scale. Fifty years ago, protected areas were almost entirely a national responsibility; now many are seen as a concern at many levels of jurisdiction, from local to international. Historically, protected areas were only concerned with protection; now there is also a need to focus on conservation, sustainable use and ecological restoration. And where previously most pro-tected areas were strictly and legally protected as national parks or nature reserves, now park planners argue that they should be complemented by other kinds of protected areas or managed land/seascapes in which people live, biodiversity flourishes, and natural and cultural resources are used sustainably.

Protected areas are often seen as hermetically sealed "bubbles," designed to be out of reach of human development and environmental destruction. This concept was the basis of the rash of protected area designations 50 years ago. Simply put, governments facing the magnitude of the environmental crisis had to find a way to ensure the protection of "ecosystems of priority importance". The first protected area designations were made to ensure that, whatever human development might occur, some places would remain untouched. In other words, protected areas have been designed, at least during the last 50 years, to be "islands of conservation in an ocean of destruction".

Whether on land, at the coastal edge, or on the high seas, if the concept of protected area as fortress conservation was acceptable in the 20th century, we can see now that it is ecologically, and even logically, unviable. Protected areas cannot be "untouchable islands", isolated from the rest of the world. Like every other part of the biosphere, protected areas as part of a global matrix, depend on a wide variety of factors for their survival. Protected areas must be connected with the global land and seascape, and interact with it, so as to ensure correct ecosystem functioning, as well as species distribution and survival. It would be foolish to think that a national park (as the most well-known type of protected area) won't be affected by impacts in its surrounding landscape or, vice versa, that the presence of a protected area won't affect or influence the surrounding ecosystems.

Protected areas need to be connected – or reconnected – to the surrounding landscape. It is said that protected areas are a key part of achieving sustainable development. But sustainable development means harnessing ecosystem services, and managing and maintaining ecosystems to produce those services for the biosphere. This intrinsic definition of sustainable development implies a partnership between development and conservation, and not a protection of conservation against development.

More and more international initiatives recognize the importance of integration between conservation and ecologically sensitive development. People, through economics, culture and other human-induced factors, are part of any viable conservation scheme. Here UNESCO's World Network of Biosphere Reserves provides a series of practical examples of how protected areas (in this case the biosphere reserve cores), linked by buffer zones and a transitional area to the wider land or seascape, can promote conservation as part of sustainable human development. Similarly, the Wetlands of International Importance, listed under the Ramsar Convention, are based on ensuring conservation through wise use, or wise practice. Initially based on the conservation of waterfowl, the Ramsar Convention has evolved to match sustainable development principles, including integrating human, social, cultural and economic parameters with the conservation imperatives.

The aim to link protected areas with surrounding ecosystems is precisely in line with the "Benefits beyond boundaries" theme of the Vth World Parks Congress. Discussions on this theme are intended to produce the following outcome:

> Better awareness amongst protected area managers, and protected area agencies, of the need to establish, understand and manage protected areas in the context of the surrounding landscape/seascape matrix.

Underlying the achievement of this outcome, there are four key areas of linkages: ecological, economic, institutional and cultural. But questions continue to be raised on the underlying theme of the effectiveness of linkages in promoting better protected areas. The discussion of corridors in this volume, as well as the recent studies published in the literature (e.g., the inefficiency of corridors in conserving birds in Canadian forests; Hannon and

Schmiegelow, 2002 – *Ecological Applications*, 12), draw attention to the uncertainty of how effective linkages really are, and that there is rarely one perfect or instant solution.

Critical to an understanding of linkages is a good science basis, coupled with an understanding of the bio-cultural nature of Earth systems. Talking about linkages in the landscape and seascape will bring to a wider public the need to set protected areas in context, and make sure that everyone clearly understands that protection alone is not enough. To take a culturally related example, what would be the meaning of a Romanic church inscribed on the World Heritage list if its surroundings were destroyed by inappropriate buildings, highways, tunnels and bridges?

For these protected areas to survive, it is vital to understand that they are not untouchable islands – they are affected by changes in the surrounding landscape. The critical link that will help us to survive is the simple understanding that protected areas, as they have been designed, are part of the solution to human and other species survival, but certainly not THE (only) solution.

Peter Bridgewater
Secretary General of the Ramsar Convention on Wetlands

Sebastià Semene Guitart
Director, Centre for Biodiversity – IEA (Andorra)
Coordinator of the Secretariat of the Linkages Stream for the Vth WPC 2003

PREFACE TO THE FIRST EDITION

In June 1994, our family camped for a week in Brachina Gorge in the Flinders Ranges National Park in South Australia. In this isolated rocky valley, with a colony of the beautiful, but endangered, Yellow-footed Rock Wallaby less than 200 metres from our camp site, I started browsing through recent literature on the theme of corridors, landscape connectivity and wildlife conservation. It was only five years since I had previously reviewed the available literature to prepare a small booklet on this theme, with particular application to nature conservation in south-eastern Australia (Bennett 1990a). Now, the goal was to update that review and include international examples, in response to a request from the IUCN Forest Conservation Programme for a book that would provide information and guidelines on this subject.

Indicative of the intense interest and activity in this area of conservation biology, there has been a wealth of new material over the last decade. This includes several published conference proceedings, critical reviews, and a variety of papers reporting field studies, computer simulations and application of conceptual principles to land-use planning. There is also a rapidly growing number of situations in which 'corridors' of various types are being incorporated into conservation strategies and land uses. Consequently, what set out to be a short project turned into a much larger undertaking and resulted in the present volume.

Two particular challenges were evident while reviewing literature and writing the manuscript. First, those reading this book will approach the topic from a number of viewpoints. Those that might be described as having a primarily scientific perspective are likely to be most interested in a theoretical understanding of the role of corridors in the dynamics of species populations in heterogeneous environments, and in the scientific evidence in support of their function. Others, whose perspective is primarily that of conservation, may have greater interest in the conservation values of linkages and information pertaining to practical issues of design, management and land-use planning. The structure and content of the book have been planned to encompass both theoretical and applied aspects of this topic, but with particular emphasis given to the role of linkages in the conservation of biodiversity.

A second challenge relates to the differing spatial scales at which linkages are incorporated in conservation plans. In intensively-developed landscapes, attention is often directed to local networks of habitat corridors that link small natural areas. In other situations, the focus of those involved in conservation planning is on major links between conservation reserves and on the maintenance of connectivity within large geographic areas. At a broader scale, others are concerned with protecting national and continental networks for conservation. Recognizing these diverse levels of application, I have selected examples and case studies to illustrate the role of linkages at both local and broad spatial scales, and have sought to identify principles that are relevant across a range of spatial scales.

A goal in writing this book has been to provide an international perspective by using examples from throughout the world. Inevitably, the content is biased by the geographic experience of the author (and mine is limited primarily to Australian and Canadian ecosystems), the predominance of the scientific literature from western 'developed' countries, and my limitation to information published in English. However, a number of people provided information or reprints, responded to letters, or discussed ideas at various times – thus broadening my perspective. In this regard I am grateful to: Roy Bhima (Malawi); Christine Dranzoa (Uganda); Debra Roberts (South Africa); Alan Tye (Tanzania); A. Johnsingh (India); Lenore Fahrig, Susan Hannon, Kringen Henein, Gray Merriam and Marc-André Villard (Canada); Paul Beier, Randy Curtis, Richard Forman, Lawrence Hamilton and William Newmark (USA); Francoise Burel (France); Richard Ferris-Kaan and Nigel Leader-Williams (UK); Jana Novakova (Czech Republic); Jakub Szacki (Poland); Don Gilmour (Switzerland); Colin O'Donnell (New Zealand); Jocelyn Bentley, Peter Brown, Sharon Downes, Patricia Gowdie, David Lindenmayer, Lindy Lumsden, Ralph MacNally, Doug Robinson, Denis Saunders, Lee Thomas, Kathy Tracy, Rodney van der Ree, Paul Ryan, Rob Wallis and Grahame Wells (Australia).

Don Gilmour, Co-ordinator of the IUCN Forest Conservation Programme, has been supportive throughout the project, and I greatly appreciate his patience in waiting for the final manuscript. For helpful comments on draft manuscripts, I am grateful to Ralph MacNally, David Lindenmayer, Denis Saunders, Nigel Leader-Williams, Doug Robinson, Kathy Tracy, Mary Bennett, Rodney van der Ree, Ken Atkins and Grahame Wells. Thanks also to Geoff Barrett, Simon Bennett, Lindy Lumsden, Ian Mansergh and Charles Silveira who generously allowed the use of their photographs. Production of the book was ably facilitated by Elaine Shaughnessy and Simon Rietbergen (IUCN).

Last, but certainly not least, I owe a great debt of appreciation to my family for their sustained support, encouragement and assistance in many ways. They have been remarkably patient and tolerant of the time I have spent on this project, frequently at the expense of family activities. Thanks Rilda, Mark and Graham.

Andrew Bennett
July 1997, Melbourne

PART 1

DEFINING THE ISSUES

1 RESPONDING TO AN ISSUE OF GLOBAL CONCERN

In south-eastern Costa Rica, biologists work with indigenous landholders to develop sustainable forest management along a broad gradient of tropical rainforest, from the coastal lowlands to the mountain range. In the wet beech forests of New Zealand, ornithologists survey the density of endemic forest birds in unlogged tracts of forest between two mountain ranges. Among intensive farmland in the Netherlands, landscape ecologists measure the length of hedgerows that connect small farm woods where bird populations have been censused. In the rangelands of Tanzania, wildlife managers document the pathways followed by herds of Wildebeest and Zebra during seasonal migratory movements. Across rural districts of southern Australia, community volunteers drive along country roads to assess and map the quality of remnant strips of roadside vegetation.

What do these activities have in common? Is there a common thread among these diverse actions in different countries across several continents? The examples noted above each illustrate a way in which scientists, planners, local communities or concerned individuals are promoting measures to assist the movements of animals or to maintain the continuity of species populations and ecological processes in the face of habitat change. Their efforts are part of a practical response to the global issue of habitat destruction, fragmentation and isolation in human-dominated landscapes.

Habitat change in human-dominated landscapes

The Earth is presently experiencing changes to its natural environments that are unprecedented in historic times. Destruction and degradation of natural habitats are widespread and profound and their implications for the conservation of biological diversity and the sustainability of natural resources are of global significance. Humankind is responsible for an episode of species' decline, endangerment and extinction of enormous proportions, and widespread deterioration in the quality of air, water and soils – the basic resources on which all of life depends. Such degradation of the natural environment is not a new phenomenon, but it is the rapidity and global scale at which change is now taking place that causes great alarm (Brown 1981; Myers 1986; Lunney 1991; Houghton 1994). Much current attention, for example, is centred on the massive decline in tropical forests and the loss of biodiversity that this entails for these biologically rich environments. A recent estimate placed the rate of deforestation of tropical closed forest at 10.7 million ha per year (Houghton 1994), an area *more than twice* that of Switzerland or Costa Rica, or three times the size of the Netherlands, being cleared *every year*. However, it is not only tropical countries that are experiencing deforestation and habitat loss; similar change is occurring in many countries, including those where extensive clearing has already taken place. In Australia, for example, the rate of clearing of native vegetation over the decade 1983–1993 was estimated to be 500,000ha per year (Department of the Environment, Sport and Territories 1995).

Closely coupled with the issue of broadscale loss of natural habitats is the challenge of maintaining and conserving biodiversity in landscapes now dominated by human land use. In many such landscapes, large natural tracts are becoming scarce or no longer exist. Remnants of the natural environment increasingly occur as a mosaic of large and small patches, survivors of environments that have been carved up to develop new forms of productive land use for humans. These natural fragments range from large blocks that may be set aside as nature reserves, to tiny remnants surrounded by intensive land use. Together they provide the habitats upon which the conservation of much of the flora and fauna in developed landscapes ultimately depends. Throughout the world, reserved areas dedicated to conservation are relatively few in number and scattered in location. Success in conserving Earth's biodiversity will largely depend on the capacity of plants and animals to survive in fragmented landscapes dominated by humans.

Understanding the consequences of habitat change, and developing effective strategies to maintain biodiversity in developed and disturbed landscapes, is a major challenge to both scientists and land managers. In the scientific community there has been strong growth in the relatively new discipline of conservation biology. Although there is substantial overlap with other areas such as wildlife management, forestry, landscape ecology, population genetics and much of traditional population and community ecology, a key element in conservation biology is its fundamental focus on reversing the decline in biodiversity and extinction of species on Earth. To be effective it must integrate scientific skills with applied management and policy in order to achieve practical outcomes that have long-term benefits for species and biological communities. Issues addressed in conservation biology encompass broad themes such as the status, management and recovery of threatened species, the viability of small populations, the impacts of habitat loss and disturbance on plants and animals, the design of protected area systems, and the dynamics of threatening processes on populations and communities.

For land managers, the challenge is to design and implement land-use strategies that will ensure the conservation of natural resources in the face of competing demands for land use. This is especially important for government agencies responsible for the administration and management of large areas of land, but also relevant to community groups and individuals managing small parcels of land in fragmented landscapes subject to a wide range of land uses.

Linking habitats to enhance wildlife conservation

One of the earliest practical recommendations for land use to arise from studies of habitat fragmentation was the proposal that fragments that are linked by a corridor of similar suitable habitat are likely to have greater conservation value than isolated fragments of similar size (Diamond 1975; Wilson and Willis 1975). This initial recommendation was based entirely on theoretical considerations, primarily stemming from island biogeographic theory. Subsequently, protection or provision of continuous corridors of habitat to link isolates such as nature reserves, woodlands or patches of old-growth forest have been widely recommended as conservation measures to counter the impacts of habitat reduction and fragmentation.

The concept of corridors as a conservation measure has been highly successful in catching the attention of planners, land managers and the community and a wide range of 'wildlife corridors', 'landscape linkages', 'dispersal corridors', 'green belts', 'greenways' and other forms of connecting features have been proposed, drawn into conservation plans, or are now under active construction or management. These encompass a range of spatial scales and a variety of levels of sophistication – from artificial tunnels and underpasses that assist animals to move across local barriers such as roads and railway lines, to major tracts of undisturbed natural forest that link reserves at high and low elevations.

In many ways, the acceptance of corridors as a concept for biodiversity conservation has outpaced scientific understanding and the collection of empirical data (especially experimental data) on the requirements of species and communities and their potential use of linkages. The implementation of linkages of various types has proceeded with little practical information to guide their design, location and management. At the most basic level, our knowledge of the scale of movements of many animal species, their habitat requirements, tolerance of disturbance processes and factors that constrain or enhance their movement through human-dominated landscapes, is limited. There is even less understanding of the role that linkages might play in the conservation of plant species and communities.

Why has there been such widespread interest in corridors as a conservation measure? First, the concept is intuitively appealing as a practical measure that responds directly to the isolating effects of habitat fragmentation (i.e. if isolation of habitats is the problem, then linking them together is the solution). In this sense it is also a visible solution to a visible problem. Habitat fragmentation is generally a strikingly obvious process, especially when viewed from the air or from an aerial photograph (Fig. 1–1). Equally, habitat corridors are a visible sign of efforts to 'mend' the fragmented landscape ('bandages for a wounded natural landscape', Soulé and Gilpin 1991). Second, the concept of providing linkages for conservation can be applied at several scales: it is relevant both to local conservation efforts and to regional or national strategies. In local environments, habitat links can be protected, managed or restored at the level at which individuals or community groups are able to carry out conservation works. It is feasible for local communities to actually 'do something about' managing linkages in their local environment and to see visible environmental change as a result. Other global environmental issues such as greenhouse warming, population growth, loss of tropical forests and desertification of arid lands, often seem outside the scope of individual or community action.

Corridors and controversy

The explosion of interest in corridors has not been without scepticism, criticism and debate (Noss 1987; Simberloff and Cox 1987; Harris and Gallagher 1989; Harris and Scheck 1991; Nicholls and Margules 1991; Stolzenburg 1991; Hobbs 1992; Simberloff *et al.* 1992; Andrews 1993; Bonner 1994; Hess 1994), and the conservation benefits potentially gained from corridors have become a contentious issue. Criticisms have centred around three points (see Chapter 4 for further discussion):

- whether sufficient scientific evidence is available to demonstrate the potential conservation benefits of corridors;

- whether the potential negative effects of corridors may outweigh any conservation value;

- whether corridors are a cost-effective option in comparison with other ways of using scarce conservation resources.

There is now an intense scientific interest in this topic that is proceeding on several fronts. Several scientific symposia have addressed the theme of corridors and linkages (Hudson 1991; Saunders and Hobbs 1991); reviews have been published (Bennett 1990a; Thomas 1991; Hobbs 1992; Noss 1993; Lindenmayer 1994; Wilson and Lindenmayer 1995); and there is a growing stream of scientific literature presenting new data from computer modelling (Henein and Merriam 1990; Soulé and Gilpin 1991; Baur and Baur 1992; Burkey 1995) and field studies (Beier 1993, 1995; Lindenmayer and Nix 1993; Bennett *et al.* 1994; Dunning *et al.* 1995; Haas 1995; Hill 1995; Machtans *et al.* 1996; Sutcliffe and Thomas 1996). Other scientists have emphasized the need for experimental studies to provide conclusive evidence of the value of corridors (Nicholls and Margules 1991; Inglis and Underwood 1992).

But have the criticisms and the scientific debate about corridors addressed the fundamental issues? Several points are relevant here. First, much of the debate has had a narrow focus on a particular type of linkage (i.e. continuous corridors) and on a particular type of movement (direct dispersal of animals between two fragments). The scope of the topic must be broadened to the more useful issue of maintaining connectivity in developed landscapes (Box 1–1). Second, most studies of animal movements and their use of habitat linkages are at the local scale – the level of fencerows, roadsides and hedgerows – dealing with small populations that are generally separated by distances of a kilometre or less. It is at this scale that much of the evidence for the use and benefits of linkages has been obtained and, likewise, knowledge of the factors influencing design and management of linkages. Even at this scale, experimental studies pose extraordinary difficulties (Nicholls and Margules 1991) and a long

Fig. 1–1 Fragments of forest vegetation retained amongst farmland at Naringal East, south-western Victoria, Australia. (Photo: S. Bennett).

Box 1–1   Corridors or connectivity: what is the real issue?

Controversy and critical debate over the issue of 'corridors' has had a narrow focus. It has concentrated on continuous linear strips of habitat and whether direct dispersal movements of animals through such strips will improve the conservation status of otherwise-isolated populations. Other types of connecting habitats, such as stepping stones or habitat mosaics; other types of movements, such as daily foraging or migratory movements; and other ways that movements can facilitate continuity, have largely been ignored by critics. In many ways, the debate has missed the point.

The fundamental issues at stake are the effective conservation of populations and communities and the maintenance of ecological processes in landscapes that have been heavily disturbed and fragmented by human activities. A key question can be framed:

'Are populations, communities and natural ecological processes more likely to be maintained in landscapes that comprise an interconnected system of habitats, than in landscapes where natural habitats occur as dispersed ecologically-isolated fragments'?

Few ecologists would argue for the latter case. There can be little doubt that movements of animals and plants and the flow of wind, water, materials and biota between habitats is a key element in the functioning of natural ecosystems (Forman 1995; Wiens 1995). A second question can then be posed:

'What is the most effective pattern of habitats in the landscape to ensure ecological connectivity for species, communities and ecological processes?'

There is considerable room for debate and analysis on this latter question and it is in this context that corridors, along with other habitat configurations that enhance connectivity, can be reviewed. Consequently, the emphasis of this book is on 'connectivity' rather than 'corridors' *per se*. The primary thesis of this book is that landscape patterns that promote connectivity for species, communities and ecological processes are a key element in nature conservation.

time scale is required to obtain meaningful results. However, from a conservation perspective, many important opportunities to protect and manage linkages are at the landscape or regional scale, such as major links between conservation reserves to assist their long term viability. It is impossible to carry out experimental studies at this scale and the time frame over which the benefits of connectivity to conservation reserves must be assessed is decades and centuries, not years.

Meanwhile, interest and onground activities by land managers around the world have continued apace. The design and development of new linkages continues in a multitude of ways, from small revegetation projects by local communities to ambitious continent-wide schemes that aim to redesign the way that humans live in and use the land. The need for ecological linkages is now recognized as a fundamental principle in land-use planning and land management in developed landscapes (Smith and Hellmund 1993; Forman 1995;

Jongman 1995; Dramstad *et al.* 1996). However, many land managers are desperately seeking information and the best available advice on how to design, implement and manage habitat linkages that will be effective in conserving biodiversity in their environment. They must make decisions now concerning future land use, before options are limited or foreclosed by further development (Hobbs 1992).

Connectivity

The emphasis of this book is on the value of 'connectivity' rather than the merits of corridors *per se* (Box 1–1) The primary thesis is that landscape patterns that promote connectivity for species, communities and ecological processes are a key element of nature conservation in environments modified by human impacts. Accordingly, it is useful at this stage to discuss what is meant by 'connectivity'. This theme is developed further in Chapter 4.

The concept of connectivity is used to describe how the spatial arrangement and the quality of elements in the landscape affect the movement of organisms among habitat patches (Merriam 1984, 1991; Taylor *et al.*1993; Forman 1995). At the landscape scale, connectivity has been defined as 'the degree to which the landscape facilitates or impedes movement among resource patches' (Taylor *et al.* 1993). It is critical to recognize that a landscape is perceived differently by different species and so the level of connectivity varies between species and between communities. A landscape or local area with high connectivity is one in which individuals of a particular species can move freely between suitable habitats, such as favoured types of vegetation for foraging, or different habitats required for foraging and shelter. Alternatively, a landscape with low connectivity is one in which individuals are severely constrained from moving between selected habitats (Fig. 1–2). A particular landscape or region may, at the same time, provide high connectivity for some organisms, such as mobile wide-ranging birds, and low connectivity for others such as snails or small sedentary reptiles.

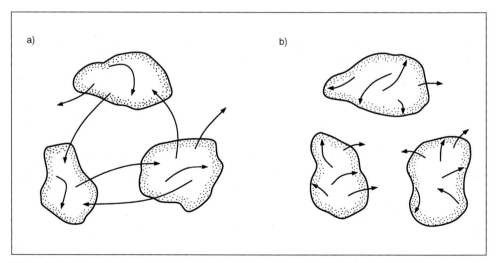

Fig. 1–2   A patchy landscape may, at the same time, offer a high level of connectivity for one species (a), and a low level of connectivity for another species (b) that has difficulty moving amongst habitats.

There are two main components that influence potential connectivity for a particular species, community or ecological process – a structural component and a behavioural component (Bennett 1990a). The structural component of connectivity is determined by the spatial arrangement of different types of habitats in the landscape. It is influenced by factors such as the continuity of suitable habitat, the extent and length of gaps, the distance to be traversed, and the presence of alternative pathways or network properties. It refers to the mappable, spatial arrangement of habitats for which a number of quantitative indices have been proposed (e.g. measures of circuitry, mesh size, fractal dimension) (Forman and Godron 1986; Forman 1995).

The behavioural component of connectivity relates to the behavioural response of individuals and species to the physical structure of the landscape. It is influenced by factors such as the scale at which a species perceives and moves within the environment, its habitat requirements and degree of habitat specialization, its tolerance of disturbed habitats, the life stage and timing of dispersal movements, and the species' response to predators and competitors. Consequently, even though living in the same landscape, species with contrasting behavioural responses (to habitat disturbance for example) will experience differing levels of connectivity.

Throughout this book, the terms 'link' and 'linkage', rather than corridor, are used to refer to arrangements of habitat that enhance connectivity for species, communities or ecological processes (Box 1–2). The term 'corridor' has been used in a variety of ways and can have a number of different interpretations. Further, it is important to emphasize throughout that connectivity can be increased by a range of habitat patterns, not only by continuous corridors of habitat. For clarity, a number of terms used in this book are set out in Box 1–2.

Scope of this book

First and foremost, this volume is intended to be an information source for practitioners – for those scientists, planners, land managers, conservation agencies, community groups, students or individuals who are grappling with the question of how wildlife can be conserved within developed landscapes; and who ask what role linkages might play. Its goal is to furnish practitioners with an understanding of why measures that enhance landscape connectivity are important, how such linkages can benefit the conservation status of wildlife species, and the important issues that need to be considered in incorporating and implementing these concepts into conservation strategies. To this end, a large number of examples and case studies are featured, drawn from many countries throughout the world. They are intended to place these issues in the reality of wildlife conservation in diverse environments that are facing an array of different circumstances and challenges. The text is extensively referenced throughout to provide readers with access to the source literature for examples and case studies, and as an entry into this growing field in conservation biology.

The material in the book is biased towards animal populations and assemblages, and the use of the term 'wildlife' refers in this context primarily to indigenous species of vertebrate and invertebrate animals. Although there is substantial evidence for the value of linear features and other linkages as habitat for plants, there is limited evidence of their role or importance in the dispersal of plants through the landscape (see Pollard *et al.* 1974; Helliwell 1975; Forman 1991, 1995; McDowell *et al.* 1991; Fritz and Merriam 1993 for an

Box 1–2   Corridors, linkages and other terminology

A number of terms such as 'habitat corridor', 'movement corridor', 'wildlife corridor', or 'dispersal corridor' have been used in the scientific literature and, indeed, even the term 'corridor' has been defined in a variety of ways. Different definitions can imply different habitat structures or forms of use, so that it is not always clear what is meant. I have chosen to use the terms 'link' or 'linkage' as general terms to minimize this uncertainty, and, in particular, to emphasize that connectivity can be increased by a range of habitat configurations, not only by corridors. For clarity, the use of terms in remaining chapters in this book is as follows.

- **Link, linkage**: General terms referring to an arrangement of habitat (not necessarily linear or continuous) that enhances the movement of animals or the continuity of ecological processes through the landscape.

- **Linear habitat**: A general term referring to a linear strip of vegetation. Linear habitats are not necessarily of indigenous vegetation and do not necessarily provide a connection between two ecological isolates.

- **Habitat corridor**: A linear strip of vegetation that provides a continuous (or near continuous) pathway between two habitats. This term has no implications about its relative use by animals.

- **Stepping stones**: One or more separate patches of habitat in the intervening space between ecological isolates, that provide resources and refuge that assist animals to move through the landscape.

- **Landscape linkage**: A general term for a linkage that increases connectivity at a landscape or regional scale (over distances of kilometres to tens of kilometres). Typically, such linkages comprise broad tracts of natural vegetation.

- **Habitat mosaic**: A landscape pattern comprising a number of patchy interspersed habitats of different quality for an animal species.

introduction). This volume also gives scant attention to linkages such as greenways, urban parks, recreational trails and other linear features whose primary objective is for human recreation or aesthetic enjoyment. A valuable introduction to the design of such landscape features is given in the works by Little (1990), Smith and Hellmund (1993) and Ahern (1995). The focus of this volume is on the importance of landscape connectivity for the conservation of biodiversity. However, the potential overlap in values, and also the potential conflict between linkages designed for recreation and the requirements for wildlife conservation, are issues that warrant further consideration.

The thesis of the book develops through three parts: defining the issues, assessing the values of linkages, and evaluating the role of connectivity in conservation strategy.

Defining the issues

The dynamic process of habitat loss and fragmentation has profound implications for the conservation of flora and fauna throughout the world. Major consequences for wildlife are a loss of species from fragments and entire landscapes, changes to the composition of faunal assemblages, and changes to ecological processes involving animal species (Chapter 2). Isolation of habitats, a fundamental consequence of the process of fragmentation, also influences the status of animal populations and communities in developed landscapes. Minimizing the effects of isolation by enhancing landscape connectivity is one way to counter the adverse effects of fragmentation. Pragmatic and theoretical approaches that address the status and conservation of wildlife in heterogeneous environments (Chapter 3) each implicitly recognize the importance of maintaining habitat patterns that allow animals to move through modified landscapes.

Values of linkages

Landscape connectivity may be achieved by several main types of habitat configurations that function as linkages for species, communities or ecological processes. The spatial and temporal scales over which animals require connectivity is also an important consideration. Proposed advantages and disadvantages of linkages are summarized and attention is given to the concerns that have been raised with regard to habitat corridors (Chapter 4). Linkages are used as pathways by animals undertaking a range of movements, including daily or regular movements, seasonal and migratory movements, dispersal movements, and range expansion. Studies of the use of linkages are reviewed to evaluate the ways in which they enhance the conservation of animal species and communities (Chapter 5). Linkages also contribute to other ecological functions in the landscape and, in particular, have an important role in providing habitat for plants and animals in human-dominated environments (Chapter 6).

Connectivity and conservation strategy

The final section considers how the concept of landscape connectivity can be most effectively incorporated into conservation strategy and actions. The value of habitat linkages can be maximized by addressing biological issues relating to location and dimensions, composition and quality of habitats, and behavioural ecology of the species that will use the link. Socio-political issues that affect the management of linkages must also be considered in the development and implementation of practical actions (Chapter 7). The role of linkages in conservation strategies is then explored in the context of an integrated landscape approach to conservation. Attention is also given to criteria for assigning values and priorities to linkages (Chapter 8). Finally, a range of case studies are presented (Chapter 9) to complement examples throughout the text, and to illustrate the diverse ways in which land managers are planning, implementing, or presently managing linkages for conservation.

Summary

The loss and fragmentation of natural environments and their implications for the conservation of flora and fauna are of global significance. The provision of 'corridors' to link otherwise-isolated habitats was one of the earliest practical recommendations arising from studies of habitat fragmentation. The concept has proved attractive to planners, land managers and the community, but the merits of corridors have become a subject of debate. This book addresses the broader theme of landscape connectivity and its role in nature conservation. The primary thesis is that landscape patterns that promote connectivity for species, biological communities and ecological processes are a key element in nature conservation in environments modified by human impacts.

2 HABITAT FRAGMENTATION AND THE CONSEQUENCES FOR WILDLIFE

Habitat loss and fragmentation have been recognized throughout the world as a key issue facing the conservation of biological diversity (IUCN 1980). As the global population increases, less and less of Earth's surface remains free from human interference. Human activities have modified the environment to the extent that the most common landscape patterns are mosaics of human settlements, farmland and scattered fragments of natural ecosystems. Most conservation reserves, even large reserves, are becoming increasingly surrounded by intensively modified environments and in the long term appear destined to function as isolated natural ecosystems.

Before considering the theoretical basis and practical evidence for the importance of landscape connectivity in conservation, it is necessary to review the issue of habitat loss and fragmentation as the underlying problem to be addressed. Changes in the status of wildlife populations and communities resulting from the destruction and fragmentation of their habitats has been the primary stimulus to land managers to take practical action to maintain or restore connectivity of habitats in developed landscapes. The objective of this review is to provide a basis for understanding and evaluating the potential role of landscape connectivity in the conservation of biota. This chapter briefly considers in turn:

- changes to landscape patterns arising from fragmentation;

- the effects of fragmentation on wildlife populations and communities;

- the implications of isolation for species and communities.

Fragmentation and changes to landscape pattern

Habitat fragmentation is a dynamic process that results in marked changes to the pattern of habitat in a landscape through time. The term 'fragmentation' is generally used to describe changes that occur when large blocks of vegetation are incompletely cleared leaving multiple smaller blocks that are separated from each other. The process of fragmentation has three recognizable components (Fig. 2–1):

- an overall *loss* of habitat in the landscape (habitat loss)

- reduction in the *size* of blocks of habitat that remain following subdivision and clearing (habitat reduction); and

- increased *isolation* of habitats as new land uses occupy the intervening environment (habitat isolation).

We may wish to identify the consequences of each component separately to fully understand the impacts of fragmentation, but it is important to recognize that they are each closely linked as part of the process of habitat change (Box 2–1). The dynamic nature of

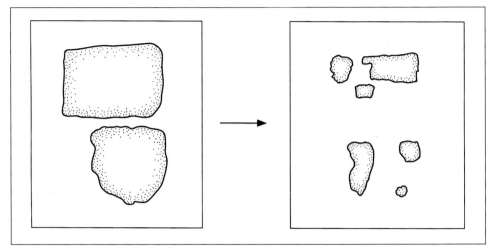

Fig. 2–1   The process of habitat fragmentation has three components: (a) an overall loss of
habitat; (b) a reduction in the size of remaining habitats; and (c) an increased isolation
of habitats.

fragmentation is most strikingly observed where a series of 'snapshot' views of landscape
pattern are available for successive intervals (Box 2–1) (see also Curtis 1956; Webb and
Haskins 1980; Saunders *et al.* 1993).

Changes to landscape patterns arising from fragmentation can be readily identified and
described by measuring attributes such as the total area of remaining natural habitat, the
size-frequency distribution of fragments, the shapes of fragments, the mean distance between
fragments, and the level of contrast between habitats and adjacent land uses. These changes in
spatial pattern and arrangement of habitats also set in train a series of other changes as
ecological processes are modified in response to the changing habitat geometry. Such
ecological changes can have far-reaching effects on the flora and fauna, the soil and water
resources, and on human ecology (Forman and Godron 1986; Saunders *et al.* 1987, 1991;
Forman 1995). The consequences of changes in landscape pattern on ecosystem processes is a
fertile field for research that has direct relevance to conservation management (e.g. Lovejoy *et
al.* 1984; Hobbs 1993a).

Total amount of habitat

Unless accompanied by active replacement or regeneration, habitat fragmentation invariably
involves an overall loss of habitat on a landscape scale. The pattern of habitat loss and
reduction is most visibly obvious where there is a sharp contrast between the vegetation
structure of the fragments and the altered landscape, such as for woodland vegetation in
grassy farmland.

However, habitat fragmentation is not always obvious: in some situations, habitat loss,
reduction and isolation may be significant in extent but not visibly apparent. For species
dependent on old-growth forests, ongoing timber harvesting results in increasingly fewer
areas of old undisturbed forest. However, because there is usually subsequent forest regeneration, the decline in areas with 'old-growth' features such as large old trees, large logs and deep
moist litter, may not be readily perceived by the untrained eye within the continuous expanse

of forest. Likewise, fragmentation and replacement of native grasslands by swards of exotic pasture grasses may not greatly change the appearance of a grassy plain, but has major ecological effects.

In a typical example of fragmentation, the landscape is initially dominated by natural vegetation with disturbance from human land use creating small clearings or inroads along edges. As the disturbance proceeds, the number and size of clearings increases, the natural vegetation becomes subdivided and isolated and the total area of natural habitat declines. A critical point is reached when the disturbed land, rather than natural vegetation, becomes the dominant feature in the landscape and the fragments are increasingly isolated. As the total area of natural vegetation declines, a change occurs in the balance of ecological processes that shape the structure and function of biotic communities in fragments. Processes arising from surrounding land uses become increasingly more important than internal processes as the driving influence on the status of the flora and fauna (Saunders *et al.* 1991; Haila *et al.* 1993b).

The hydrologic cycle is one example of an ecosystem process that is strongly influenced by the total amount of natural habitat in the landscape. Rainfall patterns, soil infiltration rates, runoff and flooding are all sensitive to the amount and nature of the regional vegetation cover. In south-western Western Australia, for example, a major effect of land clearing for agriculture has been a documented rise in the levels of water tables resulting from a reduction in evapotranspiration by trees and shrubs (Hobbs 1993a). The rising water table brings salt to the soil surface and an estimated 62,500ha of land is going out of agricultural production each year (Hobbs 1993a). Nature reserves and woodland fragments are also vulnerable to this degradation.

Sizes of habitat patches

Fragmentation, by definition, implies a reduction in the size of remaining blocks of habitat. At first, extensive tracts may be subdivided into a few large parcels. As the process continues, the mean and modal size of remaining fragments decline. Typically, the size-frequency distribution of remnants in fragmented landscapes is strongly skewed towards small blocks. For example, on the Fleurieu Peninsula of South Australia where only 9% of the 1500km^2 region now supports natural vegetation (Williams and Goodwin 1988), 67% of the remaining 544 forest patches are less than 10ha and only three are larger than 500ha (Fig. 2–2). The same skewed distribution is found generally for the sizes of national parks and nature reserves that increasingly are becoming isolates surrounded by developed land (Hopkins and Saunders 1987; Shafer 1990). Of a total of 1270 nature reserves in the Netherlands in 1982, only nine (less than 1%) were larger than 4000ha whereas 275 (22%) were less than 40ha (van der Maarel 1982 cited in Shafer 1990).

Large tracts of habitat are a scarce and precious resource. It is easy to produce many small patches, but large tracts are essentially irreplaceable and have many intrinsic ecological values. Among those attributes positively correlated with size of habitat tract are the diversity of vegetation types, the likelihood of occurrence of rare or specialized habitats, the richness of plant and animal species, the size of populations and the sustainability of natural disturbance regimes. In particular, the maintenance of natural patch-dynamic processes in fragmented landscapes is critically dependent on there being tracts of sufficient size to sustain a mosaic of habitats that correspond to different states. The presence of a natural mosaic of fire-induced vegetation classes, for example, is dependent on a fragment being sufficiently large that a

Box 2–1   Forest fragmentation in south-western Victoria, Australia

A study of land use, forest fragmentation and historical change to the mammalian fauna in a 20,000 ha study area in south-western Victoria, Australia, provides an example of the process of habitat loss and fragmentation (Bennett 1990c). Prior to European settlement, commencing in the 1840s, the area was heavily forested and used seasonally or infrequently by Aboriginal people. The dense forest vegetation and infertile soils were not favoured for subsequent pastoral settlement, and forest clearing was initially slow. Most forest loss has occurred during the 20th century, particularly after 1940.

The process of forest fragmentation has had three components: an overall loss of forest, a progressive fragmentation of surviving forest stands into smaller blocks, and an increasing spatial isolation of fragments through time. In 1942, about 51% of the area remained forested; by 1971 forest cover had been reduced to 12%; and by 1980 it was approximately 9% of the study area. The forest vegetation has been replaced by farmland used mainly for dairy farming and beef cattle production. In 1942, most forest cover was interconnected, but by 1980 forest cover comprised many small and isolated fragments, of which 92% were less than 20 ha and none was larger than 100 ha (Bennett 1990c). Remnant forested strips along roadsides and streams (not shown in the diagram) connect many fragments and ameliorate the isolating effect of intervening farmland (Bennett 1988; 1990c).

Changes associated with habitat loss and fragmentation not only relate to the spatial pattern of the vegetation. The structure and composition of the vegetation are also affected by land uses associated with forest clearing. Almost all remaining forest vegetation is privately owned and most has been greatly modified by altered fire regimes, extensive felling of trees for fuel wood, grazing by domestic stock, and weed invasion. Forest patches subject to sustained grazing by domestic stock progressively lose their native understorey leaving the tree layer as the main natural element remaining. In 1983, most of the study area was burned by a severe wildfire that consumed almost all forest vegetation in its path, and also resulted in nine human fatalities, the death of 19,000 stock and loss of 157 houses.

At least 33 species of native mammals are known to have occurred in this area, of which six species are no longer present and several others are now rare. Several native species have partially adapted to the modified farmland environment, but most now depend on the mosaic of remnant forest vegetation for their continued persistence in the area. Six species of introduced mammals have established feral populations in the area, including new predators (Red Fox, Cat) and competitors (Black Rat, House Mouse, European Rabbit) for native species. None of the remaining patches are of sufficient size to maintain viable populations of native mammals in the long term. Persistence of the native mammal fauna in this rural landscape depends on the extent to which the forest fragments can function as an integrated system of natural habitat (Bennett 1990c).

Box 2–1 (cont.)

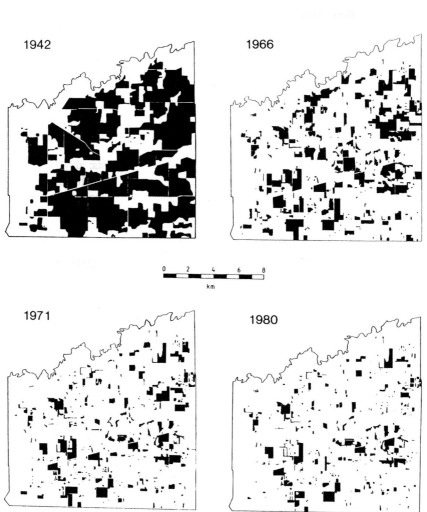

Change in forest cover at Naringal, south-western Victoria, Australia, illustrating the process of habitat loss and fragmentation in a rural environment. The study area is approximately 20,000ha in size. From Bennett (1990c) with permission, CSIRO Publishers, Australia.

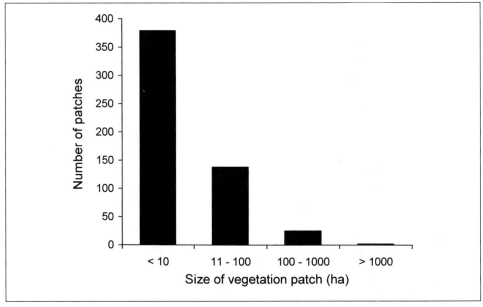

Fig. 2–2 **Size-frequency distribution for remnant patches of natural vegetation on the Fleurieu Peninsula, South Australia. The bias towards small habitats (even with a logarithmic scale) is characteristic of fragmented landscapes. Data from Williams and Goodwin (1988).**

single fire does not reduce all of its vegetation to the same stage. The maintenance of natural disturbance regimes is particularly important for the long-term viability of national parks and conservation reserves (Pickett and Thompson 1978; Baker 1992).

Isolation of habitat patches

Isolation of fragments is also a fundamental consequence of fragmentation. Patches of woodland become isolated by cleared farmland; urban forests are separated by streets, houses and roads; old-growth forests are surrounded by regenerating forest; heathland remnants disappear among pastures; and nature reserves are surrounded by zones of intensive human activity.

How can we measure isolation of fragments? In a spatial sense, isolation can be measured by a variety of indices such as the distance to the nearest larger habitat fragment, the amount of suitable habitat within a defined radius, or the presence of linking habitats in the intervening space (Forman and Godron 1986; Askins *et al.* 1987; Forman 1995). It is essential that isolation is also understood in a functional sense by relating it to the particular species or ecosystem process under consideration. A fragment that is effectively isolated for a small woodland rodent may easily be reached by migratory birds or forest bats.

Ecosystem processes that are most sensitive to isolation effects are those that depend on some vector for transmission through the landscape. Seed dispersal, pollination of plants, predator-prey relationships, and the dispersal of parasites and disease, are examples of processes that may be greatly disrupted by isolation if their animal vectors can not readily move through the landscape.

Composition of habitats

Fragmentation and loss of habitats in developed landscapes is not a random process. Clearing, cultivation and pastoral land use are biased toward those areas that have the most fertile soils or are most accessible, such as plains and fertile river valleys. Conversely, national parks, nature reserves and other patches of retained natural vegetation frequently are located on steep or rocky areas, infertile soils, or swamps and floodplains, because such areas are more difficult to develop and least valuable for productive uses (Leader-Williams *et al.* 1990; Pressey 1995). These trends in land use mean that some vegetation communities are often 'missing' or poorly represented in reserve systems, whereas others are proportionately over-represented. For depleted communities, small fragments in developed landscapes are particularly important because often they are the only remaining examples of the vegetation, and they may be repositories of rare plants and animals (McDowell *et al.* 1991; Prober and Thiele 1993; Shafer 1995).

Changes to shapes of habitats

The shapes of natural patches, such as lakes and wetlands, rocky outcrops, treefall openings and heathlands are usually curved or irregular. In contrast, fragments, regenerated patches, tree plantations and nature reserves arising from human land uses, generally have straight boundaries and are often rectilinear in shape (Forman and Godron 1986; see Box 2–1).

The aspect of fragment shape that has greatest impact on ecological and environmental processes is the ratio of the perimeter length to area, and hence of exposure to 'edge effects' (Forman and Godron 1986; Yahner 1988; Angelstam 1992; Murcia 1995). An increase in perimeter to area ratio means that a greater proportion of the natural environment is close to the edge and therefore is exposed to ecological changes that occur there (Fig. 2–3). In intensively-developed landscapes, linear habitats and small fragments with high edge ratios often form the bulk of remaining natural habitats.

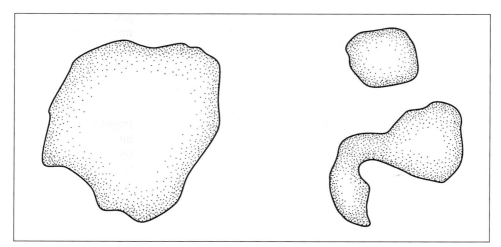

Fig. 2–3   Small fragments with a high ratio of perimeter to area are more vulnerable to edge disturbance processes than are large fragments. In small fragments, the disturbed zone (stippled) may extend throughout most or all of the fragment leaving little habitat free of influences arising from edge effects.

A growing number of studies have documented a variety of changes, both to physical processes and biological processes, that occur at edges. These include changes in microclimatic conditions (wind speed, temperature, humidity, solar radiation), changes to soil nutrient status and other soil properties, invasion and competition from organisms in surrounding lands, elevated levels of predation and parasitism, and human incursion and disturbance (Lovejoy *et al.* 1986; Angelstam 1992; Hobbs 1993a; Scougall *et al.* 1993; Young and Mitchell 1994). Edge effects are considered further in Chapter 7 as an important issue in the design and management of linkages.

Sharpness and contrast across habitat boundaries

The sharpness of habitat edges and the contrast between adjacent habitats are generally accentuated in developed landscapes. There is usually a marked contrast in the structure and floristic composition of vegetation at the interface between natural areas and developed land, such as forest-farmland ecotones (Fig. 2–4). The term 'hard edge' has been used to describe such situations in which the level of contrast between two habitats inhibits many organisms from readily moving across the edge (Wiens *et al.* 1985). Alternatively, natural boundaries are often 'soft edges' across which animals may readily move. Streamside vegetation, for example, is usually distinct from that on adjacent slopes in temperate forests, but there is a gradual rather than abrupt transition between forest types. Similarly, the transition between successional age classes in forests are relatively soft edges.

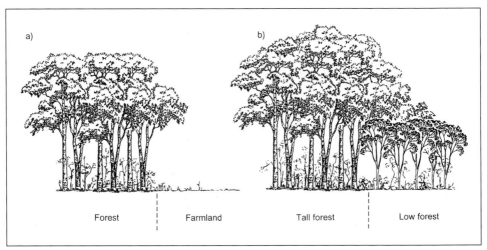

| Forest | Farmland | Tall forest | Low forest |

Fig. 2–4   **The contrast in habitat structure at the interface between (a) natural vegetation and cleared land such as farmland is usually much greater than that between (b) two adjacent natural habitats.**

Effects of fragmentation on wildlife

Throughout the world, concern about the effects of habitat fragmentation and isolation on native fauna has stimulated a large number of studies on animal species or assemblages in fragmented landscapes. For an introduction to this field, Table 2–1 provides examples of studies of mammals, birds, reptiles and amphibians, and invertebrates from six continents.

Table 2–1   Examples of studies on the effects of habitat loss and fragmentation on different faunal groups in six continents.

Continent	Mammals	Birds	Reptiles and amphibians	Invertebrates
Africa	East 1981; Struhsaker 1981; Western & Ssemakula 1981	Diamond 1981; Stuart 1981; Newmark 1991		
Asia		Diamond *et al.* 1987; Thiollay & Meyburg 1988		
Australasia	Kitchener *et al.* 1980b; Suckling 1982; Bennett 1987, 1990b,c; Pahl *et al.* 1988; Laurance 1990; Arnold *et al.* 1991, 1993	Kitchener *et al.* 1982; Howe *et al.* 1981; Howe 1984; Loyn 1985a, 1987; Saunders 1989, 1990; Lynch & Saunders 1991; Saunders & de Rebeira 1991; Barrett *et al.* 1994	Kitchener *et al.* 1980a; Kitchener & How 1982; Sarré *et al.* 1995; Hadden & Westbrooke 1996	Main 1987; Ogle 1987; Keals & Majer 1991; Margules *et al.* 1994
Europe	Dickman 1987; Dickman & Doncaster 1987; Verboom & van Apeldoorn 1990; Szacki & Liro 1991; Kozakiewicz *et al.* 1993; Bright 1993; Fitzgibbon 1993	Moore & Hooper 1975; Opdam *et al.* 1984; van Dorp & Opdam 1987; Ford 1987; Haila *et al.* 1993a; McCollin 1993; Tellería & Santos 1995	Laan & Verboom 1990; Mann *et al.* 1991; Dickman 1987	Shreeve & Mason 1980; Mader 1984; Tscharntke 1992; Kindvall & Ahlen 1992; Thomas & Jones 1993
North America	Matthiae & Stearns 1981; Middleton & Merriam 1981, 1983; Henderson *et al.* 1985; Beier 1993; Bennett *et al.* 1994; Newmark 1995; Bolger *et al.* 1997	Galli *et al.* 1976; Whitcomb *et al.* 1981; Ambuel & Temple 1983; Blake & Karr 1984; Lynch & Whigham 1984; Freemark & Merriam 1986; Askins *et al.* 1987; Soulé *et al.* 1988; Bolger *et al.* 1991; Villard *et al.* 1995	Jones *et al.* 1985	Harrison *et al.* 1988; Taylor & Merriam 1996
South America	Lovejoy *et al.* 1984; da Fonseca & Robinson 1990	Leck 1979; Lovejoy *et al.* 1984, 1986; Bierregaard *et al.* 1992; Willson *et al.* 1994; Stouffer & Bierregaard 1995a,b	Lovejoy *et al.* 1984	Lovejoy *et al.* 1984; Klein 1989

The ecological consequences of habitat fragmentation are diverse and a variety of authors have reviewed this topic from different perspectives (Saunders *et al.* 1991; Bierregaard *et al.* 1992; Haila *et al.* 1993b; Hobbs 1993a; Fahrig and Merriam 1994; Wiens 1994). Here, the process of fragmentation is recognized as having three main types of impacts on the fauna of remnant habitats:

- loss of species in fragments;

- changes to the composition of faunal assemblages;

- changes to ecological processes that involve animal species.

Loss of species

Fragmentation sets in train a process of species loss at a local (habitat fragment) and landscape level. Such loss of species can occur in response to each of the three types of change associated with the process of fragmentation: overall loss of habitat, reduction in size of fragments, and increased isolation of fragments.

There is clear evidence of species loss on a landscape and regional scale in areas where clearing and fragmentation have removed much of the natural vegetation (Matthiae and Stearns 1981; Saunders 1989; Bennett 1990b; Bennett and Ford 1997). However, it is often difficult to directly attribute species losses to an overall decline in habitat because of other potentially contributing factors (such as hunting, persecution as pests, introduction of disease and new predators, habitat modification) that are also associated with human land use. Clearly, though, regional species loss is a process that occurs over time as separated populations dwindle, decline, and disappear one by one. It is of critical importance to recognize that there is a time lag between changes to habitats and the time when the full implications of those changes are experienced by animal communities.

The most common evidence of species loss accompanying landscape fragmentation relates to the reduction in size of fragments when larger tracts are subdivided into two or more smaller isolated blocks. The resultant fragments are each smaller and together comprise less area than the original tract because intervening vegetation has been cleared. There is now a wealth of evidence that shows that smaller areas generally support fewer species than larger areas of the same vegetation type. A highly significant relationship between the number of species present and the size of habitat fragments has been demonstrated for many taxa, including forest and woodland birds (Galli *et al.* 1976; Opdam *et al* 1984; Ambuel and Temple 1983; Blake and Karr 1984; Mc Collin 1993); mammals (Kitchener *et al.* 1982; Suckling 1982; Bennett 1987; Laurance 1990); reptiles and amphibians (Kitchener *et al.* 1980a; Caughley and Gall 1985; Kitchener and How 1982; Laan and Verboom 1990); and invertebrates (Shreeve and Mason 1980).

Three explanations have been proposed for this widely observed species-area relationship (Connor and McCoy 1979):

- a small fragment contains a smaller 'sample' of the original habitat, and consequently it is likely to have sampled a more limited range of the fauna than a larger area;

- with decreasing area there is usually a reduced diversity of habitats for animals to occupy and consequently the number of species may reflect the habitat diversity available;

- smaller areas generally support smaller population sizes and therefore fewer species are able to maintain viable populations than in a large tract.

Most of these studies have compared patches of varying size at a single point in time. More limited are data sets from experimental studies in which observations were collected before fragmentation followed by subsequent monitoring after the event (Lovejoy *et al.* 1984, 1986; Margules *et al.* 1994), or from studies where comparison is made between fragments and 'control' areas of similar size and habitat within larger tracts (Howe 1984; Bolger *et al.* 1991; Newmark 1991). These latter studies have shown that not only is there a loss of species due to changes in size, but that the isolating effect of fragmentation can result in further loss. In urban San Diego, California, USA, birds dependent on chaparral shrubland were censused in small isolated canyons of varying size (0.3–68ha of chaparral habitat) and the number of species in these remnants was compared with a species-area relationship derived from sample plots in large continuous tracts of chaparral (Bolger *et al.* 1991). The results clearly demonstrated that the isolated fragments, especially those less than 10ha in size (80% of those studied), were impoverished in comparison with similar plots in continuous habitat. Further, the length of time that each canyon had been isolated was also an important predictor of the number of species expected to occur. Thus, not only does isolation result in a loss of species, but further species can be expected to disappear as the years go by.

Species loss in fragments is not immediate upon isolation. The ongoing decline of populations and species numbers in remnants following isolation has been termed 'faunal relaxation' and is directly comparable to the gradual loss of species that has occurred on landbridge islands following isolation by rising sea levels (Wilcox 1980; Diamond 1984). The dynamic nature of species loss has been most clearly shown by studies in which remnants have been censused at two or more intervals following isolation, with a demonstrated loss of species during the intervening period (Butcher *et al.* 1981; Diamond *et al.* 1987; Leck 1979; Saunders 1989; Recher and Serventy 1991). They clearly demonstrate that the number of species present immediately following isolation is greater than that which can be sustained in the long term (Box 2–2).

For example, an 87ha remnant of wet tropical forest in Ecuador, the Rio Palenque Field Station, was increasingly isolated from surrounding forest during the 1970s. Of 170 species of forest-dependent birds recorded in the reserve from previous ornithological studies, 44 species (26%) disappeared in the six years between 1973–1978, and a further 15 species were in such low numbers in 1978 that they are also likely to disappear (Leck 1979). These population declines refer to forest-dependent species; many birds of open areas, forest edges and regrowth remain common and may even be increasing as forests in the region are cleared and isolated (Leck 1979). Similar rapid loss of bird species has been reported from King's Park, an isolated bushland reserve of less than 300ha in the city of Perth, Western Australia (Recher and Serventy 1991). Over the 60 year period from 1928 to 1986, 20% of bird species have become locally extinct and a further 11% have declined in abundance.

Species loss following fragmentation and isolation is not limited to small fragments only. It has also been documented from mountain ranges, large reserves and national parks (Picton

Box 2–2   Loss of breeding birds from an isolated Javan woodland, Indonesia

The Bogor Botanical Gardens on the Indonesian island of Java is an 86ha woodland comprising both native and exotic tree species. The gardens were isolated when surrounding woodlands were destroyed around 1936, and the nearest habitats for forest birds are now at least 5–10km distant. A total of 62 species of birds was recorded breeding in the gardens during the period from 1932–1952, and this provided a basis for comparison with bird species recorded from 1980–1985 (Diamond *et al.* 1987). Twenty species formerly present now no longer breed in the gardens, four are close to extinction, five more have declined substantially and about half (33 species) have maintained their populations. As a consequence of the isolation of the gardens from nearby habitats, small populations of woodland birds have declined and disappeared with little opportunity for immigrants to halt the decline. Those that have survived are primarily species that are able to live in the intensively-used countryside that surrounds the gardens (Diamond *et al.* 1987). The selective loss of species means that this woodland fragment now supports an impoverished community that 'mirrors' the surrounding land use, rather than providing an effective refuge for forest-dependent species.

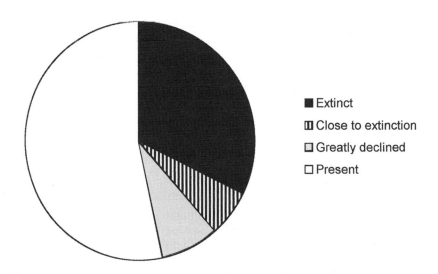

■ Extinct

Ⅲ Close to extinction

☐ Greatly declined

☐ Present

Change in the status of breeding bird species in the Bogor Botanical Gardens, Java, Indonesia between 1932–52 and 1980–85. The diagram illustrates the status in 1980–85 of 62 species recorded breeding in 1932–52. Data from Diamond *et al.* (1987).

1979; Newmark 1987; Newmark *et al.* 1991). For example, comparison of historical records with recent sightings of three orders of mammals (Lagomorpha, Carnivora, Artiodactyla) in 14 national parks in western North America showed that the number of extinctions has greatly exceeded the number of colonizations since park establishment (Newmark 1995). At least 15 of the 38 species (39%) in these orders have experienced local extinction in at least one national park. Further, the *rate* of extinction was inversely correlated with park area; smaller parks have experienced a higher rate of extinction of mammal populations since establishment than have large parks.

A natural experiment that has demonstrated loss of species occurred with the flooding of Lake Gatun during the construction of the Panama Canal in the 1920s, when many former hilltops were converted into islands in the lake. Among these was the now well-studied Barro Colorado Island (Willis 1974; Karr 1982a,b). Of approximately 108 breeding species recorded on the island, about 45 species have disappeared following this 'natural isolation experiment'. Some of these losses, but not all, can be attributed to habitat changes on the island. However, it is likely that many other species may have disappeared unnoticed because intensive studies on Barro Colorado began long after it was transformed from a hilltop into an island (Diamond 1984).

Changes to the composition of faunal assemblages

Different species of animals respond to habitat destruction and fragmentation in different ways. Differences in home range area, body size, food resources and foraging patterns, nesting and shelter requirements, as well as tolerance to habitat disturbance and sensitivity to altered microclimates, each influence the idiosyncratic response of each species to fragmentation. The outcome is that after isolation the composition of faunal assemblages in fragments differs from that in large intact habitats. Is it possible to predict the outcomes of changes to animal assemblages in remnants? An important goal for conservation biologists and wildlife managers is to understand what types of species are most prone to extinction in remnant habitats and why they are sensitive, so that management for conservation can be more effectively directed (MacNally and Bennett 1997).

When biologists first examined the occurrence of species in remnants it quickly became apparent that the composition of small species-poor remnants was not a random selection from the pool of species available in extensive habitats. In particular, studies of birds in woodland and forest remnants suggested that fragment size has a strong influence on the identity of the species that occur. For many species, the frequency of occurrence (also known as the incidence function) increases with increasing size class of habitat patches (Moore and Hooper 1975; Lynch 1987; Ogle 1987). For example, an extensive survey of 433 woods in Great Britain, ranging across six orders of magnitude in size (from 0.001 to 100ha), examined the frequency of occurrence of bird species in each size class. Birds such as the Blackbird, Song Thrush and Wood Pigeon occurred in all size classes, though occurring in a greater proportion of larger woods. In contrast, species such as the Great Spotted Woodpecker, Tawny Owl and Marsh Tit were essentially found only in large woods (Fig. 2–5) (Moore and Hooper 1975).

The hypothesis that there may be a relatively predictable sequence of occurrence of species in fragments was further supported by examination of the pattern of occurrence of birds, mammals and reptiles on true islands and on naturally insular habitats such as mountain tops.

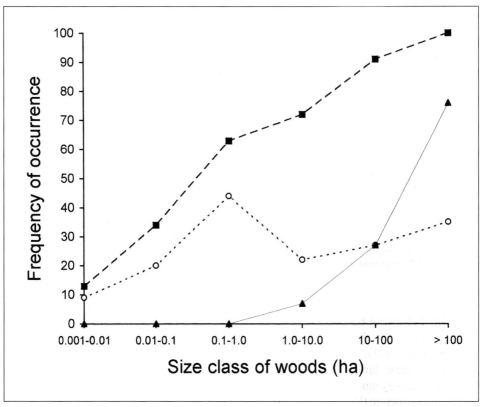

Fig. 2–5   Frequency of occurrence of three species of birds in relation to the size of woodland patches in Britain. The Blackbird (■) occurs with increasing frequency as woodland size increases, the Great Spotted Woodpecker (▲) is primarily found in large woods, whereas the occurrence of the House Sparrow (○) is not clearly related to the size of the wood. Data from Moore and Hooper (1975).

These isolates have had a longer time for the full effects of isolation to be experienced. There is a consistent tendency for the assemblage of species on species-poor isolates to be a subset of that present on larger, species-rich isolates (Jones *et al.* 1985; Patterson 1987; Cutler 1991). Patterson (1987) coined the term 'nested subset' to describe this pattern (Fig. 2–6). Limited data from habitat fragments suggest a similar pattern. Assemblages of birds in rural woodlots in Idaho, USA (Blake 1991), in small rainforest isolates in New South Wales, Australia (Howe *et al.* 1981), in oak forest fragments in Spain (Tellería and Santos 1995) and chaparral-dependent birds in urban canyons in San Diego, USA (Bolger *et al.* 1991) have also shown a nested pattern of occurrence.

Although alternative explanations are possible for this phenomenon, a gradient in proneness to extinction has generally been thought to be the most likely mechanism for the nested subsets pattern, with species 'dropping out' in a relatively ordered sequence. This view is supported by observations that distributional patterns of reptiles and non-flying mammals, which generally have lower dispersal abilities than birds, show a better 'fit' to a nested pattern than do birds (Jones *et al.* 1985; Cutler 1991).

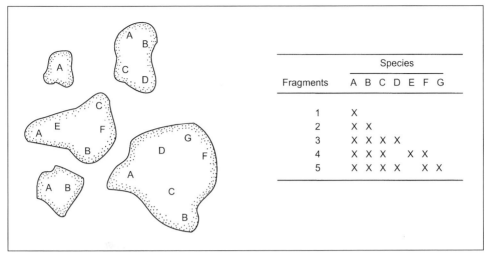

	Species						
Fragments	A	B	C	D	E	F	G
1	X						
2	X	X					
3	X	X	X	X			
4	X	X	X			X	X
5	X	X	X	X			X	X

Fig. 2–6   Diagrammatic representation of a nested subset. Species-poor fragments generally contain a nested subset of species that are present in richer fragments. (A-H represent animal species).

Isolated chaparral habitats in San Diego, USA, have experienced a rapid loss of species since isolation, with the greatest loss being of those birds that naturally occur at low density (Bolger *et al.* 1991). Because the probability of dispersal and recolonization of isolated habitats by these birds is low, it appears that vulnerability to extinction based on low population density (and hence number present in small patches) has the strongest influence on community structure (Bolger *et al.* 1991). In contrast, the mobility of woodland birds in Idaho is relatively high (many are neotropical migrants) and here the nested pattern of occurrence was attributed to differential ability to breed successfully in woods of different sizes (Blake 1991). It seems that while the pattern of occurrence of many species in fragments is non-random, there may be a number of biological processes operating.

A different approach to developing generalisations about the composition of assemblages in fragments has been to compare ecological characteristics of species that are vulnerable to, or tolerant of, habitat reduction and isolation. Several trends are discussed below but there is still much to learn before reliable predictions can be made. In particular, there is a need to develop a better understanding of the relationship between patterns arising from area-based stochastic processes and those driven by external influences in the environment.

First, habitat generalists and species that favour or tolerate disturbed habitats (such as edges) are likely to be common in small remnants. Numerous studies in eastern North America (Galli *et al.* 1976; Ambuel and Temple 1983; Lynch and Whigham 1984; Blake and Karr 1984) have highlighted the occurrence in small woods of 'edge species' of birds such as the Common Grackle, Gray Catbird, Indigo Bunting, Starling, House Wren and Brown-headed Cowbird. Conversely, 'forest interior' species such as the Wood Thrush, Ovenbird, Scarlet Tanager, Black and White Warbler and White-breasted Nuthatch are more likely to occur in larger tracts. Similar trends were found for nature reserves (ranging from 34–5000ha in size) surrounded by farmland in Western Australia (Humphreys and Kitchener 1982). The percentage of birds, mammals and reptiles that regularly use disturbed environments (such as farmland, disturbed woodland and roadsides), was disproportionately high in smaller nature reserves. Conversely, species that require natural habitat comprised a greater proportion of the assemblage in the largest reserves.

Second, there is a growing body of evidence to suggest that the species that are most sensitive to habitat fragmentation are those that occur naturally at low densities, or that have some innate dependence on interior habitats (Terborgh and Winter 1980; Diamond 1984; Soulé *et al.* 1988; Laurance 1990). These may include:

* large-bodied animals that have large area requirements;

* species that are high in the food chain, such as owls, diurnal raptors, snakes and large carnivorous mammals;

* species that have specialized food or habitat requirements, such as seasonally varying or patchily distributed foods.

Because of their low population density, small fragments may support only a few individuals or breeding pairs, or for some species the available area may be insufficient for even a single breeding pair (Box 2–3). These tiny isolated populations are vulnerable to

---

Box 2–3   Area requirements of rainforest raptors in French Guiana

If nature reserves and protected areas are to preserve the full complement of species, it is essential to know the requirements of those that are most vulnerable to insularisation. Quantitative data relevant to the design of natural reserves in tropical rainforests of South America comes from a study of one such group – rainforest raptors, including vultures, kites, eagles, falcons, hawks and other birds of prey (Thiollay 1989). The distribution and density of these forest-dependent birds of prey were assessed in a series of large plots, of 2500ha and 10,000ha, in primary undisturbed rainforest in French Guiana.

Twenty-seven species of raptors (of a total of 54 species recorded from the country) normally occur in primary rainforest in French Guiana. From 14–21 species were recorded in plots of 2500 ha but only 12–16 of these species had at least one resident pair with most of its home range included in the study plot. In the 10,000ha plot, 23 species were recorded, of which 21 were represented by only one to eight pairs.

The patchy distribution of raptor home ranges, even in this extensive undisturbed rainforest, and the large area required by pairs of many species means that a vast area will be required to adequately protect an entire assemblage of forest raptors. Based on this distributional data, a rainforest reserve of at least 1 million ha (10,000km^2) will be needed to protect the complete raptor community (Thiollay 1989). The extent of unbroken rainforest in French Guiana, with 70,000km^2 uninhabited, means that such an opportunity is still possible. These data also confirm that Manu National Park, a large protected area of 1,600,000ha in Peru, is of the right order of magnitude to conserve entire assemblages of rainforest animals.

---

stochastic processes, including random fluctuations in environmental, demographic and genetic processes, and may rapidly disappear (see Box 3–1).

An array of external influences (such as changing land use in the surrounding environment, introduced predators) and internal changes within remnants (such as vegetation succession) can also have a strong influence on the vulnerability of species to local extinction. Consequently, the relative composition of faunal assemblages in fragments may change substantially over time, even though the size of the habitat isolate remains unchanged (Butcher *et al.* 1981; Diamond *et al.* 1987; Recher and Serventy 1991). Bird censuses were undertaken in a 23ha section of the Connecticut Arboretum, New London, Connecticut, USA, during 11 breeding seasons between 1953 and 1985 (Butcher *et al.* 1981; Askins *et al.* 1987). The composition of the avifauna of this hardwood forest displayed substantial variation over this period. Between 1953 and 1976, eight species of forest birds disappeared or declined and there was a significant decline in the abundance of long-distance migrants. At the same time the occurrence and abundance of species characteristic of suburban environments increased, in parallel with extensive suburban development and forest destruction in the vicinity (Butcher *et al.* 1981). Subsequently, from 1976 to 1985, the downward trend for long-distance migrants was reversed. An increased abundance of these species was attributed to nearby reafforestation and increased use of the maturing forest (Askins *et al.* 1987).

Changes to ecological processes in fragments

Ecological processes that form part of the natural functioning of ecosystems (including predator-prey relationships, competitive interactions, seed dispersal, plant pollination, nutrient cycling, maintenance of successional mosaics by disturbance), are frequently disrupted or modified by fragmentation. These changes can be driven by influences from *within* fragments or by influences from environments *surrounding* the fragment. To date, our knowledge of how fragmentation has affected ecological processes is limited but it is through such changes to the way that natural communities operate that habitat fragmentation will have its greatest impact on biodiversity conservation. It is likely, for example, that we will increasingly become aware of secondary extinctions of plants and animals in fragments as the full implications of ecological changes take effect over time. The following examples illustrate some of the diverse ways in which changes to ecological processes potentially have profound implications for the conservation of the flora and fauna of fragmented landscapes.

Seed dispersal

The term 'keystone species' is used to describe species whose loss would have widespread ecological effects. For example, the loss in fragmented environments of animals that have a key role in pollination or seed dispersal will have negative effects on the status of numerous plant species and their decline, in turn, may have diverse ecosystem effects across the entire ecosystem.

The Southern Cassowary, a large (up to 80 kg) flightless bird of the tropical rainforests of northern Australia and Papua New Guinea, is one example of a keystone species that has an important role in seed dispersal in tropical forests. This frugivore consumes several hundred species of fleshy fruits of the rainforest community (Marchant and Higgins 1990; Crome and Bentrupperbaumer 1993). In the wet tropics of northern Australia, the Southern Cassowary is the only known dispersal vector for over 100 species of rainforest plants that bear large fruits with big seeds. The seeds are voided intact as the animal moves throughout its extensive home range, thus spreading them through the forest landscape.

The distribution of the Southern Cassowary is becoming fragmented and isolated as tropical forests in the coastal lowlands are cleared and land development increases. It is also subject to other direct threats such as road kills, hunting, and predation by feral pigs (Crome and Bentrupperbaumer 1993). The loss of this frugivore and its seed dispersal function from tropical forest fragments has potentially widespread and long-term effects on forest composition and vegetation dynamics. It is now the focus of an integrated conservation and recovery program in at least one locality, with the goal of restoring its habitat and enhancing its conservation status (Crome and Bentrupperbaumer 1993).

Predator-prey relationships

The loss of large predators from fragments, and the consequent changes in the abundance and ecological impacts of prey species, have been identified as having potentially major effects on the structure of plant and animal communities in isolates (Terborgh and Winter 1980; Soulé *et al.* 1988). In the USA, Soulé *et al.*(1988) used the term 'meso-predator release' to describe the increased abundance of smaller omnivores and predators in the absence of large dominant

---

Box 2–4   Nest predation and its relationship with landscape pattern in Sweden

Much attention has recently been given to the question of whether animal populations in fragments are subject to higher levels of predation than comparable populations in large continuous habitats. Evidence has been presented to show that in some situations, particularly for small fragments in farmland, levels of predation on the nests of woodland birds are elevated close to woodland edges (Wilcove 1985; Angelstam 1986; Andrén and Angelstam 1988). This has been attributed to generalist predators that live in the surrounding farmland matrix also preying on nests close to the woodland edge.

In Sweden, predation by corvids on eggs in artificial nests was studied in a series of landscapes along a gradient in forest cover ranging from mainly forest to mainly agricultural land (Andrén 1992). Both the density of corvids and the intensity of nest predation increased as the proportion of agricultural land in the landscape increased. However, the identity of the nest predators on artificial nests placed in forest vegetation varied greatly in relation to the landscape pattern. The two forest-living corvids, the Common Raven and European Jay, mainly preyed on nests in large forest fragments. The Jackdaw and Black-billed Magpie mainly preyed on nests placed in cleared agricultural land, while the Hooded Crow, a habitat generalist, preyed on nests in both forest and agricultural land.

The density of Hooded Crows was highest in landscapes with a mixture of both agricultural land and forest. It was this generalist species that was identified as the most important member of the corvid family causing increased predation pressure close to forest edges and in small forest fragments (Andrén 1992).

predators. Meso-predators such as the Raccoon, Gray Fox and Cats are often common in small isolated habitats, especially in near-urban environments, and have been associated with increased mortality of ground-living and ground-nesting birds in isolates (Matthiae and Stearns 1981; Soulé *et al.* 1988; Harris and Gallagher 1989).

Similar observations on the 'release' of prey species in the absence of large predators have been noted for Barro Colorado Island, Panama (Terborgh and Winter 1980), where it was suggested that high densities of Collared Peccaries and Coatis may be associated with high levels of nest predation. An experimental test of this hypothesis, based on the loss of eggs from artificial nests, showed that predation of nests on Barro Colorado Island was significantly greater than in adjacent mainland forest, especially for those nests placed at ground level (Loiselle and Hoppes 1983).

Nutrient cycling

Dung beetles and carrion beetles of the family Scarabidae are specialist feeders in dung and carrion. They bury nutrient-rich dung and carrion as food for their offspring and in doing so they incidentally increase the rate of soil nutrient cycling. In tropical Amazonian forest in Brazil, fewer species of beetles, lower population densities and smaller individuals were recorded in small fragments than in comparable control sites in adjacent intact forest (Klein 1989). Experimental studies revealed a lower rate of dung decomposition in the smallest (1ha) fragments compared with intact forest, a result that was consistent with the observed changes in beetle numbers.

The beetles' activities also influence other ecological processes in the tropical forest, so that changes in beetle numbers in fragments may have further secondary effects (Klein 1989). For example, by eating and burying dung the beetles kill nematode larvae and other gastrointestinal parasites of vertebrate animals. In addition, burial of seeds within dung may prevent them being preyed upon by small rodents and could assist in seed survival and dispersal (Klein 1989).

Nest parasitism

Increased levels of nest parasitism of bird populations in wooded fragments has been associated with an increased abundance of the Brown-headed Cowbird, a nest parasite of small woodland birds, following a dramatic expansion of its range in eastern USA this century. The clearing of forests for agricultural land has provided additional habitat for this open-country bird, and an enhanced winter food supply from grain crops and artificial feeders has allowed its numbers to increase. Parasitism of nests close to forest edges by Brown-headed Cowbirds has been advanced as a potential cause of the decline and disappearance of forest-interior birds in small fragments (Ambuel and Temple 1983; Brittingham and Temple 1983; Terborgh 1989). At least one rare species, Kirtland's Warbler, would now be extinct from nest parasitism were it not for an annual campaign to remove the Brown-headed Cowbird from its breeding habitat in Michigan, USA. During the 1960s, before management intervention, cowbirds were parasitizing 70% of nests, with the result that annual breeding success of the warblers was insufficient to offset natural mortality (Terborgh 1989).

High levels of nest parasitism have also been reported for other woodland species. In a study in Wisconsin, 65% of all nests found along the edge of woodlands were parasitized (Brittingham and Temple 1983). It is feared that the reduced breeding success of parasitized species in fragments, in conjunction with other stresses such as increased nest predation, may tip the balance for many species and contribute to regional declines in fragmented landscapes (Wilcove 1985; Terborgh 1989). The situation is exacerbated because a number of parasitized species, such as Hooded Warbler and Worm-eating Warbler, were not historical hosts of cowbirds, but have come into contact in recent times due to the range expansion of the cowbird.

Nest parasites themselves can suffer extinction following the decline of their host species – an example of a secondary extinction or 'trophic cascade' (i.e. the effects of ecological change flowing on to influence other levels of ecological organisation). The Brush Cuckoo, a nest parasite of forest birds, has disappeared from the Bogor area in Indonesia along with two of its likely host species, the Pied Fantail and Hill Blue Flycatcher (Diamond *et al.* 1987) (Box 2–2).

Is isolation of habitats important?

Isolation of remnant habitats is a fundamental consequence of habitat fragmentation. However, the nature of the isolation of habitat fragments differs from that of true islands surrounded by water, with which fragments have often been compared. When large tracts are subdivided, the remaining small fragments are isolated by a new form of land use. Differing forms of land use act as variable filters on the movements of animals through the landscape. Some land uses pose little resistance to movement, while others can be an effective barrier to all interchange. Intensively-managed crop lands, for example, may have a stronger isolating effect on a small rodent than does a similar expanse of abandoned farmland with scattered trees and regenerating woody shrubs. Similarly, an urban housing development is likely to have a more severe isolating effect for woodland butterflies than a lightly-wooded golf course. The extent to which animal populations in fragments are isolated from those in nearby habitats varies greatly in relation to land use and the biology of the species of concern.

How important is isolation in the conservation of wildlife in fragmented landscapes? This is a key question of both theoretical and practical interest and of immediate relevance to land management for conservation. If populations have a high probability of survival in isolated fragments, or if they have a high capacity to move through the surrounding modified matrix, then the spatial arrangement of habitats in the landscape is of little importance. In such circumstances, habitat links will be of limited value because population continuity is not hindered by land use. On the other hand, if there is a distinct risk that isolated populations *will* decline and species movement *is* restricted by surrounding land use, then spatial arrangement of habitats is of great importance. In these circumstances, habitat links that promote movement of animals and continuity of populations through the landscape will be of benefit to population persistence. Priority in conservation strategy must then be given to preserving and managing *systems* of habitat with a spatial pattern that will maximize the opportunity for movement and interchange.

How many species and situations correspond with the positions outlined above? There is no simple answer. It is clear that animal species and assemblages respond in a variety of ways to isolation, and to different levels of isolation; and that a particular form of land use poses differing levels of isolation to different species. Evidence from studies of a range of animal groups show that isolation has negative effects on the distribution and occurrence of many (but not necessarily all) species.

First, convincing evidence of the detrimental effects of isolation is shown by experimental studies that compare the fauna of remnant habitats before and after their isolation from an extensive area of habitat (Stouffer and Bierregaard 1995a,b), or compare communities in isolated fragments with those in matched 'control' areas of similar size in extensive habitat blocks (Howe 1984; Bolger *et al.* 1991, 1997; Newmark 1991). The loss of birds from isolated chaparral fragments in California was discussed above, and similar losses were demonstrated for native rodents in the same fragments (Bolger *et al.* 1997). Another example comes from Tanzania, where forest understorey birds were found to be sensitive to isolation of tropical forest fragments (Newmark 1991). All but the largest of nine isolated fragments had significantly fewer species present than was recorded from comparable census effort in extensive tropical forest (Fig. 2–7). Further, the number of species in the fragments was also influenced by the *degree of isolation*: after controlling for forest size, the number of understorey species decreased with increasing distance from extensive forest.

There are numerous other examples that illustrate how the degree of isolation, frequently measured as the spatial distance from other populations or habitats, also affects various animal species.

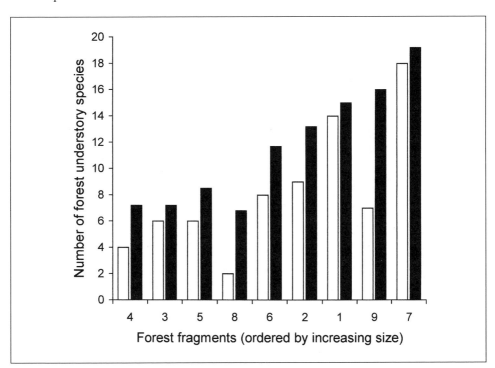

Fig. 2–7   **Effect of isolation of tropical forest fragments on the richness of understorey birds in the East Usambara Mountains, Tanzania. The number of species captured in nine fragments of tropical forest (open bars) was significantly less than the mean number of species captured with equivalent sampling effort in extensive forest (closed bars), except for fragment 7. Data from Newmark (1991).**

- Spruce Grouse in the Adirondack Mountains of New York, USA, were more likely to occur in coniferous bog patches close to occupied patches than in similar, but more distant, patches (Fritz 1979).

- Rocky outcrops (mine tailings) in the Sierra Nevada, USA, that were close to other outcrops were more likely to be occupied by Pikas (a rabbit-like mammal) than were those more isolated (Fig. 2–8) (Smith 1974).

- In Switzerland, the occurrence of the Middle Spotted Woodpecker in remnants of oak woodland was related to the size of the woods and distance to the nearest wood larger than 40ha. Those that were isolated by more than 9km were not occupied (Muller 1982 cited in Opdam 1991).

- The rare Bay Checkerspot Butterfly was more likely to occur on remnant serpentine grasslands close to a large source area, than on distant remnants of similar suitable habitat (Harrison *et al.* 1988).

- In managed pine forests of South Carolina, USA, Bachman's Sparrows were more likely to colonize forest clear-cut close to known source populations than those that were distant from the source (Dunning *et al.* 1995).

- In the Netherlands, the abundance of female Bank Voles in farmland woods was significantly influenced by the distance from a woodland source greater than 25ha in size (van Apeldoorn *et al.* 1992).

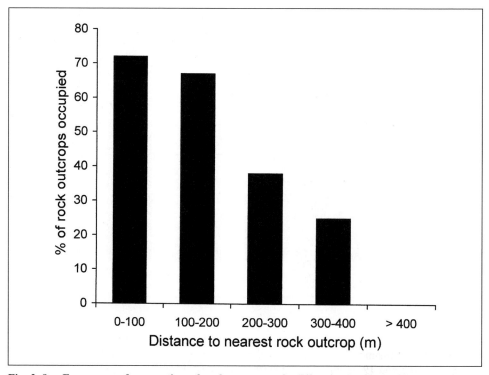

Fig. 2–8 **Frequency of occupation of rocky outcrops by Pikas in the Sierra Nevada, USA, in relation to distance from nearby habitats. Data from Smith (1974).**

Box 2–5 Effects of isolation on the recovery of a rare butterfly in Britain

In Britain, the Silver-spotted Skipper inhabits heavily grazed calcareous grasslands. When rabbits were killed by myxomatosis in the 1950s, patches of suitable grassland became overgrown and the distribution of the Silver-spotted Skipper declined to fewer than 46 localities in 10 refuge regions (Thomas *et al.* 1986). Re-introduction of domestic stock to graze these grasslands, and the recovery of rabbit populations, led to improved habitat quality for the butterfly and slow recolonization of patches of suitable grassland.

Between 1982 and 1991, there was a 30% increase in the number of occupied patches, involving at least 29 colonizations and 10 patch extinctions (Thomas and Jones 1993). The probability of *colonization* during this period increased with patch size and decreased with isolation from the nearest populated patch. That is, the grassland patches most likely to be colonized by butterflies were those that were large or those close to a nearby butterfly population. Spatial isolation from a neighbouring population was the most important influence. Many grassland patches of suitable size and habitat were available, but none further than 10km from an occupied patch were colonized. Conversely, the probability of *extinction* between 1982 and 1991 decreased with patch size and increased with isolation from the nearest patch population (Thomas and Jones 1993). Extinctions were more frequent on those patches that supported small populations in 1982 (i.e. less than 225 individuals); there were no extinctions on patches with initially larger populations in 1982 (225–800 or 800–3000 individuals).

The conservation and recovery of this rare butterfly depends on the availability of *systems* of suitable grassland patches. Its capacity to recover further and to occupy more of the vacant patches of suitable grassland (more than 100 vacant patches exist), depends on its ability to disperse via 'stepping stone' patches that are separated by less than 10km (preferably much less). Thus, isolation from source populations has a major controlling influence on the spatial dynamics of the Silver-spotted Skipper.

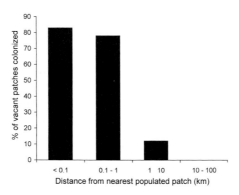

Frequency of colonization of vacant grassland patches by the Silver-spotted Skipper between 1982 and 1991 in relation to their distance from a nearby butterfly population. Data from Thomas and Jones (1993).

The influence of degree of spatial isolation has also been highlighted by studies that have shown significant relationships between species richness in isolates and the proximity to nearby habitat. A number (but not all) studies of the birds of forest and woodland remnants have reported that some measure of isolation, together with fragment area, provides a better prediction of species richness than does area alone (Howe *et al.* 1981; Whitcomb *et al.* 1981; Howe 1984; Opdam *et al.* 1984; Askins *et al.* 1987; van Dorp and Opdam 1987; Newmark 1991; McCollin 1993). For example, fragment area was the best single predictor of the number of woodland birds in 36 fragments in the Rhine Valley in the Netherlands (Opdam *et al.* 1984), but three different measures of isolation were also significant predictors in a multiple regression model. Distance to the nearest wood greater than 25ha, distance to the nearest large forest tract, and the total area of woodland within a radius of 3km, each accounted for further variation in the number of bird species over and above that attributed to woodland size. In other words, for woods of a given size those that are close to other woods are likely to support more species of woodland birds.

Why does isolation affect populations and communities of animals?

The underlying interpretation of the effect of degree of spatial isolation on species in fragmented or insular habitats is that changes have occurred because animals have been restricted or prevented from dispersing between isolates. Indeed, it has been stated that for fragmented populations, dispersal is the 'key to survival' (Opdam 1990). The reduced ability of animals to move through the landscape has a number of major consequences; it limits their capacity to supplement declining populations, to recolonize habitats where extinctions have occurred, or to colonize newly suitable habitats. Empirical evidence in support of this hypothesis has been clearly provided for a range of species (birds, butterflies, crickets) by the demonstration of significant negative relationships between the rate of recolonization of fragments and their isolation from nearby habitat (Verboom *et al.* in Opdam 1991; Thomas and Jones 1993; Kindvall and Ahlen 1992). In each case, the rate at which animals recolonized unoccupied fragments was higher for those closer to source areas (Box 2–5).

There is also strong theoretical support for the contention that the capacity of animals to move through the landscape is fundamental to conservation of natural ecosystems. The major theoretical and conceptual bases for understanding the status of populations and communities in patchy environments each recognize, either implicitly or explicitly, the importance of animal movements. This is the theme of the next chapter.

Summary

Habitat fragmentation is a dynamic process that has three main components: an overall loss of habitat in the landscape, reduction in the size of remaining blocks, and increased isolation by new forms of land use. Changes to the pattern of habitats in the landscape result in changes to ecological processes that in turn affect the status of the flora and fauna. Effects of habitat fragmentation on wildlife include: loss of species in fragments, changes to the composition of faunal assemblages, and changes to ecological processes that involve animals. Isolation of habitats is a fundamental consequence of fragmentation. A range of evidence shows that isolation, and the degree of spatial isolation, have negative impacts on many populations and communities. The negative effects of isolation are attributed to the decreased opportunity for movement of animals to and from other habitats.

3 APPROACHES TO UNDERSTANDING THE BENEFITS OF CONNECTIVITY

Why is connectivity beneficial? Why have many scientists and land managers, from around the world, concluded that managing habitats and linkages to reduce the isolation of wildlife populations has benefits for nature conservation? It is pertinent to review four approaches (not mutually exclusive) that recognize, either implicitly or explicitly, that the capacity of animals to move through the landscape is fundamental to biodiversity conservation. The first approach is pragmatic – based on knowledge of the natural history of species and communities and from practical experience in wildlife management. The other three are major conceptual bases associated with scientific understanding of how organisms live in patchy environments; namely, the equilibrium theory of island biogeography (MacArthur and Wilson 1967; Diamond 1975), models of the dynamics of subdivided populations (Hanski 1989; Gilpin and Hanski 1991; Opdam 1991), and principles of landscape ecology (Forman and Godron 1986; Noss and Harris 1986; Turner 1989; Forman 1995; Hansson *et al.* 1995).

In briefly reviewing these approaches, the goal is not a critical assessment of their theoretical merits or validity for conservation biology. Rather, it is to highlight that the best efforts that ecologists have made to understand how animals live in fragmented environments emphasize the necessity for movements of individuals and species between fragments for effective long-term conservation to be achieved. The potential benefits of such movements (and hence of connectivity) suggested by each approach are noted below. They are also summarized in Chapter 4 (Table 4–2) where the question of the relative advantages and disadvantages of linkages is treated in greater detail.

Natural history and wildlife management

Field biologists who spend much time observing, studying and managing animal populations in the wild gain a wealth of practical knowledge and understanding of the species and communities they observe. Such pragmatic knowledge, derived from experience, has great influence in shaping the principles upon which land management is based and in many situations is a more powerful influence on land managers than scientific theories and models.

Several different types of observations have convinced many field biologists of the need to enhance landscape connectivity by incorporating linkages of various kinds. First, knowledge of the migratory movements of many species, especially waterfowl and large mammals, has stimulated national and international efforts to protect migratory pathways. This management may take the form of identifying and protecting critical stopover points, or ensuring that intensive land use does not pose an ecological barrier to movement along traditional routes.

Second, observations of the impacts of local barriers (such as highways, oil pipelines, railway lines and canals) on the movements and mortality of animals have been a strong stimulus to managers to implement and evaluate artificial measures such as tunnels, underpasses or bridges to assist movements across the barrier (Harris and Gallagher 1989;

Langton 1989; Bennett 1991; Forman and Hersperger 1996). Movements that are restricted or blocked may be seasonal migrations, or movements by wide-ranging animals within a large home range.

Third, knowledge of the natural history of animals that move between different habitats on a daily or regular basis to obtain necessary resources (such as birds that feed and roost in different areas) points to the need for adequate landscape connectivity for them to meet their daily requirements and to survive in environments modified by human land uses (Saunders and Ingram 1987; Wauters *et al.* 1994).

Finally, observations that local populations of game species (such as Fox Squirrels and Wild Turkeys in USA), could recolonize after being 'shot out' in small habitats led game biologists to recognize the importance of 'travel lanes' as a principle in wildlife management (Harris and Gallagher 1989).

Such knowledge of natural history and the insights gained from practical management experience highlight the potential conservation benefits to be gained from linkages in terms of:

- assisting animals to cross local barriers, and to maintain local movements through environments that are ecologically inhospitable;

- assisting species to maintain traditional migratory movements between different geographic areas;

- allowing species to recolonize habitats by increasing dispersal and immigration.

Equilibrium theory of island biogeography

The equilibrium theory of island biogeography was developed by MacArthur and Wilson (1963, 1967) in response to observations that islands contained fewer species than mainland areas of comparable size. The equilibrium theory proposed that the number of species occurring on an island tends towards an equilibrium level determined by a dynamic balance between the rate of colonization of new species and the rate of extinction of species resident on the island. The rate of colonization is determined primarily by the degree of isolation of the island from mainland source areas, while the rate of extinction is determined primarily by island area. The number of species on the island should remain approximately constant (i.e. an equilibrium number), but the composition of the faunal assemblage should change, or show 'turnover', with time.

It was quickly realized that isolates of habitat on the mainland, such as mountain tops, lakes, forest fragments and nature reserves, might also be viewed as 'islands' surrounded by a 'sea' of unfavourable habitat. Thus, the equilibrium theory became the first theoretical framework for interpreting the distribution and dynamics of fauna in remnants of habitat. It has stimulated a large body of research into the consequences of habitat fragmentation and isolation for animals (for reviews see Simberloff 1974; Gilbert 1980; Shafer 1990).

The potential importance of isolation in determining the number of species that an isolate or remnant might support at equilibrium suggested that measures to reduce isolation and increase the rate of colonization would have a significant conservation benefit. Accordingly, stepping stones or preferably continuous corridors of habitat to facilitate movements of animals between isolates were recommended in design strategies for nature conservation (Diamond 1975; Wilson and Willis 1975). Further, the presence of corridors to facilitate colonization of animals might also supplement declining populations before they actually reached extinction, in this way slowing down the rate of species extinction. This has been termed the 'rescue effect' (Brown and Kodric-Brown 1977).

Thus, island biogeographic theory predicts that increased movement of animals between fragments will enhance the conservation status of fragments by maintaining a higher level of species richness at equilibrium (Fig. 3–1). This is achieved by:

- increasing the rate of colonization of species to the isolate, and

- supplementing declining populations, thus slowing the rate of species' extinctions.

The theory of island biogeography has lost favour among conservation biologists, largely because natural isolates and habitat fragments differ fundamentally from true islands in the way that they are isolated. In contrast to lakes or oceans that surround true islands, the developed land that surrounds habitat isolates supports a modified flora and fauna and has land uses that interact with the biota within the fragment (Saunders *et al.* 1991; Wiens 1995). Thus, while colonization and extinction dynamics (based on area and isolation) may remain as important influences, a more comprehensive framework is required that also recognizes the role of ecological processes and impacts arising from the surrounding matrix in shaping the assemblage within habitat fragments.

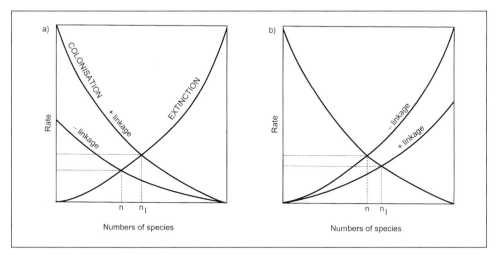

Fig. 3–1   The contribution of linkages to the species richness of an habitat isolate as predicted by the equilibrium theory of island biogeography. The number of species at equilibrium (n) is a balance between the rate of colonization of species to the isolate and the rate of species extinctions. The presence of a habitat link increases the species richness at equilibrium (n_l) in two ways: (a) by increasing the rate of colonization and (b) by decreasing the rate of extinction. Redrawn from Bennett (1990a).

Dynamics of subdivided populations

Natural environments are not homogeneous but rather are composed of habitats that vary spatially and temporally in their quality and suitability for animal species (Wiens 1976, 1989; den Boer 1981; Dunning *et al.* 1992). A species may occur naturally as a series of 'local populations' (*sensu* Hanski and Gilpin 1991) that occupy patches of suitable habitat that are separated from similar populations by areas of poorer quality. Similarly, in fragmented landscapes a species may occur as a series of local populations in remnant habitat patches that are isolated by surrounding unsuitable land. Together such a set of local populations forms a regional population. Small populations are particularly sensitive to disturbance and stochastic (or random) variation (see Box 3–1), and consequently each local population is potentially vulnerable to extinction. However, as long as there is sufficient movement between local populations to supplement declining populations before they disappear, to add new genes, or so that the rate of recolonization exceeds the rate of extinction of local populations, the regional population can persist. This general concept of a set of subdivided populations interacting at a landscape or regional scale has been outlined using a variety of models and terminology (Fahrig and Merriam 1994), but it is most commonly referred to as a 'metapopulation' or 'population of populations' (Harrison *et al.* 1988; Hanski 1989; Hanski and Gilpin 1991; Merriam 1991; Opdam 1991; Verboom *et al.* 1991).

Two main forms of metapopulation models are most relevant to the conservation of animal species in fragmented landscapes (Fig. 3–2).

- The 'island-mainland' or 'core-satellite' model is based on the presence of a large mainland population that provides a source of colonists for the surrounding local populations of varying size and degree of isolation (Harrison *et al.* 1988). In this model, the mainland is rarely likely to experience extinction but local extinction and recolonization may regularly occur on surrounding isolates.

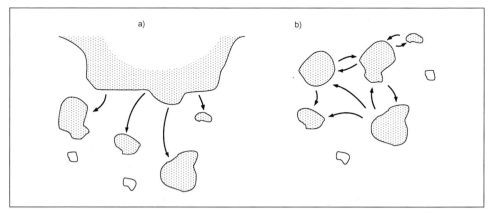

Fig. 3–2   **Diagrammatic representation of two metapopulation models. (a) The island-mainland model in which a large tract of habitat acts as a source of colonists for local populations in small habitat patches. Local extinctions and recolonizations are assumed to occur in small habitat patches but not in the mainland. (b) The patchy population model based on a diverse set of local populations that all may experience extinction and recolonization. Shading represents occupied patches, clear are unoccupied patches, and arrows indicate movements.**

Box 3–1   Threats to the persistence of small populations

The primary impacts of habitat loss and fragmentation on wildlife populations are a reduction in population size and increased isolation from other populations. Small and isolated populations are more vulnerable to decline than are large populations. Documented examples of species' extinctions have frequently shown an initial pattern of major range reduction and fragmentation followed by successive extinctions of local populations until none are left (e.g. Petterson 1985).

Why are small populations vulnerable to decline and extinction? First, both small and large populations are subject to on-going disturbance processes in the landscape, such as continued habitat loss and fragmentation, increased predation from introduced predators, degradation of habitats, and altered food supply. A large population size and a widespread distribution are likely to provide a better buffer against these deterministic processes.

Second, small populations are more sensitive than large populations to at least four sources of chance variation (Shaffer 1981; Soulé 1986; Simberloff 1988; Caughley 1994).

- *Demographic stochasticity* refers to random variation in population parameters such as birth rate, death rate and sex ratio. For example, if a small population of a short-lived species experiences, by chance, a low birth rate in two successive years, the immediate probability of survival of the population may be greatly reduced.

- *Genetic stochasticity* refers to random genetic processes that can lead to a loss of genetic variation and a reduced capacity for a population to resist recessive lethal alleles, or to respond to changing environmental conditions. Inbreeding depression, genetic drift and a founder effect can all contribute to a loss of genetic variation in small populations.

- *Environmental stochasticity* is the random variation in environmental processes that can affect a population, such as fluctuations in temperature, rainfall, food resources, and populations of predators and competitors.

- *Natural catastrophes* such as floods, fire, drought, hurricanes and earthquakes, occur at irregular intervals and can have a major effect on population survival. Wildfire, for example, is a natural but irregular event in many forest ecosystems. Localized populations of animals may be eliminated but in extensive tracts of forest there are always small refuges that are not burned. However, in fragmented environments, small isolated remnants can be totally burned and the local population of a species eliminated.

- The 'patchy population' model does not assume the presence of a mainland population but is based on a set of isolated local populations that each have a finite probability of extinction (Harrison 1991; Merriam 1991; Opdam 1991). The size of each local population and the spatial arrangement within the set of such populations are the main determinants of colonization and extinction, and therefore of the dynamic distribution and status of the species at the regional scale. Depending on the level of dispersal between local populations, such patchy populations will vary along a gradient between a 'typical' metapopulation and what is, in effect, a single dynamic population.

The essential elements of a metapopulation are a set of distinct local populations that are connected by movements of animals. Extinctions and colonization occur within the local populations, resulting in a pattern of distribution that changes over time (Opdam 1991; Villard *et al.* 1992). However, movement of animals between local populations can not occur unless the animals have some way of actually getting there. The ability of animals to move through the landscape is crucial to the way a metapopulation functions (Hansson 1991; Taylor *et al.* 1993). If local populations are isolated and movement between them is limited, the likelihood of recolonisation following local extinction events will be low. Alternatively, if local populations are connected allowing more frequent movements, extinctions should be less frequent and recolonization more rapid, thus tending to increase the stability of the total population at the regional level (Fahrig and Merriam 1994). Consequently, habitat configurations that assist movements of animals through the landscape will have benefits for the overall persistence of the species.

In the real world, patches of habitat vary greatly in the resources they provide for animals and in the disturbance they experience. Consequently, some populations can be regarded as 'sources' that produce a nett surplus of animals that are available as potential colonists to other habitat patches. On the other hand, 'sinks' are those populations in which mortality exceeds natality and the persistence of the population depends on a regular influx of immigrants (Pulliam 1988; Pulliam and Danielson 1991; Dunning *et al.* 1992). There are, as yet, limited data on the relative frequency of sources and sinks in natural environments but theoretical models suggest that the relative proportions of each and the level of dispersal between them, may have a significant influence on regional population dynamics and species conservation.

The metapopulation concept has largely replaced island biogeography as a theoretical basis for understanding the dynamics of animal populations in fragmented environments. While it has value as a conceptual framework, there is limited evidence of its practical value and predictive ability in wildlife management and conservation biology (but see Harms and Opdam 1990; Opdam *et al.* 1995). Particular challenges include the need for models that incorporate real-world variation in patch size, quality and the dispersal ability of species through the landscape (Fahrig and Merriam 1994). There is also a need to carefully define what constitutes extinction and colonization (see Haila *et al.* 1993a) and to gain a better appreciation of the actual likelihood of species turnover at scales that are relevant to conservation in a particular region. Colonization and extinction events may regularly occur in very small fragments in farmland (Fahrig and Merriam 1994) but this is unlikely to be true (or possible) for nature reserves that form the core of a national conservation network.

The metapopulation approach, therefore, recognizes the importance of movements of animals among patches of habitat and disjunct populations in order to:

- supplement local populations that are declining;

- recolonize habitats where populations have become locally extinct;

- colonize new habitats as they become available.

This is a species-level approach and the benefits of connectivity are measured in terms of the persistence of viable populations of the target species in the landscape or region.

Landscape ecology

Landscape ecology is an emerging discipline that seeks to develop an integrated, holistic understanding of environments at the scale of whole landscapes. It recognizes that all landscapes, those largely natural in form as well as those heavily modified by humans, are mosaics of different types of habitats. The focus is on spatial patterns within such landscape mosaics, how spatial patterns influence ecological processes and how the landscape mosaic changes through time (Forman and Godron 1986; Merriam 1988; Turner 1989; Hansson and Angelstam 1991; Forman 1995; Hansson *et al.* 1995). Thus, landscape ecology provides a broad framework for exploring the ecological function of habitat fragments in developed environments and the benefits of connectivity and interchange between fragments in sustaining local and regional population dynamics (Noss 1983, 1987; Forman and Godron 1981, 1986; Harris and Gallagher 1989; Forman 1991, 1995).

Movements of animals, water and wind through landscape mosaics, and the flow of materials, energy and nutrients that are transported in this way, are central to how the overall landscape functions and to its ecological sustainability (Hobbs 1993a; Forman 1995). These flows through the landscape are clearly influenced by the spatial pattern and composition of different habitats. Consequently, changes in landscape patterns by clearing and fragmentation, by increased isolation or the imposition of artificial barriers, or by restoration and revegetation, have strong influences on movement patterns – not only of animals but also on the flow of other biotic and abiotic components such as plants, weeds, seeds, fertilizer, snow, dust, salt and so on.

The flow of species and materials through the landscape occurs in a variety of ways. In some situations movements may be direct, crossing any boundaries that are encountered. A fox moving through farmland, for example, may move directly across open fields, through cropland and into a woodland, readily crossing the boundary between each habitat type. However, in many situations movements of animals, water and wind tend to follow the same type of habitat or landscape element, and minimize the crossing of boundaries. Consequently, by virtue of their homogeneity and their high structural connectivity, continuous linear habitats potentially have a key role as conduits for the flow of species and materials through the environment (Cantwell and Forman 1994). Stream systems are a good example. They are continuous linear habitats that effectively channel the movement of water, sediments and aquatic invertebrates for large distances in a downstream direction through the landscape, while the active movements of fish and aquatic mammals allow these animals to move upstream also, against the current.

It is important to note that linear habitats and other connecting habitats (or linkages) in the landscape, have broader ecological roles than just assisting the transport of animals and materials through the environment. They are an integral part of the landscape and contribute to its structure and function in other ways also (Fig. 3–3) (Forman 1991, 1995).

- *Habitat for plants and animals.* There is abundant evidence that linkages such as riparian vegetation, hedgerows and broad forested strips between reserves provide habitat for a wide range of plants and animals. Numerous examples are discussed in Chapter 6.

- *Filters or barriers to the movement of certain species.* Naturally-linear features such as streams can form a boundary to animal home ranges, to populations and even to taxonomic units (subspecies or species) when there is effective isolation of populations on either side. There are striking examples of major rivers, such as the Amazon in South America, that form boundaries between subspecies of animals (Ayres and Clutton-Brock 1992). Isolation by natural barriers is a part of natural landscape processes. In contrast, disturbance corridors of human origin (such as highways, canals, pipelines, railway lines, transmission clearings) are imposing an ever-growing network of partial or complete barriers through the landscape (Klein 1971; Oxley *et al.* 1974; Singer 1975; Campbell 1981; Mader 1984, 1988; Bennett 1991; Askins 1994). The isolating effect on wildlife populations that results from these linear disturbance strips is a major conservation concern.

- *Sources and sinks for environmental and biotic effects.* Linear habitats and other linkages interact in numerous ways with their surrounding environment. They may provide shelter, nesting sites or refuge for species that live in the surrounding environment (and thereby act as a sink); or animals within the linear habitat may move out to forage in adjacent habitats (and thereby they act as a source). Road systems, for example, are a source of chemical and physical pollutants from cars and they may introduce invasive plants and animals into environments that the road passes through (Bennett 1991). Conversely, riparian vegetation is well known as a buffer or sink that limits the flow of chemicals, nutrients and particulate matter into streams (Binford and Bucheneau 1993).

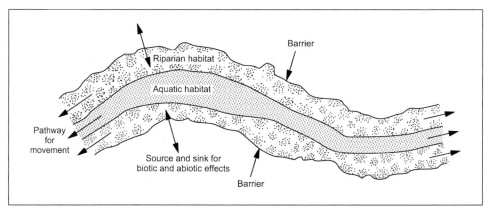

Fig. 3–3   **Diagrammatic representation of a stream illustrating four main functions of a linkage in the landscape. The riparian and aquatic zones: (i) provide a habitat for plants and animals; (ii) provide a pathway for movement of animals through the surrounding environment; (iii) pose a barrier or filter to the movements of certain animals; and (iv) are a source and sink for interactions with the surrounding environment. From Bennett (1990a).**

Landscape ecology is based on the premise that both natural environments and developed environments are mosaics, and that if we wish to conserve species and communities we must understand their capacity to live within and move through such mosaics. In relatively natural landscapes the capacity of animals to move influences not only the status of populations in different habitat patches but, because animals are also vectors for the flow of energy, nutrients and other biota (such as parasites, seeds and spores), their movements also influence ecological processes in the environment. It can be expected, therefore, that in human-dominated landscapes the ability of animals to move among habitat patches also has a strong influence on sustainability of populations and ecological processes.

Summary

The major conceptual approaches that underpin present understanding of how animals live in fragmented landscapes, each implicitly recognize the necessity for animals to be able to move between habitat and resource patches if their effective long-term conservation is to be achieved. Pragmatic observations by field biologists recognize that in certain circumstances animals must be assisted to traverse inhospitable environments and to cross ecological barriers on daily, regular or migratory movements. The equilibrium theory of island biogeography predicts that increased movements of animals will sustain a greater species richness in isolates by enhancing the rate of species colonisation and reducing the rate of species extinctions. Metapopulation models take a species-level approach and advocate the importance of movements between habitat patches to supplement local populations that are declining, to recolonize habitats where local populations have disappeared, and to colonize new habitats as they become available. Landscape ecology seeks to understand how land mosaics are structured, how they function and how they change over time. The flow of energy, nutrients, biota and abiotic matter through the mosaic depends on three primary vectors; wind, water and animals. Movement of animals, therefore, is not only critical to the survival of local populations, but also to the ecological function of the wider landscape.

PART 2

VALUES OF LINKAGES

4   CONNECTIVITY AND
       WILDLIFE CONSERVATION

The first part of this book has addressed the issues and theoretical considerations that have led many people – scientists, planners and land managers – to recognize the importance of maintaining connectivity for species, communities and ecological processes within developed landscapes. The theme of this second part is the values of linkages that achieve such connectivity. Attention is given to different types of linkages that promote landscape connectivity, to the benefits of linkages in assisting movements of animals, and to the role of linkages as ecological elements in the landscape.

This chapter considers how connectivity can be achieved in the landscape by different types of habitat configurations and emphasizes the importance of considering both the spatial and temporal scales at which connectivity is required. It concludes by summarising and discussing the proposed advantages and disadvantages of linkages.

Corridors, stepping stones and other habitat configurations to enhance connectivity

How can landscape connectivity be maintained most effectively for a particular species or community? Are there certain arrangements or configurations of habitats that are more effective than others? Do all species require specific linkages to move through developed landscapes?

Animal species vary greatly in their level of habitat specialisation and their tolerance to habitat disturbance and change. These attributes are important influences on how they perceive a particular landscape and the level of connectivity that it affords. Some species are tolerant of human land use and are able to live in, and freely move through, a patchwork of degraded natural habitats and anthropogenic environments. Such species generally do not require special structures or arrangements of habitat to maintain connectivity. For example, Cabbage White Butterflies readily move through disturbed environments, and even highly-developed landscapes may not be hostile to their dispersal (Fahrig and Paloheimo 1988). In contrast, there are many organisms that are sensitive to habitat change and degradation and whose survival and movements are limited in heavily-disturbed landscapes. Bird species dependent on the tropical forest understorey are an example of those with limited tolerance, that find cleared land an almost impenetrable barrier (Newmark 1991). For these species, survival and maintenance of connectivity in disturbed landscapes depends on the provision of suitable habitat.

A primary distinction can be drawn, therefore, between species that require no particular type or pattern of habitat to maintain landscape connectivity and those that do require some type and arrangement of suitable habitat. Few species fall into the former category: those that do are unlikely to be of concern from a conservation perspective because of their wide tolerance of disturbed environments. Subsequent discussion in this book relates primarily to species in the latter category, that are not ubiquitous in disturbed landscapes. These species can be envisaged as occurring along a gradient of tolerance to habitat disturbance.

Landscape connectivity can be achieved for animal species in two main ways (Fig. 4–1): by managing the whole landscape mosaic to promote movement and population continuity, or by managing specific habitats within the landscape to achieve this purpose. Clearly, the most desirable alternative is for the whole landscape to be managed in a way that maintains connectivity for species, communities and ecological processes. This approach is especially suitable for species that perceive the landscape as a mosaic of habitats of varying suitability, none of which are hostile. These animals may not live or reproduce in all parts of the mosaic but are able to move among most habitats to obtain access to resources such as food and shelter, or to move between local populations.

Alternatively, for species that perceive the landscape as comprised of suitable patches of habitat set within a matrix of generally unsuitable or hostile environments, landscape connectivity depends on the availability and arrangement of suitable habitats. Either continuous habitat corridors or discrete stepping stones of favoured habitat may assist individuals to move through the inhospitable matrix. This approach depends on identifying and managing specific habitats for wildlife.

Habitat mosaics

In some situations, such as the sustainable use of rangelands for pastoral activities or forests used for timber production, human land use results in modification, rather than total removal and loss, of natural habitats. Frequently, the result is a habitat mosaic in which the boundaries between undisturbed vegetation and the modified states may be poorly defined and occur as mosaics or gradients rather than as sharp discontinuities (Fig. 4–1a). A primary distinction between 'suitable' and 'unsuitable' habitats in the landscape is not obvious; rather, many species use a range of habitats, at least to a limited extent. This type of habitat mosaic has also been termed a 'variegated habitat' (McIntyre and Barrett 1992; McIntyre 1994), as an alternative to the more common concept of fragmented habitats (Box 4–1).

Connectivity in such landscapes depends on species using the mosaic of natural and modified vegetation to move between resources or local populations. Movement is not dependent on an arrangement of strips or patches of favoured habitat, but on use of the whole mosaic. Parts of the mosaic will be suitable for a particular species to live in, other parts may be unsuitable to live within but do not inhibit movements, while some parts may be relatively inhospitable.

Management of the whole landscape as a habitat mosaic is likely to be an effective way to provide connectivity in situations where:

- a large part of the landscape will remain in a natural or semi-natural form;

- the species or communities of concern have a high level of tolerance to existing land uses;

- the goal is to protect wide-ranging species that require large areas of habitat.

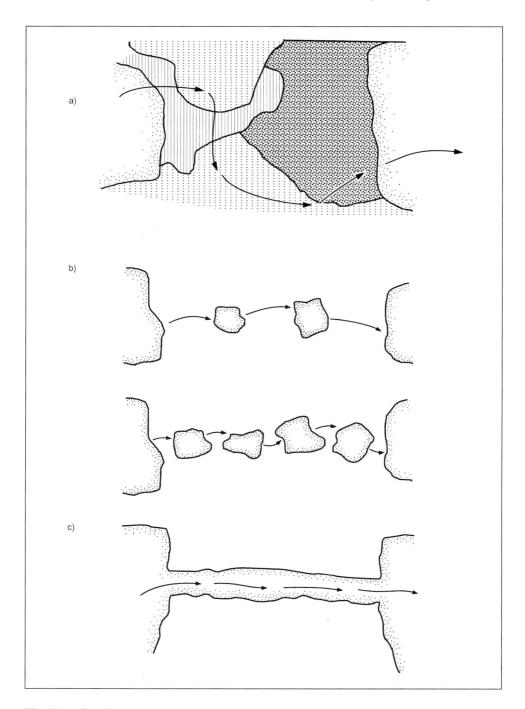

Fig. 4–1   Landscape connectivity may be achieved in two main ways: (a) by managing the entire
landscape mosaic to facilitate movement; or (b) and (c) by maintaining specific
habitats that assist movement through an inhospitable environment. These patterns of
habitat may be in the form of (b) stepping stones of various sizes and spacing, or (c)
habitat corridors that provide a continuous connection of favoured habitat.

Box 4–1   Birds in a variegated habitat, New England Tablelands, Australia

In the New England tablelands of New South Wales, Australia, the agricultural landscape does not conform to the 'isolates of habitat in a sea of developed land' model, typical of many other rural regions of Australia where less than 10% of the natural vegetation remains. Rather, much of the farmland retains a scattering of sparse tree cover and native grassland amongst forest and woodland patches of varying size, disturbance and management history (McIntyre and Barrett 1992; Barrett *et al.* 1994; McIntyre 1994). In total, about 50% of the tablelands retains tree cover in various forms, together comprising what has been termed a 'variegated habitat' for the flora and fauna.

Of a total of 137 species of land birds known from the region, about half (68 species) are regarded as common within the rural habitat mosaic. Others have declined in status, some have become locally extinct, while others are believed never to have been common in this area. Barrett *et al.* (1994) suggested that an important priority for conservation of the avifauna is to maintain a mosaic of semi-natural habitats within the farmland environment, rather than directing attention to securing a few large reserves. Only 17 species are believed to be especially dependent on large blocks of greater than 400ha and many of these have distributions that are marginal to the region. The majority of the present avifauna can be conserved by working with landholders to maximize the health of the woodland patches, many of which are greatly disturbed and degraded from grazing by stock and dieback of trees. Patches of woodland larger than 20ha are particularly valuable. Landscape connectivity for most birds can be achieved by maintaining the diffuse mosaic of forest, open woodland and scattered trees (Barrett *et al.* 1994).

An outlook across a variegated landscape in the New England Tablelands region, New South Wales, Australia. Tree cover occurs as a mosaic rather than as distinct patches and strips. (Photo: G. Barrett).

It is a less effective or unsuitable approach in landscapes that have been substantially modified, especially for species intolerant of disturbance or for maintaining connectivity for communities and processes (Table 4–1).

The concept of a landscape habitat mosaic is a promising framework for understanding the dispersion of animals in forests used sustainably for timber production (Franklin 1989, 1992; Simberloff 1993). Timber harvesting typically results in a spatial mosaic of recently-harvested coupes, patches of young and old regeneration, strips of unharvested forest along streams and on steep slopes, and some remnants of intact older forest. Although much of the forest is modified into different states, it is not completely cleared and replaced with an inhospitable matrix as occurs in agricultural croplands or suburban environments. Even though regenerating forests may not provide all of the resources that a particular species needs to survive (such as large hollow-bearing trees), they may pose little resistance to the movement of many animals between protected areas of forest where these resources are available. The whole mosaic can be managed to maintain connectivity for wildlife while permitting a level of resource harvest.

Table 4–1 Summary of the potential effectiveness of different types of linkages in landscapes that have experienced differing levels of environmental disturbance.

Symbols indicate that the linkage is likely to be: *** an effective approach; * somewhat effective; or – unlikely to be an effective approach.

Type of use	Type of linkage		
	Habitat mosaic	Specific habitats	
		Stepping stones	Habitat corridors
A. Less-disturbed landscapes			
Species tolerant of habitat disturbance	***	***	–
Species intolerant of habitat disturbance	*	*	***
Wide-ranging and mobile species	***	***	*
Communities and ecological processes	***	*	***
B. Greatly-disturbed landscapes			
Species tolerant of habitat disturbance	*	***	*
Species intolerant of habitat disturbance	–	*	***
Wide-ranging and mobile species	*	***	*
Communities and ecological processes	–	–	***

Habitat corridors

An effective habitat corridor provides a continuous, or near continuous, link of suitable habitat through an inhospitable environment. Such corridors have been variously termed 'wildlife corridors', 'dispersal corridors', or 'movement corridors' where they are known to be used by animals for movement (Harris and Scheck 1991; Newmark 1991; Simberloff *et al.* 1992; Noss 1993).

Habitat corridors are likely to be a more effective means of promoting landscape connectivity (Table 4–1):

- where a large part of the landscape is modified and inhospitable to native species;

- for species that are habitat specialists or have obligate dependence on undisturbed habitats;

- for species that have a limited scale of movement in relation the distance to be traversed. In these situations, the habitat corridor must provide resources to sustain resident individuals or a population;

- where the goal is to maintain continuity of populations between habitats, rather than simply fostering infrequent movements of individuals;

- where the goal is the continuity of entire faunal communities;

- where maintenance of ecosystem processes requires continuous habitat for their function.

There are many everyday examples of habitat corridors that link fragments of natural vegetation at the local scale in developed landscapes. Linear features such as hedgerows, fencerows, plantations, remnant roadside vegetation, streamside strips and unlogged strips of forest can all function as linkages. Similarly, broad tracts of natural vegetation that link nature reserves or other large natural areas at the landscape, regional, or even continental scales, also function as habitat corridors (they are here termed landscape linkages).

A distinction between different types of habitat corridors based on their origin (Forman and Godron 1986) is useful because it indicates the likely composition and quality of the habitat for wildlife. Corridors of different origin also differ in the type of ongoing management that they require.

Natural habitat corridors, such as streams and their associated riparian vegetation (Fig. 4–2), usually follow topographic or environmental contours and are the result of natural environmental processes.

Remnant habitat corridors, such as strips of unlogged forest within clear-cuts, natural woodland along roadsides, or natural habitats retained as links between nature reserves, are the result of clearing, alteration or disturbance to the surrounding environment.

Regenerated habitat corridors occur as the result of regrowth of a strip of vegetation that was formerly cleared or disturbed. Fencerows and hedges composed of plants that originate from rootstocks, soil-stored seed, or seeds dispersed by wind or birds, are examples.

Planted habitat corridors, such as farm plantations, windbreaks or shelterbelts, many hedgerows and some urban greenbelts have been established by humans. They frequently are composed of non-indigenous plant species, or exotic plants.

Disturbance habitat corridors include railway lines, roads, cleared transmission lines and other features that result from sustained disturbance within a linear strip. The connecting feature is a line of disturbed land that differs from the surroundings. Many disturbance corridors, such as powerline easements (Fig. 4–3), have detrimental consequences for natural environments (Rich *et al.* 1994).

Fig. 4–2 Streams and their associated riparian vegetation are examples of natural habitat corridors that result from natural environmental processes. (Photo: A. Bennett).

Stepping stones

Stepping stones of suitable habitat enhance connectivity in developed landscapes for species able to make short movements through disturbed environments (Fig. 4–1b). Connectivity is achieved by a sequence of short movements or 'hops' from stepping stone to stepping stone along the length of the linkage, or by the combined dispersal movements of numerous individuals moving between populations resident within a chain of stepping stone habitats (Box 4–2).

Fig. 4–3   Transmission line clearings are examples of disturbance corridors that are maintained by continued human intervention. Near Ottawa, southern Ontario, Canada. (Photo: A. Bennett).

Stepping stones are likely to be an effective approach to maintaining landscape connectivity:

- for species that regularly move between different resource patches in the landscape (such as temporally varying food sources, or spatially separated nesting and foraging habitat);

- for species that are relatively mobile and able to move substantial distances in relation to the intervening distance between fragments;

- for species that are tolerant of disturbed landscapes, although not necessarily able to live within the modified zone;

- where the objective is to maintain continuity of ecological processes that depend on animal movements and the animal vectors are capable of movement across gaps.

In the same manner as habitat corridors, stepping stone habitats have different origins. They may be *natural* patches, such as a chain of wetlands across a region or patches of moist rainforest within surrounding drier forests. Small *remnant* patches of vegetation or incomplete sections of remnant linear habitats can also function as stepping stones. Alternatively, stepping stone habitats may be of human origin, such as plantations, artificial ponds or a sequence of urban parks across a metropolitan area.

Connectivity at different scales

Spatial scale

The natural world is complex with a host of ecological processes operating at different spatial and temporal scales. If the goal of biodiversity conservation is to preserve viable natural communities and the integrity of ecological processes, then conservation strategies in developed landscapes must ensure that effective connectivity is maintained at a wide range of spatial scales (Noss and Harris 1986; Noss 1991).

At the simplest level, it is obvious that different groups of animals display markedly different levels of mobility and operate in the environment at different spatial scales. Birds, bats and flying insects have greater mobility than non-flying species such as geckos, centipedes or terrestrial rodents. Large-bodied animals tend to move further on a regular basis than do smaller species, and carnivores generally forage over a wider range than sedentary herbivores. These different scales of movement mean that there is a need for suitable linkages between resources at a scale relevant to each species.

Even within similar groups of species, closer examination reveals a range of different movement patterns at a range of scales. Within a community of forest birds, for example, whether in Africa, South America or Asia, there are likely to be species that correspond to the following categories:

- resident species that are relatively sedentary, living within the same habitat year-round;

- residents that move regularly between several habitats to obtain different resources (food, shelter);

Box 4–2   How do animals move through linkages?

Animals undertake several types of movements through linkages, each of which may enhance continuity between populations and contribute to maintenance of ecological processes in patchy environments (Bennett 1990a).

First, individual animals may undertake single direct movements between resource patches, using linkages to pass through inhospitable environments. Such direct movements along the entire length of a link are likely to be made by large animals, or those that regularly move at a greater spatial scale than the dimensions of the linkage. A mammalian predator foraging within an agricultural landscape, for example, may move through a habitat corridor in a few minutes. Animals using tunnels to cross local barriers, or moving daily between nesting and foraging habitats, also undertake direct movements.

Second, movements through linkages may be punctuated by one or more pauses. Individuals that forage as they move may pause several hours, while migratory birds or mammals may pause for days or weeks, using the link as 'stopover' to forage or rest before continuing the journey (see Boxes 5–2, 5–3). However, the same individual moves the entire distance through the link.

Third, where a species is resident within a linkage, numerous short movements of individuals to and from, and within the link, can achieve effective population continuity. The combined effects of numerous movements results in demographic exchange and gene flow between patch populations connected in this way. Reproduction within the linkage habitats provides an additional source of dispersing animals and adds to overall population size. For linkages of sufficient size and habitat quality to support resident populations (especially broad landscape links), this form of movement is the most effective way that the link can function. It is the only way that linkages can function effectively where the scale of movement of organisms is small in relation to the intervening distance, or where the goal is the continuity of entire plant and animal communities.

- species that display irregular movements between habitats to exploit seasonally-varying resources such as fruits and nectar;

- species that undertake annual migrations, either to nearby areas (e.g. altitudinal migrants) or to different geographic regions.

In addition, the life-history requirements of many species of animals mean that individuals move at different spatial scales during different stages of their life. Frogs generally spend the first part of life as a tadpole in water, then disperse to terrestrial habitats and later may migrate between terrestrial and aquatic environments for breeding. Migratory species undertake long distance migrations at regular periods during their lives. Most species of birds and mammals have a phase when individuals disperse from the natal range, typically moving several orders of magnitude farther than daily movements.

Box 4–2 (cont.)

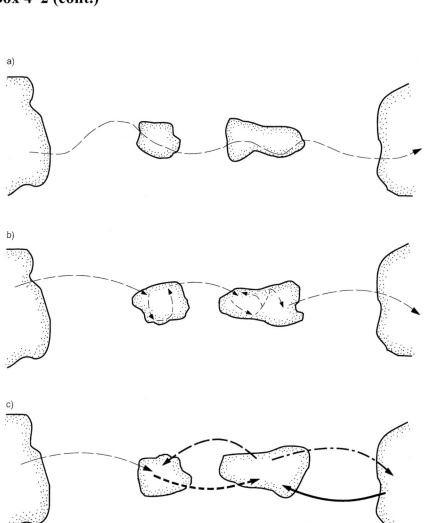

a)

b)

c)

Diagrammatic representation of three main ways in which linkages facilitate continuity between populations: (a) direct movement by single individuals; (b) movement by a single animal punctuated by pauses of various lengths within the link; and, (c) gene flow through a population resident within the linkage, resulting from the combined movements of a number of individuals.

The essential point is that for animal species and communities to thrive in landscapes heavily modified by people, connectivity within the landscape must be sufficient for individuals to move to obtain the resources they need at different stages of life. There is no general solution for a linkage that will meet the requirements of all species. A link that is effective for one species may be ineffective for others that move at different scales. Different types of ecological linkages are needed for movements spanning different scales. The type, quality and scale of the linkage must match the needs and scale of movement of the target species.

In Table 4–2, examples are presented of different forms of habitat configuration that can enhance connectivity across three main scales: the local scale (less than 1km); the landscape scale (from 1–10s of kms); and the regional or biogeographic scale (100s – 1000s of kms). At the local scale, for example, a range of linear habitats such as hedgerows, roadside vegetation, or forest corridors may assist animals to move from metres to kilometres through modified lands. This is the scale at which movements through linkages have most frequently been observed (Chapter 5). To maintain connectivity for animal species and ecological processes at the landscape scale, perhaps between conservation reserves, an appropriate habitat corridor may be a river with wide riparian vegetation or a broad strip of natural vegetation deliberately reserved for this purpose. At the biogeographic scale, natural features such as major river systems or mountain ranges can provide continuity of habitat (Bridgewater 1987).

Table 4–2   Landscape configurations to enhance connectivity for animal populations at different spatial scales.

Landscape configuration	Local scale (1 km)	Landscape scale (1 – 10s kms)	Regional or biogeographic scale (100 – 1000s kms)
Habitat corridor	hedgerows; fencerows; streams; roadsides; forest corridors; underpasses	rivers and associated riparian vegetation; broad links between reserves	major river systems; mountain ranges; isthmus between land masses
Stepping stones	patches of plants; small woods; plantations; chains of small wetlands	series of small reserves; woodland patches in farmland; urban parks	chains of islands in an archipelago; wetlands along waterfowl flight paths; alpine habitats along a mountain chain
Habitat mosaics	patchily cleared vegetation in farmland; mosaic of gardens and parks in cities	mosaics of regenerating and old-growth forest in forest blocks	regional soil mosaics supporting different vegetation communities

There is a clear need to develop a better understanding of the use of linkages at different scales by different species. Most documented examples have been at the local scale where animals have been observed using habitat corridors or stepping stones to move short distances through cleared land, generally in agricultural settings. Yet it is at the landscape, regional and continental scales that connectivity is particularly important in conservation strategy. It is at this scale that many proposals for land management are being made – linkages between conservation reserves, or the development of regional conservation networks (Harris and Scheck 1991; Ahern 1995; Jongman 1995; Kubeš 1996) (see Chapter 9 for examples).

Temporal scale

The temporal scale is also important in planning for landscape connectivity. Natural environments are not fixed, but change through time – although this is not always recognized in management programmes. Changes to habitats may result from natural processes as part of vegetation succession (such as changes in understorey structure in response to fire), or from disturbance regimes arising in the surrounding environment. The latter changes, such as weed invasion, overgrazing by domestic animals, and harvesting of natural resources, are increasingly important in heavily modified landscapes.

These changes mean that particular habitat patches or types of resources change in suitability over time for animal species, so that some populations will fluctuate in density or disappear. For individuals and populations to make full use of resources at the appropriate time there must be adequate connectivity to allow them access to those resource patches. Populations must be able to 'track' the shifting pattern of suitable habitats through time (Thomas 1994). For some invertebrates, such as butterflies, habitat suitability may change quickly over a few years; while for vertebrates dependent on old trees in forests, changing suitability of habitats may extend over several centuries. Long-term planning is required to ensure that adequate connectivity is incorporated into land management in developed landscapes.

Habitats *within* linkages are also dynamic and change in quality through time. This means that the ability of a linkage to fulfil its role changes and that active management may be needed to sustain its function over time. Stepping-stone patches of grassland, for example, that provide a pathway for butterflies to recolonize a shifting habitat mosaic (see Box 2–5) may themselves become unsuitable and limit movements of individuals to other patches. Active management to maintain habitat quality or to provide alternative stepping-stone pathways must be developed.

Advantages and disadvantages of linkages

Practical measures to promote connectivity of habitats in disturbed landscapes are being widely adopted in land management, but the concept is not without criticism and debate. As outlined in Chapter 1, concerns have centred on three main points (these have been particularly directed at 'corridors'):

- there is insufficient scientific evidence to demonstrate the benefits of corridors;

- corridors and other linkages may have negative effects that outweigh any benefits;

- corridors may not be a cost-effective option in comparison with other ways of using scarce conservation resources.

It is important that these points are considered. They are each addressed below, although from the broader perspective of evaluating landscape connectivity, rather than habitat corridors *per se*.

Inadequate scientific evidence

The proposed advantages and disadvantages of linkages have been canvassed by numerous authors (Ambuel and Temple 1983; Noss 1987; Simberloff and Cox 1987; Bennett 1990a; Henein and Merriam 1990; Soulé 1991; Soulé and Gilpin 1991; Hobbs 1992; Simberloff *et al.* 1992; Newmark 1993; Lindenmayer 1994; Wilson and Lindenmayer 1995). The main points on each side, from the perspective of biodiversity conservation, are summarized in Table 4–3 (adapted from Noss 1987). The potential benefits of linkages for human recreation and landscape aesthetics, for example, are not included here (see Forman 1991; Ahern 1995).

Table 4–3 Reported advantages and disadvantages of linkages for biodiversity conservation.

Reported advantages	Reported disadvantages
1 Assist the movement of individuals through disturbed landscapes, including: • wide-ranging species that move between habitats on a regular basis; • nomadic or migratory species that move between irregular or seasonally-varying resources; • species that move between habitats at different stages of their life-cycle.	1 Increase immigration rates to habitat isolates which could: • facilitate the spread of unwanted species such as pests, weeds and exotic species; • facilitate the spread of disease; • introduce new genes which could disrupt local adaptations and co-adapted gene complexes (outbreeding depression), and promote hybridization between previously disjunct taxonomic forms (races, sub-species).
2 Increase immigration rates to habitat isolates which could: • maintain a higher species richness and diversity; • supplement declining populations, thus reducing their risk of extinction; • allow re-establishment following local extinction; • enhance genetic variation and reduce the risk of inbreeding depression.	2 Increase exposure of animals to: • predators, hunting or poaching by humans, or other sources of mortality (e.g. road kills); • competitors or parasites.
3 Facilitate the continuity of natural ecological processes in developed landscapes.	3 Act as 'sink habitats' in which mortality exceeds reproduction, and thus functions as a 'drain' on the regional population.
4 Provide habitat for many species including: • refuge and shelter for animals moving through the landscape; • plants and animals living within linkages.	4 Facilitate the spread of fire or other abiotic disturbances.
5 Provide ecosystem services such as maintenance of water quality, reduction of erosion, and stability of hydrologic cycles.	5 Establishment and management costs could reduce the resources available for more effective conservation measures, such as the purchase of habitats for endangered species.

Evidence in support of the proposed benefits of linkages is the theme of the next two chapters. In Chapter 5, examples are presented of the way in which linkages may assist the movements of animals through disturbed landscapes. This is followed by examples of studies that illustrate the types of conservation benefits gained from such movements. Subsequently, in Chapter 6 the benefits of linkages as habitats for species and communities are reviewed, as is their wider role in the ecosystem.

While it is essential that the benefits of linkages be scientifically demonstrated as a basis for their use in land management, it is also appropriate to approach this issue from a different perspective. We can also ask 'Is there sufficient scientific evidence to demonstrate that the *loss* of ecological linkages has *no detrimental effect* on the conservation of species and communities in fragmented landscapes?' This question is equally relevant because in most proposals to conserve linkages, decisions must be made about the management priority and resources to be given to habitats that *already exist*. That is, in most situations the linking habitat already exists but is not designated or managed as a link. The issue then relates to how such linking habitats should be managed in the future. Acceptance of the view that linkages have no merit because their scientific value has not been adequately demonstrated could, unfortunately, lead to loss of existing natural vegetation by neglect or lack of concern. A paucity of scientific data is not evidence against linkages, but a case for pursuing further and better studies to resolve the issue (Hobbs 1992). Several further points warrant consideration.

- Habitat connectivity is a characteristic feature of natural environments. Protection and restoration of connectivity is not an artificial change to the landscape: rather, it is the loss of connectivity and the isolation of natural environments that is an artefact of human land use (Noss 1991);

- The 'precautionary principle' demands that where knowledge is limited, the prudent alternative is to retain existing natural linkages in case they are beneficial (Hobbs 1992);

- The weight of evidence shows that isolation of populations and communities, through loss of intervening habitat, has a detrimental effect (Chapter 2).

Disadvantages may outweigh the advantages

A number of potential problems associated with habitat corridors have been identified (Table 4–3), which several workers suggest may outweigh the proposed benefits (Ambuel and Temple 1983; Simberloff and Cox 1987). These are important issues. They range from the possible spread of weeds, pests and disease, to the question of linkages acting as sink habitats in which high levels of mortality 'drain' the overall population. Several points are relevant.

- Environmental problems are most likely to accrue for linkages of human origin, especially if they attempt to link areas not naturally connected. Disturbance corridors, such as cleared powerline easements through natural forest, are examples where there may be significant negative effects (Rich *et al.* 1994).

- There is little evidence, as yet, in support of some concerns such as increased mortality in linkages or spread of disease. This does not mean these issues should be dismissed; rather, empirical studies and monitoring of existing linkages are required to evaluate these concerns.

- It is difficult to assess whether problems associated with linkages may compromise all, or only some, of the functions of a linkage. Weed invasion for example, is a problem typical of linear habitats (Loney and Hobbs 1991), but it may have little effect on the use of a linear habitat by canopy birds. Alternatively, a particular group of species may be greatly disadvantaged by poaching or hunting in a landscape link, but this may not affect its use by other organisms.

- The relative importance of these issues varies between linkages of different forms, dimensions and management history. Many concerns can be adressed through management, and by the location and dimensions of habitats protected as linkages (Chapter 7).

Linkages may not be a cost-effective option

This issue is difficult to address in general terms because it requires a case-by-case approach to assessing costs and benefits for particular situations. Clearly, examples do arise where this concern is valid, where proposed linkages are likely to have limited value for nature conservation in comparison with alternative uses of conservation resources. Several points can be made in relation to this issue.

- Use of conservation resources on linkages that have limited biological value can be minimized by carefully evaluating proposals prior to committing resources. A number of criteria for assessing the relative conservation priority of different linkages are outlined in Chapter 8, and a checklist of issues to be considered is also presented.

- Situations where linkages may not be cost-effective are likely to arise when habitats must be entirely re-established because the natural connecting vegetation has been destroyed. In such circumstances, not only is there the cost of revegetation, but also uncertainty as to whether the natural ecosystem can be effectively restored.

- The outcome of a cost-benefit analysis depends on the attributes included in the assessment. To assess the benefits of linkages only in terms of their ability to facilitate direct movements of individual animals (Simberloff *et al.* 1992) is to ignore other ways in which they enhance connectivity for wildlife species (Box 4–2). It also overlooks their contribution as habitat and in maintaining ecosystem function in the local environment. These other 'non-movement' values are great for broad landscape linkages or for major riparian corridors, for example; or where connectivity is achieved through managing a mosaic of habitats across the landscape. Assessment of costs and benefits must take into account a range of such functions. In situations where vegetated links already exist, but are not designated as such, the cost relates to maintaining their ecological function in the longer term. This may be in the form of ongoing management or the cost of land purchase if current land uses are incompatible. However, there is an ecological loss if such existing vegetation, whether managed as a linkage or not, is destroyed or degraded. The cost of not managing the area as a linkage and having it subsequently degraded must also be included in the evaluation.

- Alternatives to linkages, such as deliberate translocation of animals (Simberloff and Cox 1987), must also be assessed for their relative cost and effectiveness as a wildlife conservation measure.

Summary

Landscape connectivity can be achieved for wildlife species and communities by managing the entire landscape mosaic, or by managing specific patterns of suitable habitat such as stepping stones or habitat corridors. The most suitable approach depends upon the extent of habitat modification in the landscape and on the species concerned, especially their tolerance of modified habitats. The most attractive option for maintaining connectivity is to manage entire habitat mosaics, but this is likely to be effective only where there is largely natural vegetative cover, or for species tolerant of habitat modification. Organisms move at a range of spatial scales, from metres to hundreds of kilometres. Conservation of biodiversity in developed environments requires measures that will maintain connectivity for species, communities and ecological processes at multiple scales. Maintenance of connectivity must also be addressed in the temporal scale, to allow species to 'track' changes in resource availability and habitat quality through time. The proposed benefits of enhanced connectivity result from an increased capacity of animals to move through disturbed landscapes, greater opportunities for dispersal to isolated habitats and populations, and greater likelihood of the continuity of ecological processes in patchy environments. Linkages that promote landscape connectivity may have substantial value as habitats for plants and animals, and also make an important contribution to other ecological processes in the landscape. Proposed disadvantages of linkages include their potential to spread pest species, disease or abiotic disturbance; the increased exposure of animals to predators, competitors or parasites; and the risk that assigning resources to maintenance of linkages will be less cost-effective than undertaking other conservation measures.

5   MOVEMENTS OF ANIMALS THROUGH LINKAGES

The purpose of this chapter is to examine the use of linkages as pathways for the movement of animals through inhospitable environments. First, examples are given to illustrate the different types of animal movements that can be assisted by linkages. These examples are based on data ranging from anecdotal observations through to detailed studies using radiotelemetry. It is important to note that in most cases the studies were not designed to directly examine the use of linkages. Second, a range of studies are reviewed that present evidence of the conservation benefits gained from enhanced connectivity in developed landscapes. These include experimental studies, inference from statistical models, simulation studies and associated field data, and studies of the use of tunnels and underpasses by animals.

Types of movements assisted by linkages

Movements on a daily or regular basis

The use of linkages on a daily or regular basis typically occurs when an animal shelters or breeds in one habitat and forages in other types of habitat that are separated by developed land (Box 5–1). Regular movements along habitat corridors have been reported for a number of species of cockatoos and parrots in Australia (Table 5–1). For example, the Regent Parrot nests in large tree hollows in mesic woodlands along the Murray River and feeds in nearby 'mallee' shrublands in the semi-arid environment of north-western Victoria, Australia (Burbidge 1985). During the breeding season birds commute daily between nesting habitat and foraging areas, their flight path generally above or alongside remnant roadside vegetation. The level of spatial separation between breeding habitat and blocks of foraging habitat appears to be important for this threatened species: the birds no longer nest along sections of the Murray River where clearing of mallee shrubland for farmland has resulted in separation of more than 10km between potential nesting and feeding areas (Burbidge 1985).

In Ontario, Canada, Blue Jays were observed closely following fencerows on flights of up to 4km, while carrying beech nuts from the forest to their winter caches (Johnson and Adkisson 1985). Of the birds observed, 91% followed the fencerows closely and only 9% flew over fields. The fencerows provide a travel pathway along which shelter from avian predators can be readily obtained. In Poland, movements of passerine birds between a pine forest and a lake littoral zone were found to be greater where a corridor of shrubs connected the two habitats than at a nearby site where they were separated by an expanse of grassy meadow (Dmowski and Kozakiewicz 1990). Birds were not prevented from moving to feed in the littoral zone by the absence of a connection but the shrub corridor increased the rate of movements that were undertaken, as measured by mist net captures.

Regular movements using linkages are made by wide-ranging species when their home range spans several areas of remnant vegetation, or a mosaic of habitat. Two species of large kangaroo, the Western Grey Kangaroo and Euro, include a number of patches of

Box 5–1   Flight paths of insectivorous bats in the Netherlands

Day shelters (roost sites) and nocturnal foraging areas for bats are often located far apart. In the Netherlands, observation and mapping of daily flight paths of 11 species of microchiropteran bats showed that flight paths were closely associated with linear habitats such as forest edges, paths, lanes, hedgerows and canals (Limpens and Kapteyn 1989; Verboom and Huitema 1997). Flight paths adjacent to tall wooded vegetation were those most frequently traversed throughout the summer activity period. These linear habitats were used by bats either as a direct flight path to a foraging area, as a flight path with associated foraging en route to feeding areas, or as an important foraging source in their own right.

Smaller species of bats, such as the Pipistrelle, which generally use a high frequency for echolocation and have a short sonar range, closely followed linear elements. Pipistrelles were rarely recorded in open areas such as fields. Larger species that use lower frequencies and have a longer sonar range, such as the Serotine Bat, appeared to be less restricted to linear habitats and more able to cross open spaces. Serotines were recorded from a similar proportion of sites close to linear habitats and in open field (Verboom and Huitema 1997).

Qualitative and quantitative comparisons between landscapes with different patterns of habitat have revealed differences in their use by bats. A dense network of flight paths and a larger number of bats were observed in a landscape where there was a well-developed system of linear habitats, and a much reduced extent of flight paths was observed where there were few connecting landscape elements (Limpens and Kapteyn 1989).

(a)   (b)

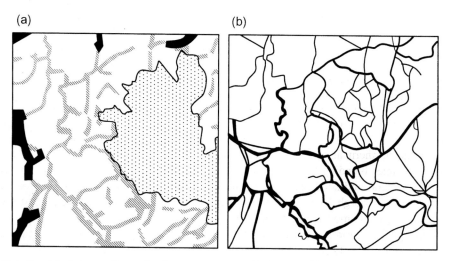

Relationship between linear landscape structure (a) and the flight paths of bats (b) in a landscape in the Netherlands with a dense network of linear habitats. Landscape structure in (a) is shown as: hatching = linear habitats with trees, stippling = woodland, and shaded = built up areas. Redrawn from Limpens and Kapteyn (1989) with permission, Vereniging voor Zoogdierkunde en Zoogdierbescherming.

remnant woodland or shrubland within their range in farmland in Western Australia (Arnold *et al.* 1991, 1993). Movements between fragments mainly follow strips of vegetation along roadsides or fencelines, or involve rapid transit across short gaps in farmland. Longer distance movements across farmland generally occur where fencelines with native vegetation and patches of trees provide stepping stones of cover. Broad stretches of cleared farmland that are too wide for animals to readily traverse set the boundaries for local populations (Arnold *et al.* 1993).

Radiotelemetry studies of Red Squirrels in Belgium (Wauters *et al.* 1994) found that adult squirrels used hedgerows to move between small woods within their home range to exploit food resources. The daily movements of the Copper Butterfly in farmland in Norway closely follow linear field boundaries, grassy banks and hedgerows, and rarely cross open fields (Fry and Main 1993).

Clearly, not all animals that regularly move between patchy resources need habitat links to facilitate their movements. Species that are tolerant of disturbed habitat or individuals that cross only short gaps in their habitat may do so readily. For example, Tawny Owls living in mainly cleared farmland in Britain were able to incorporate several small woods within their home range, apparently readily moving short distances across open land between woods (Redpath 1995).

Regular movements are also made by animals that live or forage within linear habitats. Aquatic animals such as River Otters and Platypus have elongated linear home ranges and regularly traverse up and down stream systems (Serena 1994).

Seasonal and migratory movements

Migratory movements are undertaken by a wide range of animals, primarily in response to environmental conditions that result in seasonal changes to the quality or abundance of their food resources. Migration can be defined as a 'round trip' movement within the lifespan of an individual, but typically it involves an annual departure from, and return to, a breeding area (Sinclair 1983). Other types of movement in response to fluctuating resources, that do not involve a return trip, have been termed emigration or nomadism.

Migratory movements occur at scales ranging from local movements of less than a kilometre between different vegetation types or altitudinal zones, to intercontinental movements such as those of many Palearctic and Nearctic waders that annually migrate between the northern and southern hemispheres. Neotropical migratory birds that move between summer breeding habitats in the forests of Canada and USA and overwintering habitats in central and southern America are a particularly well studied group (Keast and Morton 1980; Terborgh 1989). Altitudinal migration between habitats at higher and lower elevations is also common among some groups of animals. For example, at least 75 species of some 500 species of birds in the La Selva – Braulio Carillo region of Costa Rica undertake regular movements between montane and lowland forests (Loiselle and Blake 1992). At higher elevations in this region (1500–2000m) an even greater percentage of the bird community (40–45%) undertake such migration.

How important are linkages for migratory species? Many migratory animals are capable of moving through a range of vegetation types and generally do not require continuous corridors of favoured habitat for their journey. However, migration is not haphazard – most species follow well-defined routes, and linking habitats of various forms are used (Elphick 1995; Bildstein *et al.* 1995). The destruction of key elements of such linkages can have critical detrimental consequences for the species concerned (Box 5–2). Migratory shorebirds and waterfowl, for example, use a limited number of 'stopovers' along migration paths for feeding and shelter before continuing their journey. At these times a large proportion of the population can be concentrated in a relatively restricted area. Consequently, degradation or destruction of stopover wetland habitats, or excessive hunting at these points, can have a severe impact on migration and on overall population numbers and conservation status. Thus, game managers in North America, for example, have extensively mapped the migratory flyways of waterfowl and protection of major stopover points is a high priority (Peek 1986). Similarly, many birds of prey undertake annual north-south migrations in Europe, North America, South America, Africa and other areas, using established flight paths. Concentrations of birds occur at particular features, such as mountain ridges and passes, narrow coastal plains, isthmuses and peninsulas (Bildstein *et al.* 1995). The migrating birds are particularly vulnerable to hunters at these sites, and large numbers are deliberately killed. In these types of migratory movements, connectivity is enhanced at a broad spatial scale by protecting the strategic stopover points (stepping stones) along these continental and intercontinental migration pathways.

For large terrestrial herbivores in Africa, North America and Europe, human settlements and other developments that block traditional pathways are major impediments to migratory movements. Artificial linkages such as tunnels and highway underpasses have been employed by wildlife managers to overcome such barriers (see below). Maintenance of traditional migratory pathways for large mammals has been a primary reason for the establishment of a number of landscape linkages, especially in Africa (Baranga 1991; Mwalyosi 1991) (see examples in Chapter 9). Expansion of human settlements and agricultural croplands across migratory pathways, together with hunting and destruction of wild animals that feed in croplands, increasingly pose barriers to migration and the number of migrating animals dwindles and eventually ceases (Borner 1985; Baranga 1991). In the Tarangire National Park in Tanzania, large herds of ungulates, such as Zebra, Wildebeest, Hartebeest, Eland and Oryx, occur along the Tarangire River during the dry season but during the wet season they leave the park and disperse widely over the extensive surrounding grassy plains. Traditional migratory paths to the north are becoming blocked by large farms, other agricultural developments and human settlements, causing the movement of animals to be greatly reduced or stopped. Pathways to the east still remain open and are vital links between dry season and wet season habitats for about 55,000 migrating animals (Borner 1985). If the remaining migration pathways are eventually blocked it must inevitably decimate the herds of these species because the park, on its own, is inadequate to sustain this number of animals year-round.

Seasonal nomadic movements by species whose food resources vary in a relatively unpredictable manner may likewise be assisted by habitat corridors or stepping stone linkages. For example, frugivorous pigeons that feed mainly in rainforest patches in eastern Australia are adapted to using a resource that occurs naturally in insular patches among sclerophyll forest (Date *et al.* 1991). Remnants of rainforest and sclerophyll forest as well as patches of Camphor Laurel, an introduced fruiting tree, are used by pigeons and may provide stepping stones through farmland between the major tracts of rainforest remaining at coastal and high elevations (Date *et al.* 1991).

Table 5–1   Examples of animal movements using habitat linkages.

Species or group	Connecting feature	Description of use	Country	Reference
1 Daily or regular movements				
White-footed Mouse	fencerows	movement through farmland	Canada	Merriam & Lanoue (1990)
Red Squirrel	treerows, hedgerows	movements between feeding patches within range	Belgium	Wauters *et al.* (1994)
Eastern Chipmunk	fencerows	movements within home range	Canada	Bennett *et al.* (1994)
Cougar	canyon with degraded vegetation	regular movement between two mountain ranges	USA	Beier (1993)
Microchiropteran bats	hedges, hedgerows, lanes, paths	daily flight between roosts and foraging areas	Netherlands	Limpens *et al.* (1989)
Mountain Goat	highway underpass	regular movements to and from a natural mineral lick	USA	Singer *et al.* (1985)
Euro, Western Grey Kangaroo	roadside vegetation, small woodland patches	movement within sub-population range, encompassing multiple remnants in farmland	Australia	Arnold *et al.* (1991, 1993)
Regent Parrot	roadside shrubland	flight between nesting and foraging habitats	Australia	A. Bennett (pers. observ.)
Superb Parrot	roadside woodland	flight between nesting and foraging habitats	Australia	Webster & Ahern (1992)
White-tailed Black Cockatoo	remnant vegetation along roadside and rail line	foraging resource, movement between nesting and feeding habitats	Australia	Saunders (1980)
Pink Cockatoo	trees, patches of trees	flight from feeding flocks to nesting sites	Australia	Rowley & Chapman (1991)
Blue Jay	fencerows	flight paths to carry food to winter caches	Canada	Johnson & Adkisson (1985)
Brown Kiwi	small forest remnants	movement between habitats through cleared farmland	New Zealand	Potter (1990)

Table 5–1 Examples of animal movements using habitat linkages.(cont.)

Species or group	Connecting feature	Description of use	Country	Reference
Passerine birds	strip of shrubs	movements between a pine forest and lakeside habitats	Poland	Dmowski & Kozakiewicz (1990)
Copper Butterfly	grassy banks and field margins, wooded strips, shelter belts	feeding and movement around farm fields	Norway	Fry & Main (1993)
2 Seasonal or migratory movements				
Mule Deer	highway underpasses	movement between winter and summer ranges	USA	Reed *et al.* (1975), Ward (1982)
Indian Elephant	forested strip and river crossing	movement between sections of National Park	India	Johnsingh *et al.* (1990)
African Elephant	broad tract of uncultivated land	movements between National Parks	Tanzania	Newmark *et al.* (1991)
Mountain Pygmy-possum	rock-scree corridor and tunnel	movement of males to and from breeding habitat, dispersal of young	Australia	Mansergh & Scotts (1989)
White-naped Honeyeater	roadside woodland	seasonal migration of flocks	Australia	Middleton (1980)
Viper	hedges	movement between hibernation and summer activity areas	UK	Presst (1971)
Amphibians	tunnels under roads	movement across roads to breeding ponds	Europe	Langton (1989)
3 Dispersal movements				
Red Squirrel	hedgerows, treerows	dispersal of juveniles between woodlots	Belgium	Wauters *et al.* (1994)
Sugar Glider	forested roadside vegetation	dispersal of juveniles between forest fragments	Australia	Suckling (1984)
Long-nosed Potoroo, Bush Rat	forested roadside vegetation	dispersal between forest fragments in farmland	Australia	Bennett (1990b)

Table 5–1 Examples of animal movements using habitat linkages.(cont.)

Species or group	Connecting feature	Description of use	Country	Reference
Columbian Ground Squirrel	trails, drainage lines	dispersal between colonies, through forest habitat	Canada	Wiggett & Boag (1989)
Koala	woodland remnants, plantations, roadside vegetation, single trees	dispersal of translocated animals	Australia	Prevett (1991)
Eastern Chipmunk	fencerows	dispersal of subadults between woods, recolonisation of woods	Canada	Henderson *et al.* (1985)
Short-beaked Echidna	roadside vegetation	dispersal of juveniles from natal range	Australia	Abensberg-Traun (1991)
Cougar	stream channels, ridge lines, roads	dispersal of juveniles between mountain ranges	USA	Beier (1995)
River Otter	ditches, streams, rivers	dispersal between stream systems	USA	Forman & Godron (1986)
Bank Vole	shrubby corridor	dispersal between remnant pine forests	Poland	Szacki (1987)
White-crowned Pigeon	fragments of deciduous forest	post-fledging dispersal of birds to large areas of forest	USA	Strong & Bancroft (1994)
Western Yellow Robin	roadside vegetation	movement between remnant vegetation	Australia	Saunders & de Rebeira (1991) Merriam & Saunders (1993)
Rufous Whistler	roadside vegetation	dispersal to large remnant of native vegetation	Australia	Lynch *et al.* (1995)
Red-capped Robin	roadside vegetation	movement between remnant bushland	Australia	Cale (1990)
American Robin	wooded drainage lines	breeding dispersal between wooded shelterbelts	USA	Haas (1995)

Table 5–1 Examples of animal movements using habitat linkages. (cont.)

Species or group	Connecting feature	Description of use	Country	Reference
Ringlet Butterfly	open rides (grassy tracks)	dispersal between open fields and glades within woodland	England	Sutcliffe & Thomas (1996)
4 Range expansion				
Meadow Vole	grassy verge of interstate highway	expansion of range into new grassland areas	Illinois, USA	Getz *et al.* (1978)
Pocket Gopher	mesic microhabitat along roadside	expansion of range across desert	USA	Huey (1941)
Mink	rivers and streams	expansion of range of introduced species	Britain	Harris & Woollard (1990)
Common Mynah	highways	range expansion of an introduced species	Australia	Bennett (1991)
Cane Toad	roads and tracks	colonization of new areas, range expansion	Australia	Seabrook & Dettman (1996)
Spotted Grass Frog	roadside ditch	range expansion after accidental translocation into new geographic region	Australia	Martin and Tyler (1978)

Dispersal movements

Dispersal can be described as the one-way movement of an individual away from a home range or territory to a new area. For example, a young hopping-mouse, squirrel, or wallaby leaves its maternal home range and disperses to a new area where it establishes its own range. The use of linkages to assist dispersal of animals between otherwise-isolated patches of habitat is an important way in which they can enhance species' conservation. Immigration of new individuals can supplement a declining population to prevent its disappearance, introduce new genes to an isolated population, or allow colonization of new habitats as they become suitable.

Box 5–2   Impacts of variation in 'stopover' habitat quality for Rufous Hummingbirds along a migration corridor in western USA

The Rufous Hummingbird is one of many species of migratory land birds that breed in northern areas and undertake seasonal migration to the Neotropics where they spend the winter months. This species breeds in north-western North America and in late summer migrates south along the Cascade-Sierra Nevada and Rocky Mountain Ranges to its wintering grounds in Mexico. Individual birds require several stopovers to 'refuel' before continuing their migration. These stopovers occur in mountain meadows where individuals establish temporary territories based around patches of flowers and feed on nectar for periods of three days to several weeks to gain sufficient energy (body fat) for continued migration.

Detailed observations of Rufous Hummingbird territories, stopover durations and food resources were made at a study site in California during the southward migration over a seven year period (Russell *et al.* 1994). The quality of the stopover habitat, measured in terms of the density of flowers that provide nectar for the hummingbirds, varied widely between years. In years of low food abundance, the body mass of incoming birds was reduced and stopover durations were longer. Further, in years of poor habitat quality the overall rate of migration tended to be less, suggesting population-wide impacts (Russell *et al.* 1994).

What are the implications of variation in quality of stopover habitats? First, longer stopovers in poor years delays migration and increases the risk that birds will not complete migration within the limited flowering period of their food plants. Late-travelling birds may also be caught by storms and poor weather along the migration route. Second, in most years food is limited at stopover points and birds of low body weight unable to obtain territories are at risk of dying of starvation before refueling. Third, observations suggested that in years with poor flowering the population as a whole may decline (Russell *et al.* 1994). These observations show that high-quality stopover habitats are critical links along migratory corridors for some land birds. If *natural variation* in habitat quality has such an appreciable effect on the survival of migrating birds, then degradation or complete destruction of critical stopover points must be a cause for great concern.

Box 5–3   Stepping stone fragments for the dispersal of White-crowned Pigeons in Florida, USA

The White-crowned Pigeon is an obligate frugivore and an important seed disperser in the seasonal deciduous forests of south Florida, USA (Strong and Bancroft 1994). It is a highly mobile species that feeds on fruits of at least 37 species of trees and shrubs. In the upper Florida Keys area, it nests colonially or semi-colonially, mainly on islands in Florida Bay. Consequently, post-fledging dispersal by young pigeons involves an over-water flight of several kilometres, followed by further flight to locate habitats with suitable food resources.

Immature birds that dispersed to the mainland fed almost exclusively within the Everglades National Park or an adjacent wildlife management area. However, birds dispersing to the Mainline Keys are not able to reach large areas of protected forest within the first 72 hours of dispersal, but must pass through the heavily fragmented southern area where they preferentially selected the larger fragments (5–20ha) of seasonal deciduous forest (Strong and Bancroft 1994). These fragments appear to function as important stepping stones for immature pigeons during the first stage of dispersal to the north where large blocks of habitat are protected in reserves. The preference for larger stepping stones en route may be that they provide feeding areas with adequate cover from predators for inexperienced birds (Strong and Bancroft 1994).

What evidence is there that dispersing animals use linkages? Dispersal movements are often difficult to observe or follow unless animals are individually marked or have radio-transmitters attached. Even so, it can still be difficult to determine the actual pathway taken by the moving animal. However, a range of examples are available that illustrate how habitat links facilitate the movements of dispersing animals, especially for mammals (Table 5–1) (Box 5–3).

Arboreal mammals live above ground in the shrub or canopy tree layer and generally are dependent on networks of trees or shrubs to move through cleared land. The use of treerows and hedgerows by squirrels is well documented (see below). The Sugar Glider, a small arboreal marsupial of eastern Australia, also uses forested habitat corridors for dispersal. Studies of a population of Sugar Gliders living in fragments of eucalypt forest amongst farmland in southern Victoria showed that both males and females dispersed from their natal range at about 12 months of age (Suckling 1984). Sugar Gliders move by gliding between trees over distances of at least 50m. All of the known dispersal movements of young gliders involved movement along a forested roadside strip for distances up to 1.9km, although this also included movements of up to 200m across treeless gaps by some individuals. Four other arboreal marsupials, the Common Ringtail Possum, Common Brushtail Possum, Koala, and Feathertail Glider were also recorded in the roadside strip and probably also use it as a pathway for dispersal through cleared farmland. Large expanses of cleared farmland limit or prevent the movement of tree-dwelling mammals.

In another study in southern Australia, radio-telemetry was used to observe the movements of Koalas that were translocated into natural forest habitat on the outer urban fringe of Ballarat, Victoria, after being found in hazardous situations on highways, or at risk from dogs (Prevett 1991). Koalas used a series of habitat corridors, remnant patches of trees and single trees as stepping stones in their extensive movement through the landscape before establishing in a new home range (Fig. 5–1).

Linkages may be used for dispersal not only in disturbed environments, but also in natural environments. At a study site in Alberta, Canada, where Columbian Ground Squirrels live in colonies in grassy meadows surrounded by forest or bog habitats, animals that dispersed from their colony followed trails, drainage lines and topographic features, to create 'squirrel highways' between colonies (Wiggett and Boag 1989). Movement along these linear features is a good strategy for locating new colonies because most suitable meadow habitat is adjacent to waterways and tracks along valley floors.

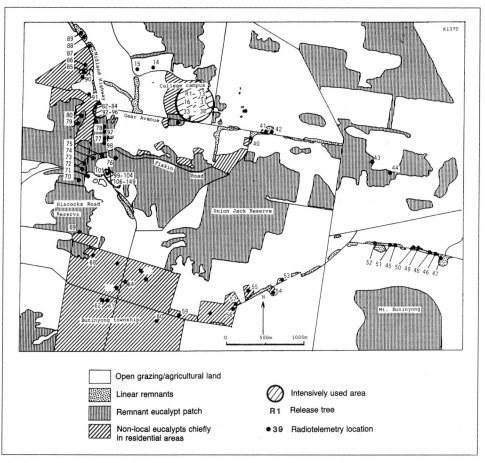

Fig. 5–1(a) **Movement path of an adult male Koala in the urban-rural fringe of Ballarat, Victoria, Australia, after the animal was translocated from an urban situation where it was harassed by dogs. Numbers represent sequential locations of the individual by radiotelemetry. From Prevett (1991) with permission, Surrey Beatty & Sons, Publishers.**

Fig. 5–1 (b) Koala (Photo: L. Lumsden).

Stream systems also form natural corridors for dispersal. Dispersal movements of River Otters in Idaho, USA, involved extensive travel along streams and river systems. Short movements overland were necessary to cross between stream systems, but such traverses were assisted by ditches and low-order streams (Melquist and Hornocker 1983; Forman and Godron 1986). In south-west Western Australia, dense vegetation along stream banks is a focus for habitat management to assist dispersal of the endangered Noisy Scrubbird. This cryptic species occupies dense low shrubby vegetation and seldom flies. Recent population expansion appears to have been assisted by dispersal along stream systems with dense vegetation (Danks 1991).

Range extension

A number of instances have been reported in which linear habitats have assisted the range expansion of animal species into areas not formerly occupied. An interesting example is the spread of the Meadow Vole, a grassland rodent, near Champagne-Urbana in Illinois, USA. Grassland vegetation adjacent to interstate highways has served as a pathway for the Meadow Vole to expand its distribution by 100km, over a six-year period, into new grassland habitat formerly isolated by forest (Getz *et al.* 1978). In most cases, however, these instances of range expansion involve the spread of introduced species, often a pest species, which has an ecologically detrimental effect. In Australia, the distribution of the Common Mynah has expanded in a radial fashion from the urban centres of Melbourne and Sydney. This introduced bird is common along the disturbed edges of main highways which have undoubtedly been the pathway for its spread (Bennett 1991). Similarly, roads and tracks enhance opportunities for introduced Cane Toads to colonize new habitats and expand their range in northern Australia (Seabrook and Dettman 1996). Mink, an introduced species in Britain, has spread rapidly in the wild. The expansion of its range occurs by dispersal along river corridors, with the initial rate estimated to have been 20km per year (Harris and Woollard 1990).

Tunnels and underpasses to assist movement across local barriers

The increasing number of hazards and barriers to wildlife in developed landscapes causes disruption to the regular or seasonal movement patterns of many animals. Railway lines, power line easements, canals, pipelines, culverts, fences and roads, hinder or prevent natural movements. Roads, in particular, pose a barrier to wildlife movements due to the expanse of cleared and altered habitat; the noise, movements and flashing lights from passing traffic; and the risk of death from passing vehicles (Bennett 1991). The extent of road systems is enormous, throughout almost all environments.

Tunnels and underpasses are a distinctive type of link that are short, direct and have the specific goal of facilitating local movements of wildlife across potential barriers (Box 5–4). The most obvious benefit from underpasses under roads, for example, is a reduction in the number of animals killed by vehicles while attempting to cross. A mounting toll of dead animals has often been the visual stimulus that has prompted action. Other conservation benefits from assisting movements across local impediments are less readily observed. These include reduced disruption to social organization (Box 5–5), maintenance of normal movement patterns, and reduced mortality during the dispersal phase in a species life-history.

Highway underpasses are now regularly used for the management of large game species such as Elk, Mule Deer and Mountain Goat in North America (Reed *et al.* 1975; Reed 1981; Ward 1982; Singer *et al.*1985; Harris 1988b). They have proved effective in assisting animals to cross highways at migration pathways, or where busy highways bisect their habitats, thus also reducing vehicle damage and human fatalities (Fig. 5–2). In Glacier National Park in Montana, USA, where a highway crossed the pathway of Mountain Goats travelling to a natural saltlick, the animals were inhibited, but not prevented, from crossing the road (Singer 1975). However, the effects of the road traffic included increased stress for the animals, the

---

Box 5–4   Underpasses to assist seasonal migration of Mule Deer in western USA

An early trial of a highway underpass for a large mammal species was made in 1970 in west-central Colorado, USA, where a regular migration pathway of Mule Deer moving between summer and winter ranges crossed interstate highway 70 (Reed *et al.* 1975). A concrete box underpass (3m x 3m x 30m), combined with highway fencing, was installed and monitored for use over four years. Most deer successfully used the underpass (an estimated 61% of the local population), with the number of individuals crossing the highway increasing by 33% per year over the four-year period (Reed *et al.* 1975).

Wider and taller 'machinery' underpasses (9m x 4.5m x 61m) were used together with a series of box underpasses on a section of interstate highway 80 in Wyoming, USA, where the highway bisected a migration path of about 1,000 Mule Deer (Ward 1982). Highway fencing and one-way gates, to allow deer trapped inside the fence to exit, were also installed. Deer were reluctant to use the underpasses in the first year and food baits were used to attract them to the passageways. Increased use in subsequent years, as in Colorado, suggested a learning pattern. The underpasses were successful in assisting the migration of Mule Deer, while also reducing road kills by 90% from monitored levels before intervention (Ward 1982).

---

risk of separation of mother and young, and increased mortality from road kills. When an underpass was subsequently constructed, less stress was observed in animals crossing and the number and seasonal duration of visits to the saltlick increased (Singer *et al.* 1985).

Experience in California and Florida, USA, has shown that underpasses assist movements of large wide-ranging species such as Cougars or Panthers (Cougar, Panther or Puma are different names for the taxon *Felis concolor*). In southern Florida, a series of 24 underpasses, each approximately 20m long and 2m high, have been specially constructed along a 64km section of interstate highway 75 where it runs through a major habitat of the Florida Panther (Smith 1993; Foster and Humphrey 1995). Thirteen bridges are also being extended to allow land crossings adjacent to wet areas. The siting of the underpasses was based on known movements and the location of previous road kills of Florida Panthers. Highway fencing has been erected to keep animals off the road and funnel them into the underpasses. Monitoring of animal movements through four underpasses over periods of up to 16 months recorded 837 crossings of 20 species, including Florida Panther, Black Bear, Bobcat and large numbers of White-tailed Deer (Foster and Humphrey 1995). Radio-tracking data for Panthers and Bobcats showed that individuals used the underpasses mainly to travel to portions of their home ranges separated by the highway.

Underpasses or tunnels have also been used to facilitate movements, or to reduce the road toll, for species as diverse as Badgers in Britain and the Netherlands (Forman and Hersperger 1996), Mountain Pygmy-possum in Australia (Box 5–5), and Common Toads and other amphibians in numerous countries in Europe (van Leeuwen 1982; Langton 1989).

Box 5–5 Rock-scree corridor and tunnel for the Mountain Pygmy-possum in Australia

The alpine habitat of the endangered Mountain Pygmy-possum is limited to less than 12km^2 in south-eastern Australia, where this small mammal inhabits rock screes and boulder fields that have suitable sub-alpine heathland vegetation. About 40% of the total population of some 2,500 individuals occurs in the Mt Higginbotham area, Victoria, which is bisected by a ski resort (Mansergh and Scotts 1989). At this site, females occupy high-quality habitats at higher elevations and males move to and from these habitats for the breeding season (Mansergh and Scotts 1990). A road and recent developments on an adjacent slope were believed to be inhibiting the seasonal movement of males and disrupting the social organization of the population. These conclusions were based on a comparison of the population demography with that of a population on a nearby undeveloped slope.

A funnel-shaped habitat corridor, 60m in length, was constructed of rocks and boulders leading to two tunnels under the road, thus restoring continuity of rock scree habitat across the development zone. A remote-sensing camera within the tunnel photographed animals using the habitat corridor within two weeks of tunnel construction. Continued monitoring revealed a significant seasonal difference in the direction of movement of animals through the tunnel. In the season following construction of the rocky habitat corridor, dispersal of males at the end of the breeding period greatly increased and overwinter survival of females increased to a level comparable to that on undisturbed slopes (Mansergh and Scotts 1989). The tunnel has had a high public profile and is known colloquially as the 'tunnel of love' (Steer 1987).

Rock-scree corridor and tunnel for the Mountain Pigmy-possum in Australia

Mountain Pygmy-possum (Photo: I. Mansergh).

Fig. 5–2 (a) **Highway underpasses combined with roadside fencing have greatly reduced the number of Elk killed on the trans-Canada highway in Banff National Park, Canada. (Photo: A. Bennett).**

Fig. 5–2 (b) **Elk (Photo: A. Bennett).**

Amphibians that cross roads to ponds or wetlands during the breeding season can be killed in large numbers. The mortality of Common Toads crossing a highway to their breeding ponds in the Netherlands was estimated to be 30% of females (van Gelder 1973). On a 3.2km stretch of road in Britain, regularly monitored throughout the year, 40% of the annual road kill of Common Frogs was recorded in a single week during the breeding season (Hodson 1960). While estimates of natural mortality are required to assess the significance of such road kills, measures that reduce direct mortality will help to alleviate one of the many pressures on amphibians surviving in developed landscapes. Tunnels and culverts for wildlife are also used under railway lines (Hunt *et al.* 1987; Yanes *et al.* 1995) and, in Alaska, oil pipelines have been elevated above the ground to provide underpasses for Caribou populations (Klein 1971; Curatolo and Murphy 1986).

It must be stressed that successful use of tunnels and underpasses by some species does *not* mean that roads and freeways can be carved through natural habitats with minimal impact on wildlife. Road systems have a host of direct and indirect detrimental effects on natural communities (Harris and Gallagher 1989; Bennett 1991; Forman and Hersperger 1996) and further dissection of natural areas must be resisted and prevented.

Experimental investigations of the values of linkages

Experimental studies provide the strongest grounds for testing hypotheses and confirming causal relationships in scientific investigations. Therefore, the most convincing evidence for the conservation benefits of linkages will come from carefully designed, manipulative field experiments. Nicholls and Margules (1991) discussed various designs to test the hypothesis that 'recolonisation will be greater in remnants that are connected to source areas by corridors than in unconnected remnants'. A suitable study design would involve clearing a continuous area of intact habitat to leave a series of equal-sized remnants, half of which (randomly assigned) are isolated and half linked by habitat corridors of equal length and width. For each of these groups of remnants, half would be subject to an experimental extinction of the target species, while the remaining remnants would serve as controls (Fig. 5–3a). The ability of the target species to recolonize remnants in each treatment would then be monitored. In a landscape already fragmented, an alternative design could involve a series of replicate remnants, half of which are connected and half isolated from a large mainland habitat (Fig. 5–3b).

While the design of such experiments may seem straightforward, the practical difficulties involved in clearing natural habitats to create remnants and habitat corridors of suitable size, or in locating suitable remnants to carry out such a study in fragmented landscapes are enormous. After examining combinations of remnants and habitat corridors and the associated covariates of remnant size and corridor length amongst a mosaic of many hundreds of remnants in the wheatbelt of Western Australia, Nicholls and Margules (1991) concluded that it was not possible to find suitable sites to adequately perform the experiment. It is even less likely that such an experimental approach can be applied to assessing the conservation value of broad landscape linkages that facilitate movements of individuals and the continuity of entire assemblages at the landscape scale. Such major links between reserves or large natural areas usually have a sample size of one, and consequently the benefits of connectivity can not be analyzed statistically (Beier and Loe 1992).

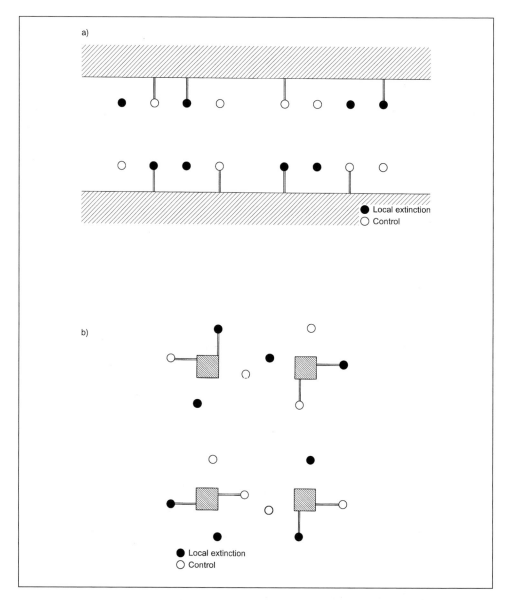

Fig. 5–3 Representation of an idealized design to test the hypothesis that 'recolonization will be greater for remnants connected to source areas by corridors than for unconnected areas'. (a) Design based on the creation of an experimental protocol from a single large habitat. The central part of the habitat has been cleared leaving a series of connected and unconnected habitat remnants for experimental manipulation. (b) Design based on a landscape already fragmented in which it is possible to locate a series of remnant habitats that are either linked or isolated from a nearby larger habitat. In each case, closed circles represent remnant habitats from which the organism under study has been driven to local extinction and open circles represent the controls. Redrawn from Nicholls and Margules (1991) with permission, Surrey Beatty & Sons, Publishers.

Some limited experimental data have come from a large field project on the effects of clearing rainforests in the Brazilian Amazon (Lovejoy *et al.* 1984; Bierregaard *et al.* 1992). This has included a study of 'army-ant followers', a guild of forest birds that obligatorily feed on insects disturbed by swarming Army Ants. Army-ant followers are sensitive to fragmentation and disappeared immediately when 1ha and 10ha fragments were isolated (colonies of Army Ants use about 30ha of forest) (Bierregaard *et al.* 1992). In one 100ha reserve that remained connected by a riparian corridor, 2km in length and 100–300m wide, the structure of the understorey bird community was not distinguishable in the first year from that in control plots in continuous forest. However, when a 250m break was cleared in the corridor (1.6km distant from the fragment) a year later, the three obligate ant-following species rapidly disappeared from the reserve (Bierregaard *et al.* 1992). After a year of regeneration in the corridor, it was reported that one of the species was beginning to recolonize (Harper in Simberloff and Cox 1987).

Systematic monitoring of understorey birds in the same fragments before and after isolation revealed a dramatic decline in both abundance and richness of insectivorous species following experimental isolation (Stouffer and Bierregaard 1995a). In the years following isolation, growth of secondary vegetation around the fragments provided increasing cover and connectivity for understorey birds, assisting them to move through the disturbed mosaic and recolonize fragments. Mixed flocks of 13 common species reassembled in 10ha (but not in 1ha) fragments by 6–9 years after isolation, but terrestrial insectivores had not recolonized (Stouffer and Bierregaard 1995a). In contrast to these insectivorous birds that were isolated by forest clearing of only 70–650m, the species composition and abundance of nectarivorous hummingbirds showed little change (Stouffer and Bierregaard 1995b). The scale of movement normally undertaken by hummingbirds, together with their habitat tolerance, allowed them to move freely through the mosaic of fragments, open areas, young second growth and intact forest to continue their use of fragment habitats.

An experimental protocol creating both isolated and linked fragments has been implemented in boreal forests of Alberta, Canada, in conjunction with timber harvesting operations (Schmiegelow and Hannan 1993; Machtans *et al.* 1996). Numbers of forest birds were monitored in two riparian buffers (100m wide) that linked forest fragments left after harvesting, and in matched control sites within larger forest. Observations were also made of movements by birds across clear-cuts that isolated the fragments. Movement rates of forest birds across open clear-cuts were significantly lower than capture rates in the forest, indicating that forest birds were inhibited by open habitat. When forested buffer strips were compared with forest controls, the corridors were found to enhance the movements of juveniles (probably dispersing individuals) and maintain (but not increase) movements of adults (Machtans *et al.* 1996). A further test of the values of these corridors will come when comparison is made between the composition of forest bird communities in linked versus isolated forest blocks.

Several attempts have been made to design experimental sets of connected and isolated habitat patches to assess the role of linkages (La Polla and Barrett 1993; Lorenz and Barrett 1990). Small patches of grassland habitat (20m x 20m) were linked by wide (5m) grassy habitat corridors, narrow (1m) corridors or no corridors (10m gap of mown grass) to examine the effects of habitat corridor width and presence on population dynamics and home range use of the Meadow Vole (La Polla and Barrett 1993). Treatments with habitat corridors supported

Box 5–6 Dispersal of American Robins between farmland shelterbelts, North Dakota, USA

Shelterbelts of trees, planted as windbreaks on farms, are used as breeding sites by tree-nesting birds in the open plains of North Dakota, USA. In a study area of some 8000ha, Haas (1995) individually marked breeding American Robins, Brown Thrashers and Loggerhead Shrikes in each of 16 clusters of shelterbelts (1–7 shelterbelts per cluster) in farmland. The only other habitats with trees in the study area were narrow lines of native woodland, 'woody draws', along creek beds or moist zones.

Movement of birds between breeding sites, both within a year and among years, were mostly within the same shelterbelt or between shelterbelts in the same cluster. However, in each year some longer breeding dispersal movements were detected. These involved birds moving from shelterbelt clusters to nest in woody draws or to nest in another cluster (Haas 1995). Movements between clusters were more likely to occur between those linked by woody draws than between isolated clusters. Although not essential for dispersal, woody draws appear to function as stepping stones that significantly increase the movement of birds through the landscape (Haas 1995). These results are particularly interesting because American Robins are regarded as open-country birds and might be expected to be much less dependent on habitat links than forest-dependent species.

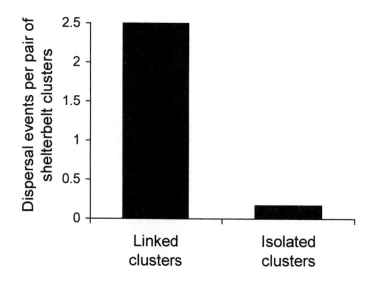

Comparison of the number of dispersal events per pair of shelterbelt clusters for American Robins: (a) between clusters linked by woody draws and (b) between those not linked. Data from Haas (1995).

significantly higher densities of voles than controls, and significantly more males dispersed between connected patches than between patches without habitat corridors. However, each patch was smaller than the home range of a single male and individuals were found to have equally moved between patches *across* treatments (3m of tilled ground) as *within* treatments.

Experimental approaches have also been used to assess the preference of animals for movement through habitat corridors of different types or quality, based on translocating animals to different situations and then monitoring their performance (Merriam and Lanoue 1990; Ruefenacht and Knight 1995). The White-footed Mouse is a common small rodent in eastern Ontario, Canada. It favours woodland vegetation but occurs widely through farm landscapes, including wooded and shrubby fencerows, farm buildings and occasionally croplands. When resident individuals and translocated individuals (to simulate dispersers unfamiliar with the landscape) were released into fencerows in Ontario, animals from both groups used fencerow vegetation for movement in preference to adjacent fields (Merriam and Lanoue 1990). Both types of animals showed a significantly greater use of fencerows with complex vegetation structure for movement than they did for simple fencerows (mainly narrow grassy strips). This preference was most pronounced for the translocated animals that were unfamiliar with the environment, suggesting a behavioural preference for habitat that provides shelter and refuge during movement.

Evidence for the value of connectivity from predictive models

Predictive models have frequently been used to describe the pattern of occurrence of animal species or the richness of faunal assemblages in remnant habitats. Typically these take the form of multiple regression models that include one or more variables each 'explaining' a significant portion of the variation in the response variable. The inclusion of measures of connectivity (such as length of adjoining linear habitats) or of isolation (such as the distance to nearby larger habitat, or the total amount of habitat within a defined radius) as significant explanatory variables in regression models indicates the importance of landscape pattern in the distribution of the species.

While the relationships revealed by such models are not necessarily causal they present strong inferential evidence of the value of landscape connectivity, especially when they are combined with practical insights into the biology of the species concerned (Boxes 5–7, 5–8 and 5–9). For example, separate field studies were made of the occurrence of the Red Squirrel in woodlands amongst agricultural areas in the Netherlands (Verboom and van Apeldoorn 1990) and of the Grey Squirrel (Fig. 5–4) in woods in rural East Anglia, England (Fitzgibbon 1993). Statistical models of these data sets predicted independently for each situation that squirrels were more likely to occur in woods that:

- were larger;

- contained suitable tree species;

- were close to a larger wood;

- were surrounded by a high density of hedgerows.

Box 5–7 Possums and Tree Kangaroos in tropical rainforest remnants, North Queensland, Australia

Arboreal marsupials in tropical rainforest in Queensland, Australia, show marked variation in their sensitivity to extinction following fragmentation of rainforest habitats (Pahl *et al.* 1988; Laurance 1990). One species, the Lemuroid Ringtail, was virtually absent from remnants; two species, the Herbert River Ringtail Possum and Lumholtz's Tree Kangaroo, showed a negative response to fragmentation compared with their occurrence in control sites in extensive rainforest; and for the remaining two species, the Coppery Brushtail Possum and Green Ringtail, the frequency of occurrence in remnants did not differ from control sites.

The sensitivity of these marsupials to extinction was negatively correlated with their ability to use secondary regrowth and riparian vegetation along the stream systems that linked most rainforest remnants. Those species most tolerant of fragmentation were frequently recorded in riparian strips. Conversely, the Lemuroid Ringtail, which was not recorded in regrowth vegetation along streams, was least able to persist in remnants despite being common in nearby extensive rainforest (Laurance 1990). These results are consistent with the hypothesis that dispersal along riparian habitat corridors is important in maintaining isolated rainforest populations of some species, by allowing patch populations to be supplemented or recolonized should extinction occur.

This hypothesis was further supported by analyses of a larger range of 16 non-flying mammals, including the arboreal marsupials, in the same study area on the Atherton Tablelands (Laurance 1991a). In general, the ability of species to use the habitat matrix surrounding rainforest fragments (such as regrowth forest, riparian strips, pastures) was the best predictor of their sensitivity to fragmentation. Species able to use the disturbed habitats in the matrix are likely to be those most able to disperse along linkages between remnants and bolster isolated populations. These results indicate that both the structural connectivity provided by riparian habitat corridors, and the behavioural tolerance of animals to these habitats, are key influences on the conservation status of mammals in rainforest fragments.

The Coppery Brushtail, an arboreal mammal relatively tolerant of forest fragmentation, was frequently recorded in streamside strips of vegetation that linked rainforest fragments. (Photo: A. Bennett).

Box 5–8 Distribution of the Dormouse in ancient woods in Britain

The Dormouse, a small mammal (up to 40g bodyweight) with specialized habitat requirements, has disappeared from approximately half of its range in Britain this century (Hurrell and McIntosh 1984). A survey of the distribution of the Dormouse in 238 woodlands in Herefordshire (Bright *et al.* 1994) found that it favoured ancient woodlands and was scarce in recent woodland. Ancient woodlands are those of a natural or semi-natural growth form that occur on sites thought to have supported woodland since 1600 AD. Ecological attributes of the Dormouse, such as low population density and a low and highly variable reproductive rate, suggest that it is likely to be vulnerable to extinction of local populations, a view consistent with its observed scarcity in small isolated woods (Bright and Morris 1990; Bright *et al.* 1994).

Analysis of survey data showed that the occurrence of the Dormouse in ancient woodland was significantly related to the size of the wood, the amount of surrounding ancient woodland, and the density of boundaries (mainly hedgerows) radiating out from the wood. Thus, the model predicts that Dormice are most likely to occur in larger ancient woodlands that are linked to similar nearby woodlands by hedgerows. The inclusion of hedgerow boundaries as a significant predictor suggests that dispersal between woods along hedgerow networks is important for the local persistence of woodland populations, and that enhancing dispersal is a key to the management and local conservation of this rare species (Bright and Morris 1990, 1991; Bright *et al.* 1994).

Dormice have little likelihood of dispersing through farmland where there are no hedgerows. Radiotelemetry studies have shown that individuals are sedentary in woodlands and are entirely arboreal in their activity. They move through the woodland canopy layer and repeatedly detour to avoid crossing open ground to reach food or other resources (Bright and Morris 1991). Habitat management now underway in woodlands includes measures such as developing networks of hazel trees as arboreal links to enhance connectivity and assist dispersal (Anon. 1993). Trial re-introductions are also planned to improve the conservation status of this species (Bright *et al.* 1994).

For arboreal mammals such as squirrels, woodlands surrounded by expanses of treeless farmland are relatively insular habitats. Hedgerows, fencerows and other woodland strips and patches that cross the intervening farmland greatly assist the movements of squirrels through the landscape. Further insights into how squirrels use hedgerows were gained by radiotelemetry studies of the home range and movements of individual Red Squirrels in fragmented woodlands in Belgium (Wauters *et al.* 1994). Adult males used tree rows and hedgerows as both foraging habitat and pathways to move between parts of their home range, which often encompassed more than one small wood. Juveniles used these habitat corridors to disperse from one wood to another to establish a new home range.

Box 5–9   Chipmunks and fencerows in eastern Canada

The Eastern Chipmunk is a common woodland animal in eastern North America. In Ontario, Canada, chipmunks occupy farm woodlots but rarely occur in crops or grassy fields. Fencerows of woody vegetation, some having large mature trees, provide a network of habitat that greatly reduces the isolation of woods within the farmland mosaic (Wegner and Merriam 1979; Henderson *et al.* 1985). Populations in farm woods vary in size and the occasional loss of local populations in small woods over the harsh winter period is likely. Experimental 'extinctions', induced by removal of animals from two woods, were followed by rapid recolonisation by individuals moving from adjacent fencerows and nearby woods through the fencerow system (Henderson *et al.* 1985).

Further studies in relation to the continuity and habitat quality of fencerows showed there was marked variation in the way that fencerows were used (Bennett *et al.* 1994). Grassy fencerows that lack wooded cover were seldom or never used but, within the network of wooded fencerows, there were frequent movements of animals between different fencerows, between fencerows and woods, and between woods. Some individuals were transients, apparently using the fencerow for direct movements through the landscape. The continuity of fencerows between woods (i.e. lack of gaps), together with fencerow structure, were significant predictors of the number of transients. Other individuals were resident within fencerows and known to breed there. The number of resident chipmunks was greatest in wide fencerows with mature woodland structure (Bennett *et al.* 1994).

The wooded fencerow system provides a high level of connectivity for chipmunks through the inhospitable farmland environment, so that they operate as a single dynamic population rather than a number of isolated populations each prone to local extinction.

A high quality fencerow used both by resident and transient Eastern Chipmunks in farmland near Ottawa, Canada. (Photo: A. Bennett).

Fig. 5–4   In East Anglia, Britain, Grey Squirrels were more likely to occur in woods that were larger, contained suitable tree species, were close to a large wood, and were surrounded by a high density of hedgerows. (Photo: A. Bennett).

Simulation models and empirical data on the values of connectivity

Computer simulation models are useful tools to explore the potential fate of animal populations under a range of circumstances. The viability of populations in habitat patches of varying size, in various spatial configurations and systems of patches, or with varying levels and quality of connectivity can be modelled (Fahrig and Merriam 1985; Fahrig and Paloheimo

Box 5–10   The White-footed Mouse in farm landscapes of Ontario, Canada

The spatial dynamics of the White-footed Mouse have been extensively studied by simulation models and field studies in farm landscapes of Ontario, Canada (Wegner and Merriam 1979, 1990; Middleton and Merriam 1981; Merriam and Lanoue 1990; Fahrig and Merriam 1985; Merriam *et al.* 1989). Overwinter mortality of this species is high in this region (80–90% of individuals) and consequently entire populations in small woods are occasionally eliminated during this severe period, or they may begin the spring breeding season with small numbers. A simulation model was used to examine whether population survival in woodland patches was related to the level of isolation or connectivity. The model predicted that populations in isolated woods would have a lower population growth rate over summer than those in connected woods and, consequently, would have a higher probability of local extinction over winter.

Field data supported this prediction. Populations in woods connected by fencerows had significantly higher growth rates than those isolated in farmland, a result attributed to enhanced dispersal into the connected patch populations (Fahrig and Merriam 1985). Other field studies demonstrated how dispersal occurs for this species. Following experimental removal of the population in a small wood, numerous dispersing individuals entered over the following spring and summer (Middleton and Merriam 1981). White-footed Mice use a range of habitats for movement through the landscape but wooded fencerows are clearly favoured (Merriam and Lanoue 1990).

In this environment, where severe winters impose high mortality, isolated populations with lower growth rates and a smaller over-wintering population are more likely to experience local extinction. Re-establishment is also likely to be slower in isolated populations than connected ones. When this pattern is extrapolated to the landscape or regional scale, a population inhabiting a system of connected patches has a higher chance of regional persistence than subpopulations in a set of isolated patches.

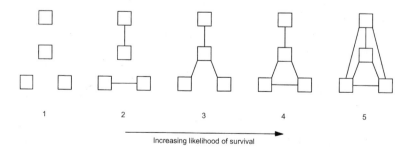

Configurations of four-patch metapopulations of White-footed Mice with differing levels of inter-patch connections. Configurations are arranged in order of increasing likelihood of survival (left to right) as predicted by the model of Fahrig and Merriam (1985). Redrawn from Merriam (1991) with permission, Surrey Beatty & Sons, Publishers.

Box 5–11   Cougars and habitat corridors in an urban-wildlands interface, California, USA

Cougars are a species of particular concern in North America because they have disappeared from much of their former range and, like other large predators, their area requirements mean they will have difficulty persisting even in some of the largest reserves (Beier 1993). This taxon has been a focal species in efforts to retain and promote linkages between large natural areas in the USA (Noss and Harris 1986; Harris and Gallagher 1989; Beier 1993).

A simulation model of the population dynamics of Cougars in the Santa Ana Mountain Range in California, together with field data on population density, home ranges and dispersal movements, has presented a strong case for maintaining habitat links if the species is to have a long-term future in this expanding urban area (Beier 1993, 1995). Computer simulations of hypothetical populations of Cougars predicted that without immigration an area of some 2200 km^2 was required to ensure a low risk of extinction over 100 years, depending on the demographic parameters used. Immigration of as few as 1–4 dispersing animals per decade would markedly increase the probability of persistence of Cougars, even in smaller areas of 600–1600 km^2.

Field studies supported this model (Beier 1993). They revealed that the Santa Ana Mountain Range of 2070 km^2 has a population of about 20 adults which is demographically unstable (Beier 1993). Cougars recently became extinct in the adjacent San Joaquin Hills (75 km^2) when it was isolated by urban development and extinction is likely in the Chino Hills, an area of 150 km^2, if development plans block a critical habitat corridor through which Cougars move to and from the Santa Ana Range (Beier 1993, 1995). Continued development in the region could reduce the overall habitat to the 1,114 km^2 of protected lands, thus adding further pressure to the regional population. The only potential source of immigrants into the Santa Ana population is via a linkage from the Palomar Range to the south, but it is already gravely threatened by disturbance and development.

Radio-telemetry of the movements of adults and dispersing subadults has clearly shown that Cougars use habitat corridors to move between large tracts of habitat (Beier 1995). Movements by males through a 1.5 km degraded corridor has sustained the otherwise-isolated Chino Hill population by allowing continued breeding with its resident females. Young dispersing animals also find and use habitat corridors. All nine subadults that were monitored moved extensively during dispersal: five of the nine found and successfully used habitat corridors and seven explored to the tips of habitat peninsulas up to 7 km in length (Beier 1995).

Given the large area of about 2000 km^2 required to support even a small population of this species, and the increasing isolation and subdivision of such tracts, the future persistence of this large predator and other such area-dependent species will depend on their ability to maintain effective connectivity between a number of blocks of habitat, each of which alone is insufficient. There is ample evidence that Cougars can find

---

Box 5–11 (cont.)

habitat corridors and will use them to move between blocks of habitat. Field studies have shown that natural travel routes such as stream channels, ridgelines and unsealed roads can be identified so that they can be protected for this purpose (Beier 1995). Cougars in this region tolerate moderate levels of disturbance within such linkages and there is evidence that effective crossings, even of busy freeways, can be managed to maintain connectivity for this species, for example by bridged underpasses at rivers combined with roadside fencing.

1988; Burkey 1989; Henein and Merriam 1990; Soulé and Gilpin 1991; Verboom *et al.* 1991; Beier 1993; Andersen and Mahato 1995; Lindenmayer and Lacy 1995; Lindenmayer and Possingham 1996). The strength of this approach is its capacity to rapidly simulate a range of hypothetical conditions, to test 'what if' scenarios, and to identify the potential sensitivity of species to different parameters.

It is also important to be aware of the limitations of this approach. Simulation models are critically dependent on the input values used for model parameters such as age-specific birth and death rates, longevity, genetic effects of inbreeding, levels of interpopulation dispersal, and so on (Lacy 1993; Lindenmayer *et al.* 1995). Of particular relevance in this context is the simulation of dispersal between (sub)populations to assess the value of habitat corridors, or habitat mosaic patterns, in sustaining species in patchy environments. In general, little quantitative data is available on animal dispersal, such as the frequency and length of dispersal movements and survival of dispersing individuals. Consequently, when using simulation models to evaluate spatial configurations of habitats, values for some of the key parameters in the model must be estimated (or guessed). For example, computer simulations of the potential survival of two high-profile forest-dependent species, Leadbeater's Possum in Australia (Lindenmayer and Possingham 1996) and the Spotted Owl in North America (Lamberson *et al.* 1994; Andersen and Mahato 1995), in relation to the spatial arrangement of suitable habitat patches, showed for both species that model outcomes were particularly sensitive to the values used for parameters representing dispersal of animals through the landscape. In both cases, the need for quantitative field data on dispersal has been identified as a high priority.

Simulation studies have greatest value when computer models can be coupled with field studies, both to calibrate model parameters and to test or confirm model predictions. Two examples are presented here in which simulation models and field studies have been used together to evaluate the importance of connectivity for species conservation. These investigations illustrate the co-ordinated use of simulation models and field investigations at two spatial levels: for a small woodland rodent within a farm landscape (Box 5–10), and for a large carnivore within a broad geographic region (Box 5–11).

Summary

There are many documented examples of animals using various types of linkages as pathways for movement. Movement on a daily or regular basis, seasonal and migratory movements, dispersal movements, and range expansion, all may be facilitated by habitat links. Four kinds of studies have revealed the range of benefits that may accrue from an increased capacity for animals to move through modified environments. Studies of the use of tunnels and underpasses by animals show that such direct links across local barriers reduce the level of mortality amongst moving animals, allow continued access to habitat resources, and may restore disrupted social structures. Experimental studies that investigate the consequences of differing levels of connectivity are difficult to undertake. Limited results provide evidence that linkages enhance the movement of animals to ecological isolates, thus improving the status of populations in isolated habitats. Predictive models based on the pattern of occurrence of animal species in patchy environments indicate that habitats with high connectivity are more likely to be occupied than those that are isolated. Thus, species able to use linkages have a greater capacity to persist in fragmented habitats. The use of computer simulation models coupled with field data for selected species provides evidence that landscape connectivity is an influential factor in determining the risk of extinction for small and otherwise-isolated populations. Overall, these studies consistently infer that high levels of habitat connectivity are associated with a greater occurrence and persistence of populations in isolated habitats.

6   LINKAGES AS ECOLOGICAL ELEMENTS IN THE LANDSCAPE

From a conservation perspective, most interest in linkages has been in their role as pathways for the movement of animals (and plants) through inhospitable environments. Little consideration has been given to their wider ecological role in the landscape and to other conservation benefits they may provide while enhancing connectivity. Forman (1991) outlined six broad categories of public policy issues that are addressed by linkage networks in the landscape: biological diversity, water resources, agriculture and wood production, recreation, community and cultural cohesion, and climate change (Table 6–1). The range of functions encompassed by these categories suggests that a focus only on animal movements limits our appreciation of the potential benefits that linkage networks may provide. Whether in the form of habitat corridors, stepping stone patches or habitat mosaics, all linkages are part of the landscape and contribute to its structure and function. To illustrate the wider role of these links in the landscape, this chapter reviews ecological values of five common types of linkages – landscape links, riparian vegetation, hedges and fencerows, roadside vegetation and forest linkages.

Particular attention in the following sections is given to the value of linkages as *habitat* for plants and animals. By providing additional habitat for species living in modified environments, linkages make a direct contribution to the conservation of biodiversity. They may substantially increase the total amount of suitable habitat and, in some cases, provide the majority of remaining habitat for wildlife (Feinsinger 1994) (Fig. 6–1). Habitat links may also be important refuges for rare and threatened species, especially in landscapes where natural vegetation has been all but removed, or where linkages are the last remnants of vegetation types that have been selectively cleared (Table 6–2) (McDowell *et al.* 1991).

Information on the pattern of occurrence of animal species in linkage habitats also provides inferential evidence of their value in maintaining connectivity through the landscape. If it can be demonstrated that a species that is reliant on natural habitats occurs within linkages in a greater frequency than in the surrounding altered landscape (where it may not occur at all), then it is reasonable to infer that these links increase its capacity for movement and population continuity through the landscape. There are many such examples of species that occur in linkages, but seldom in the surrounding lands (Box 6–1, and following sections). In most instances, however, data on actual movements of individuals or of gene flow between populations connected in this way, is not available.

Landscape linkages

Landscape linkages include a wide range of habitats that provide major links through the environment at the landscape or regional scale. They are usually substantial areas of habitat whose dimensions are measured in kilometres, and they connect across distances of kilometres to tens of kilometres or more. Examples include broad tracts of natural habitat

Table 6–1 Examples of issues in six areas of public policy (after Forman 1991) that are significantly influenced by various types of linkages and linkage networks.

Public policy area	Landscape links	Riparian vegetation	Hedgerows & fencerows	Roadside vegetation	Forest linkages
1 Biological diversity					
• Habitat for plant and animal populations	+	+	+	+	+
• Refuge for populations in harsh environments	+	+			+
• Conservation of rare species	+	+		+	+
• Movement for wide-ranging species	+	+	+	+	+
• Dispersal between isolated populations	+	+	+	+	+
• Maintenance of ecological processes	+	+	+	+	+
2 Water resources					
• Surface drainage patterns	+	+	+	+	+
• Ground water accession	+	+	+	+	
• Flood mitigation and control	+	+			
• Sedimentation and holding capacity of dams and reservoirs		+			+
• Water quality and temperature		+			+
• Nutrient levels and eutrophication		+			+
3 Agriculture and timber production					
• Soil erosion by wind and water	+	+	+	+	
• Windbreaks for crops, pasture and livestock			+	+	
• Ground water levels and condition	+	+		+	
• Timber production	+	+			+
• Firewood	+	+	+	+	+
• Fruits, berries and other natural produce	+		+		+

Public policy area	Landscape links	Riparian vegetation	Hedgerows & fencerows	Roadside vegetation	Forest linkages
4 Recreation and aesthetics					
• Wildlife observation	+	+	+	+	
• Hunting and fishing	+	+			
• Hiking, camping and recreational use	+	+			
• Landscape aesthetics	+	+	+	+	+
5 Community and cultural cohesion					
• Cultural identity of rural or suburban landscapes	+	+	+	+	
• Links with historical land use		+	+		
• Property boundaries		+	+		
• Privacy			+		
6 Climate change					
• Pathway for re-distribution of populations	+	+			+
• Habitat for species with limited dispersal ability	+	+			

Fig. 6–1   Aerial view of a rural landscape near Euroa, Victoria, Australia. Here, almost all remnant eucalypt woodland not cleared for farmland occurs as linear strips along roadsides (straight lines) and creek systems. This linked network provides important habitat for at least three threatened vertebrate species. (Photo: A. Bennett).

Table 6–2   Occurrence of rare species in linear habitats, as illustrated by the distribution of known populations of rare and endangered species of plants in different land categories in the Wheatbelt region of Western Australia.

Road and rail reserves in this region are linear habitats that usually support remnant native vegetation. Data from Hobbs *et al.* 1993.

Land category	Number of known populations
Nature reserve	79
Road reserve (Shire)	130
Road reserve (Main Roads Department)	5
Railway reserve	8
Private land	53
Vacant Crown land	30
Water reserve	20
Recreation reserve	3
Other reserves	7
Pastoral lease	1
Unknown	12
Total populations	348
Percentage on linear reserves	41%

between conservation reserves, major river systems and associated riparian vegetation, tracts of forest or forest mosaics designed to minimize logging impacts in managed forests, and habitats that provide food and refuge for species along their migratory pathways. A number of examples of landscape links between reserves, in forest management, and for the conservation of large mammals, are presented in Chapter 9.

Landscape links often encompass large areas of land, so that in addition to their role in enhancing connectivity at broad scales, they have great value in their own right as habitat for plants and animals. In many situations they support entire communities of plants and animals, including those characteristic of 'interior' habitats (Box 6–2, see also Chapter 9). Indeed, they function most effectively as linkages when they allow the continuity of plant and animal communities along their full length. These links may themselves be conservation reserves, or incorporated within reserves. In Malawi, for example, an extension was made to the Liwonde National Park in the form of a broad landscape link, approximately 6km wide and 10km in length, to connect the park with the Mangochi Forest Reserve (Bhima 1993). The link is designed to allow free movement of African Elephant between the two reserves. It also provides additional habitat (7000ha) for many other wildlife species, including large mammals such as Sable Antelope, Bushbuck, Kudu, Wart Hog, Lion and Leopard (R. Bhima, pers. comm. 1995), and consolidates a single protected area of almost 100,000ha.

Box 6–1   Rainforest insects inhabiting streamside strips in north Queensland, Australia

In the Atherton region of north Queensland, Australia, strips of rainforest vegetation along streams serve as habitat corridors between fragments of rainforest isolated by arable land. To investigate the potential conservation value of these streamside links in enhancing connectivity for invertebrates, comparison was made between the species occurring in different habitats in the landscape. Surveys for ants, dung beetles and butterflies were carried out at comparative sites in extensive rainforest vegetation, in rainforest edges, in remnant rainforest strips along streams, and in arable land (Hill 1995).

Analysis of the data collected was limited to the four species in each taxonomic group that were most abundant at the rainforest interior sites. All four of the most abundant species of ants in the rainforest interior, three of the butterflies and one of the dung beetle species were present in the streamside rainforest strips. Further, two of the species recorded from the riparian habitat corridors, a butterfly and a dung beetle, were clearly demonstrated to be rainforest 'interior' species that were significantly more abundant in the interior than the edge of extensive rainforest habitat (Hill 1995). With the exception of two butterfly species, recorded in low abundance, these examples of abundant rainforest invertebrates were not detected in the surrounding arable land, mostly cultivated for sugar cane.

These results provide evidence that streamside habitat corridors of rainforest vegetation in this area have the *potential* to facilitate dispersal and maintain connectivity through a largely inhospitable environment for a wide range of rainforest insects, including some dependent on rainforest-interior habitat.

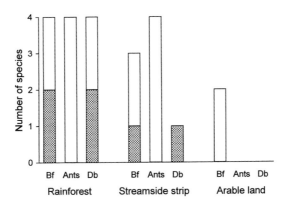

Occurrence in rainforest, streamside corridors and arable land of four species of butterflies, ants and dung beetles that were the most abundant in each taxonomic group at sites in the rainforest interior in north Queensland, Australia. The shaded portion represents species that show a significant preference for rainforest 'interior' habitat. Data are from Hill (1995).

Box 6–2   La Selva-Braulio Carrillo corridor, Costa Rica

Acquisition of land by a consortium of conservation agencies (including the Nature Conservancy, USA, National Parks Service of Costa Rica, National Parks Foundation of Costa Rica, Organisation of Tropical Studies, and World Wildlife Fund) provided initial protection for a broad landscape link between two important reserves in Costa Rica. The La Selva Protection Zone (as it was first known) is a broad band of tropical forest, 3–6 km in width, that extends for about 18km along an altitudinal gradient from the La Selva Biological Station at low elevation (30m) to the mid-upper elevation Braulio Carrillo National Park (2900m at highest point) (Pringle *et al.* 1984). Subsequently this landscape link was incorporated within the national park.

La Selva Biological Station, a 1336ha area of moist forest in the Atlantic lowlands, is a species-rich reserve used for scientific research and scientific tourism. Protection of the landscape link means that La Selva will maintain continuity of habitat with the Braulio Carrillo National Park, a large protected area of 44,000ha. About 73% of the link is primary forest with the remainder as secondary forest or young second growth, pasture and crops (Pringle *et al.* 1984). Almost the entire catchments of two rivers, the Peje and Guacimo, are within the corridor and adjacent forest reserve. The river gorges are relatively unaffected by deforestation, thus maintaining a continuous connection of primary forest despite some clearing for pasture and crops.

The protection of intact forest along an elevational gradient from 36m to 2900m, maintains the opportunity for altitudinal migration of many animal species. At least 75 species of birds within the La Selva-Braulio Carrillo region are known to be migrants that move altitudinally between breeding and non-breeding habitats (Loiselle and Blake 1992). Species such as the Emerald Toucanet, Bare-throated Umbrella Bird, Green Hermit, Three-wattled Bellbird and Silver-throated Tanager use the habitat link during their seasonal migration between mid-elevation forests and lowland forests (Pringle *et al.* 1984). Because these migrants spend several months in the lowlands, clearing of forests would threaten their survival.

The landscape link protects more than 7000 ha of tropical forest habitat that supports a high diversity of flora and fauna. There are four distinctive 'life zones' and it is estimated to contain 650 species of trees and 450 species of birds. A biological expedition in 1983 recorded numerous rare species of plants (including new species), birds, reptiles, mammals and butterflies (Pringle *et al.* 1984). The creation of an enlarged protected area also supports larger populations of animals and enhances their long-term viability. If the La Selva Biological Station was isolated by pasture (extensive clearing of tropical forest still continues) more than 90 species of birds dependent on the primary forest-interior could eventually be lost (Stiles in Pringle *et al.* 1984). The enlarged area is also important for predators. Jaguars are among more than 100 species of predatory mammals, birds and snakes known from the La Selva Biological Reserve that feed largely, or entirely, on vertebrates (Pringle *et al.* 1984).

Box 6–2 (cont.)

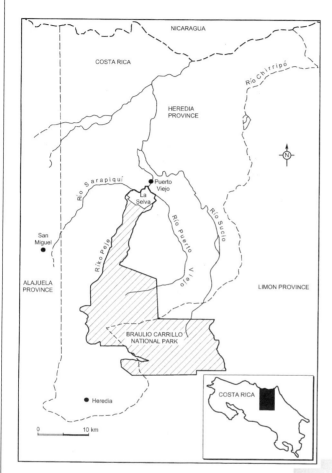

The landscape link between La Selva
Biological Station and Braulio- Carrillo
National Park in Costa Rica. Redrawn
from Timm *et al.* (1989) with permission,
United States Fish and Wildlife Service.

Major river systems and their associated vegetation have great value as habitat linkages across landscapes and regions. In Western Australia, as part of a review of nature reserves in the south coast region, four river systems were identified as having particularly high conservation values and were recommended for protection as 'corridor reserves' (Watson 1991). These riparian habitat corridors range from about 25km to more than 70km in length, and the associated natural vegetation varies up to several kilometres in width. All four link important conservation reserves. Vegetation along the Fitzgerald River, for example, links the coastal Fitzgerald River National Park, a major reserve (320,000ha) of outstanding botanical richness and endemism, with the inland Lake Magenta Nature Reserve (107,600ha) (Watson 1991). In the semi-arid north-west of Victoria, the Murray River and its associated riparian vegetation and floodplain forests function as a major biogeographic link. Many species of animals, such as the Feather-tailed Glider, Yellow Rosella, Blue-faced Honeyeater, Tree Goanna and Peron's Tree Frog, are almost entirely restricted to the mesic riverine habitats (Land Conservation Council 1987). It has clearly been the the the pathway along which they have extended and maintained their ranges in the semi-arid environment.

Many tracts of habitat that currently fill the role of landscape links, enhancing the connectivity of the natural environment and ecological processes across broad areas, are not necessarily recognized as such. There is now growing attention to identifying such areas and recognizing their importance as part of a strategic approach to conservation at the regional scale. There are different approaches to their management. Some such links are managed primarily for conservation (Box 6–2); while others are managed on the basis that local people are able to continue harvesting natural resources at an intensity that will not compromise the function of the link (see Boxes 7–4 and 8–5 for examples).

Riparian vegetation

Riparian vegetation along streams forms an hierarchical system of natural linear habitats through the landscape, from intermittent drainage lines to minor streams to major rivers. The mesic streamside environment supports a zone of vegetation that usually is structurally and floristically distinct from adjacent habitats with which it intergrades. Riparian vegetation is generally readily recognized and mapped (from aerial photographs, for example), even within continuous natural habitats, and is especially distinct from its surroundings in semi-arid or arid environments and in cleared developed landscapes.

Habitat for wildlife

Riparian vegetation is well known as a rich habitat for fauna (Fig. 6–2) (Stauffer and Best 1980; Emmerich and Vohs 1982; Harris 1984, 1988c; Redford and de Fonseca 1986; Decamps *et al.* 1987; Coles *et al.* 1989; Doyle 1990; Strong and Bock 1990; Dunham 1994; Bentley and Catterall 1997; but see Murray and Stauffer 1995). Several factors are associated with this richness.

- Riparian vegetation is at the interface between aquatic and terrestrial environments where the local diversity of habitats is frequently high. Stream edge habitats, flood plain habitats, old stream channels, and successional patterns of vegetation associated with fluctuating water levels and isolated pools, all add to the habitat diversity and array of

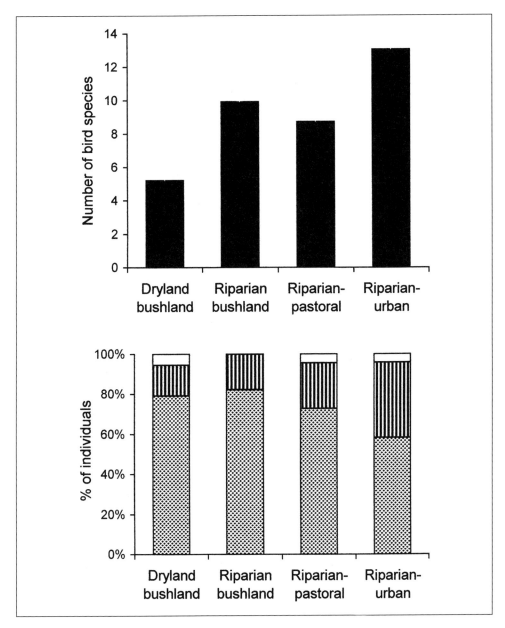

Fig. 6–2   Occurrence of bird species in winter in riparian habitats near Brisbane, Queensland, Australia. (a) Comparison of mean species richness between sites in dryland bushland, riparian bushland, remnant riparian strips in pastoral areas and remnant riparian strips in urban areas. (b) Mean percentage of individuals at each site that are forest species (stippled), generalists (vertical lines), and cleared country species (unshaded). Data from Bentley and Catterall (1997).

opportunities for fauna. There may also be a distinct ecotone between the riparian vegetation and adjacent upland vegetation, further increasing local habitat diversity.

- The adjacency of aquatic and terrestrial environments is important for species that require both environments for their life-cycle; for example, amphibians such as frogs and salamanders, and aquatic insects such as dragonflies, damselflies and mayflies. The interface between aquatic and terrestrial zones is also favoured by wetland birds, such as herons, egrets, and kingfishers, that forage in aquatic environments but shelter in terrestrial vegetation.

- Riparian ecosystems frequently support species adapted to streamside habitats, which rarely occur in adjacent habitats. These may be species that favour the band of floristically or structurally-distinct vegetation, such as forest birds associated with mesic environments (Murray and Stauffer 1995). Alternatively, there are species that use specialized habitats along streams, such as the Large-footed Myotis, an insectivorous bat that forages above the surface of the water and is rarely found away from streams (Lumsden and Menkhorst 1995).

- Fertile alluvial soils and a greater amount and seasonal availability of moisture in riparian zones contribute to a higher and more sustained productivity than in adjacent habitats. This productivity may be expressed in a number of ways. A greater structural diversity and volume of vegetation than in adjacent habitats may provide an increased range of foraging niches and microhabitats for animals (a greater number of vegetation layers, for example), and hence greater species diversity. In seasonally-drier environments, the availability of water may extend the growing season and hence the abundance, reliability and duration of food supplies for populations. It has been proposed that greater productivity and stability in riparian zones may allow these habitats to function as 'source' populations from which individuals disperse into surrounding areas (Doyle 1990).

Although linear and limited in overall extent, riparian habitats can have a major effect on regional biological diversity (Box 6–3). In dry regions, the moist productive environment along stream systems has a critical role in the regional ecology. Riparian and associated floodplain habitats support a range of species not able to survive in adjacent dry habitats, and also serve as a seasonal environment or refuge during extreme conditions for the fauna of adjacent habitats. Alluvial woodlands along the Zambezi River in Zimbabwe, for example, support higher densities of large herbivores (such as Waterbuck, Kudu, Eland, Zebra, Impala and Buffalo) during the dry season than the wet season (Dunham 1994), with particularly high densities of some species (Impala and Zebra) during drought. In Arizona, USA, riparian woodlands comprise less than 0.5% of the land area, but support a rich variety and abundance of birds (Strong and Bock 1990; Szaro 1991). Habitats dominated by Cottonwood trees were reported to have the greatest richness of birds. Indeed, it has been reported that Cottonwood-dominated riparian vegetation in the south-west (including Arizona) has the highest density of breeding birds in North America, and that destruction of these threatened habitats could result in the loss of 47% of breeding bird species in the region (Johnson *et al.* 1977 in Strong and Bock 1990).

Throughout the world, riparian vegetation often persists as remnant linear habitats or habitat corridors in heavily disturbed environments such as farmland, urban areas and among

Box 6–3   Gallery forests and the diversity of non-flying mammals in the Brazilian cerrado

'Cerrado' is the name given to the second-largest vegetation formation in Brazil, an area larger than 1.4 million km^2 (approximately 25% of the country) composed mainly of dry forests, scrubland, open savannahs and grassland. Although mean annual rainfall is relatively high (greater than 1000mm per annum), there is a pronounced dry season and the vegetation is primarily adapted to dry conditions. Threading through the cerrado are narrow strips of evergreen gallery forests along watercourses. Only a few hundred metres wide, and occupying less than a tenth of the area, they form a distinctive linear system of moister woodland and forest habitat through the landscape (Redford 1985; Redford and De Fonseca 1986).

The gallery forests are the key to the diversity and composition of the mammalian fauna of the cerrado. Only 14% of the 65 genera (100 species) of non-flying mammals known from the cerrado are *not* associated with the gallery forests – the remaining 86% are either obligate residents or opportunistically use the mesic linear habitat (Redford and de Fonseca 1986). Overall, the majority of the fauna from the cerrado vegetation formation also occur in the more mesic Atlantic or Amazon forest regions. The gallery forests increase the diversity of the mammal fauna in the cerrado in two ways: by serving as a system of mesic habitat corridors that allow forest-dwelling mammals (such as Woolly Opossum, Kinkajou, and Howler Monkeys) to extend their range into the cerrado region; and by providing food, water and refuge for species not limited to forests (such as Maned Wolves, Nine-banded Armadillos and Brocket Deer) (Redford and de Fonseca 1986). Protection of these natural linkages is a key to maintaining the diversity of the flora and fauna in this vast region. In principle the gallery forests are protected by legislation because of their important role in conserving headwaters, controlling erosion and functioning as buffer areas (Felfili 1997). However, they are often cleared for subsistence cultivation, horticulture, and for cattle. Protection from fires, often deliberately set by people, is particularly important (Redford 1985). Fire is a natural feature of dry cerrado vegetation, but too-frequent and intense fires gradually encroach into, and destroy, the moist gallery forests.

plantations of exotic tree species (Emmerich and Vohs 1982; Brooker 1983; Faanes 1984; Balát 1985; Fowler and Howe 1987; Recher *et al.* 1987; Coles *et al.* 1989; Rushton *et al.* 1994). Streamside strips make a large and valuable contribution to maintaining indigenous species in such modified landscapes, although habitat generalists are usually more likely to persist than habitat specialists or rare species. The occurrence of songbirds in riparian woodlands, or 'arroyo' vegetation, in Mexico provides a pertinent example (Warkentin *et al.* 1995). In the Chiapas region of eastern Mexico, strips of trees and shrubs, or of regrowth vegetation, mostly 5–25m in width, are retained along many streams amongst farmland cleared for cattle pasture. Censuses of birds in the arroyo vegetation revealed a high diversity and abundance, especially of Nearctic migrants (about 25% of species and 40% of individuals). However, in comparison with extensive nearby forest, resident species in the arroyo avifauna were mainly generalists and forest edge species, with only a small number of forest specialists (Warkentin *et al.* 1995). Arroyo vegetation does not support a pristine avifauna, but has a valuable role in maintaining a wide range of species through the farmland mosaic. In its absence, the fauna would be greatly depleted.

Hydrologic regulation and water quality

Streamside vegetation has other important ecological roles in the landscape. It is the interface between aquatic and terrestrial ecosystems and contributes to the function and dynamics of both. Importantly, it forms a buffer zone for the stream and mediates the exchange of water, nutrients, sediments and energy between the two ecosystems. All interactions between the terrestrial and aquatic environments involve the streamside vegetation in some way. A number of the functions of streamside vegetation in hydrologic regulation and in maintaining water quality and stream integrity are outlined below (Forman and Godron 1986; Binford and Buchenau 1993; Ward and Stanford 1995).

Hydrologic regulation

Rainfall pattern and climate are major determinants of the quantity and timing of stream flows, but streamside vegetation modifies these processes in several ways.

- Vegetation slows runoff into streams and increases the rate at which water infiltrates soil. Litter and soil associated with riparian vegetation act as a sponge to hold water, which is later slowly released, adding stability to the water supply to the stream.

- Floodplain forests and riparian wetlands adjacent to streams moderate flood levels by providing floodwater storage. The lateral spread of floodwaters slows the movement of water and exposes a greater area of soil for infiltration and subsequent release. Vegetation (shrubs, trees, trunks) also physically slows the movement of flood waters.

- Vegetation in the riparian zone transpires water to the atmosphere. In temperate zones this may have little influence on water flow in streams but in arid environments transpiration may substantially influence the quantity and duration of stream flow.

The scale of these hydrologic impacts is directly related to the amount of vegetation, and therefore the width of the riparian strip. Wide vegetated strips have a greater regulatory influence (Table 6–3) (Binford and Buchenau 1993).

Table 6–3   Attributes of riparian vegetation that enhance the protection of water quality.

Continuous strip of vegetation with few gaps
Increased width of streamside vegetation
Gentle slope of streamside bank
Dense ground layer vegetation and litter cover
Extensive root systems to bind the soil of stream banks

Filter for sediments and nutrients

Influx of excess sediments and nutrients from surrounding land is one of the main threats to the integrity of aquatic systems. Sediments, such as clay, sand and silt can blanket rocky and gravelly stream beds, thus destroying breeding areas for fish and aquatic habitats for invertebrates. Sediments increase turbidity in water and change the flow characteristics of streams by depositing sandbanks. The loss of storage capacity in reservoirs and large dams as a result of sedimentation is of great economic importance (McNeely 1987).

Excess runoff of nutrients, especially nitrogen and phosphorus, from fertilizers and human or animal waste causes artificial enrichment (eutrophication) of water bodies: this results in changes to aquatic plant and animal communities and decreased water quality. It poses health problems to humans and domestic animals. Runoff from pesticides, insecticides and herbicides from adjacent land uses has even more severe pollutant effects on aquatic ecosystems. Streamside vegetation traps and filters sediments and nutrients before they reach the stream, thus limiting their negative impacts. Filtration efficiency of riparian vegetation is greatest for gentle slopes, wide streamside vegetation, and a high density of vegetation and litter cover at ground level (Binford and Buchenau 1993).

Stabilize stream banks and beds

Erosion from stream banks and scouring of the stream channel are important sources of erosion and sedimentation when the stream channel is unstable. Streamside vegetation plays a major role in stabilising stream channels. Root systems bind and hold soil along stream banks, while foliage, trunks and debris reduce the flow velocity and alter flow patterns.

Regulate water temperature

Increased water temperature reduces the level of dissolved oxgen, which in turn reduces the rate of decomposition of organic material and the capacity to support aquatic organisms (Binford and Buchenau 1993). Riparian vegetation buffers water against changes in temperature by shading the stream surface, especially in summer months. The shading effect is greatest for shallow streams with low water volume where solar radiation causes the greatest changes in water temperature.

Aquatic habitats and productivity

Streamside vegetation and the resulting fallen trees and branches, root systems and overhanging vegetation contribute to the diversity of structural habitats and flow regimes (pools, riffles, waterfalls) in streams. In turn, these provide a wider range of microhabitats that support a greater diversity of fish and other aquatic organisms. Streamside vegetation is also an important source of energy for aquatic ecosystems. Herbaceous vegetation is rapidly consumed after falling into streams, whereas trunks and logs are a long term source of nutrients for aquatic food webs.

Retaining and protecting streamside vegetation is not a universal solution to problems of stream degradation. It has little influence on point sources of pollution, such as effluent pipes, sewers and drains. However, it does have a significant role in maintaining a healthy aquatic ecosystem. Vegetation along lower order streams is likely to have the greatest regulatory and environmental benefits because these constitute the greatest proportion of stream length and greatest length of interface between aquatic and terrestrial environment (Binford and Buchenau 1993; Forman 1995).

Hedgerows and fencerows

Hedgerows and fencerows are part of a diverse group of linear vegetated habitats that occur in rural environments throughout the world. They display great variation in origin, floristic composition and structure, but there are several common features (Forman and Baudry 1984; Burel 1996):

- they are linear in shape and usually form rectilinear networks of habitat;

- they frequently provide links between remaining natural and semi-natural habitats in rural environments;

- they are closely associated with agricultural land and their composition and structure are strongly influenced by past and present agricultural land management;

- their presence, dimensions and vegetation composition are not stable, but change through time in response to prevailing land uses and management of surrounding land.

Hedgerows are linear strips of shrubs, small trees and sometimes large trees, that have been planted by humans along the boundaries of fields (Fig. 6–3). They are widespread in Great Britain, France and other European countries, and there is a long cultural history of hedgerows providing boundaries to farmland and a barrier to the movement of stock between fields (Pollard *et al.* 1974; Forman and Baudry 1984; Dowdeswell 1987; Burel 1996). Many hedgerows are dominated by a single species or a small number of woody plant species,

Fig. 6–3   **A network of hedgerows and woodland in a rural landscape in Surrey, Great Britain. (Photo: C. Silveira).**

although grasses and herbaceous species of the ground layer and associated structures (such as ditches and raised banks) add to the floristic diversity. In many regions there are extensive networks of hedgerows amongst farmland, forming links between woods and forests retained within the rural environment.

Fencerows are characteristic of farmland in the eastern United States and southern Canada, where they also form extensive networks amongst farmland and between woodland patches. Generally, fencerows have not been deliberately planted but are narrow strips (usually less than 10m) that have developed by the regeneration and dispersal of plants in a neglected strip of land between fields. Fencerow vegetation ranges from that dominated by grasses and herbs, to narrow lines of shrubs, to broad strips with mature woodland trees (see Box 5–9). Woody plant species in fencerows are primarily those with wind or animal dispersed seeds, but wider fencerows may support species characteristic of the woodland interior (Forman and Godron 1986; Fritz and Merriam 1994).

Shelterbelts, windbreaks, tree rows and plantations are other terms for linear strips of vegetation, generally trees, that have been deliberately planted by humans for a variety of purposes, including: shelter from wind, to reduce soil erosion, as a source of timber, as wildlife habitat, and for aesthetic qualities (Forman and Baudry 1984; Bird *et al.* 1992). Their structure and composition vary greatly. They may comprise a monoculture of a single non-indigenous tree species, or a mixture of indigenous trees and shrubs that mimics natural vegetation.

Habitat for wildlife

The ecology of hedgerows has been much studied, especially in Great Britain and France (Forman and Baudry 1984; Burel 1989, 1996; Burel and Baudry 1990), and they are well known as a habitat for wildlife in rural environments (Lewis 1969; Pollard and Relton 1970; Eldridge 1971; Pollard *et al.* 1974; Osborne 1984; Rands 1986; Lack 1988). The persistence and abundance of many animals traditionally present in European farm landscapes depends upon the availability of hedgerows to provide shelter, breeding sites, refuge and foraging habitat. Almost all British mammals make use of hedgerows at varying times: some small mammals rely on hedgerow habitats for persistence in farmland (Bank Vole), others (such as Wood Mice and Field Voles) also occur in agricultural fields, and predators forage or move along hedgerows (Harris and Woollard 1990).

Much attention has been given to the use of hedgerows as a habitat for birds, particularly in Great Britain (Arnold 1983; Osborne 1984; Lack 1988; Green *et al.* 1994; Parish *et al.* 1994, 1995), and this has provided insights into their value for wildlife.

- The presence of hedgerows significantly increases the diversity of birds, especially woodland species, in farmland. Sites with hedges, ditches or linear woods have more species than comparable areas of arable land.

- The occurrence and richness of bird species is related to the dimensions and structure of the hedgerows. Species respond to different aspects of hedge structure, but in general 'bird rich' hedgerows are those that are tall and wide, have many trees and species of trees, dead timber, and a diverse structure.

- Habitats associated with hedgerows along field boundaries, such as ditches and wide grassy margins, also enhance the overall boundary strip for birds.

- Hedge intersections are favoured by many breeding birds in comparison with straight sections, probably because a greater area of habitat is available within a specified distance.

- Land use surrounding hedges is an influential factor on their use as a habitat. There is a greater species richness in hedgerows where permanent pasture occurs on either side, in comparison with those with adjacent arable lands.

Fencerow networks in North America are also used by a wide range of animal species and have a role in maintaining wildlife, albeit mostly common species, within the farmland mosaic (Petrides 1942; Dambach 1945; Wegner and Merriam 1979; Best 1983; Asher and Thomas 1985; Shalaway 1985; Henderson *et al.* 1985). Small terrestrial mammals such as shrews, voles and chipmunks live within suitable fencerow vegetation, while medium-sized mammals such as the Striped Skunk, Woodchuck, Red Fox and Raccoon use fencerows for foraging, refuge and movement. Fencerows are used as nesting habitat by forest-edge and farmland birds, but many other species use them for shelter, temporary refuge, or foraging habitat. For example, in New York State, USA, 93 species were noted from fencerows (Petrides 1942), while in Iowa, USA, 62 species were reported to use fencerows in various ways (Best 1983).

The establishment of plantations and shelterbelts, and the regrowth of brushy fencerows in farmland were advocated by early wildlife managers in North America as a strategy to increase wildlife, especially game species, in rural areas (Davison 1941; Dambach 1945). Recent studies have documented the variety of wildlife that use such planted habitats (Martin 1980; Emmerich and Vohs 1982; Yahner 1983a,b; Schroeder *et al.* 1992). For example, during two breeding seasons in southern Minnesota, USA, 87 species of birds were observed in linear shelterbelts (Yahner 1983a). To maximize their value for the avifauna, shelterbelts were recommended to be large in size, at least eight rows in width, have a diversity of tree and shrub species, not be mowed or cultivated, and that dead trees be retained as nesting and foraging sites.

Hedgerows, fencerows and plantations are seldom likely to support sustainable populations of rare or threatened species of animals, but by forming networks together with remnant natural habitats, they have a significant role in sustaining a broad range of wildlife species and enhancing biodiversity within rural environments. Consequently, the decline and loss of these networks associated with changing rural land use, particularly increased mechanization and a trend toward larger field sizes, is of great concern (Conyers 1986; Barr *et al.* 1986; Burel 1996). In Great Britain, a total of 28,000km of hedgerows was removed in the six-year period between 1978 to 1984, while only 3500km of new hedge was established (Barr *et al.* 1986).

Other ecological functions

Recent studies of the ecology of hedgerows and fencerows have emphasized their context within the landscape and their relationship with other landscape components through the flow of wind, water, nutrients, energy and biota (Forman and Baudry 1984; Burel and Baudry

1990; Fritz and Merriam 1993; Burel 1996). The importance of a landscape perspective was starkly realized in France when extensive clearing of hedgerow networks in the 1940s–60s, as part of the rationalisation of farmland boundaries, led to widespread ecological problems – soil erosion, flooding, wind damage and crop diseases (Baudry and Burel 1984). Recognition of these problems led to one of the first major multidisciplinary studies of hedgerow ecology (INRA 1976).

By influencing microclimatic conditions, hedgerows, fencerows and tree plantations exert a major modifying influence on the rural environment (Forman and Baudry 1984; Forman and Godron 1986; Bird *et al.* 1992; Forman 1995). Relative to open areas, wind speed and evaporation are reduced downwind of the shelter, while daytime temperatures, soil moisture and atmospheric moisture are increased. Shading occurs in a narrow band next to the vegetation. Evaporation is reduced downwind for distances of up to 16 times the height of the vegetation, while for wind speed the effect extends to about 28 times the height. Reduced wind speeds greatly reduce the potential for wind-based soil erosion in adjoining farmland. Hedgerows and fencerows also intercept snow and other airborne particles such as dust and aerosols: over time, an increased deposition or terracing occurs at the hedgerow.

Hedgerow and fencerow networks intercept and slow the surface runoff and subsurface flow of water across agricultural land, and so reduce the potential for soil erosion. Deep root systems assist infiltration of water into deeper ground layers, while active transpiration by the foliage of trees and shrubs pumps moisture from the ground to the atmosphere. Ditches and banks associated with many hedgerows further increase their capacity to influence movement of water.

Ecological interactions with surrounding environments also occurs through the exchange of biota, which may have either positive or negative effects. In Europe, attention is being given to the role of field margins and hedgerows as refuges for 'beneficial' predatory invertebrates, such as beetles and spiders, that prey upon agricultural pests (Thomas *et al.* 1991; Dennis *et al.* 1994).

In these and other ways, hedgerows, fencerows and plantations have ecological impacts that extend across large areas, far beyond the immediate environment of the linear vegetation. These properties can be manipulated for ecological and agricultural benefits in rural environments by careful location, orientation and spacing of vegetation, and management of the vegetation (Bird *et al.* 1992; Forman 1995).

Roadside vegetation

Road systems are transport corridors imposed on the environment by humans for the movement of people and their goods and materials. The length of road systems and the area they occupy throughout the world is immense. In mainland Great Britain, for example, road reserves were estimated to occupy 212,000ha or 0.9% of the land area (Way 1977), while in the United States the 6.3 million km of roads occupy at least 8.1 million ha (Adams and Geis 1983). Clearly, they are one of the largest and most extensive functioning systems of linear habitats on Earth. The vast network structure of road systems, their pervasive spread throughout many different environments, and the large area that they occupy, are indicative of a significant ecological effect. There is much concern about the detrimental effects of road systems, particularly their role as ecological barriers, as a source of mortality for wildlife, and as a source of disturbance to adjacent habitats and the wider landscape (Bennett 1991; Forman and Hersperger 1996). However, the extent of road systems and their high level of structural connectivity suggests that there may be advantages for species that are able to use the associated roadside habitats. Roadside vegetation, the strip of vegetation between the road surface and the boundary of the road reserve, is the focus of this discussion.

The type and quality of habitats on roadsides varies greatly, both within and between countries. In Australia, in particular, road systems are distinctive in that many roadsides support strips of remnant natural vegetation such as eucalypt forest and woodland, shrubland and grassland (Walling 1985; Arnold *et al.* 1987; Bennett 1988; Hibberd and Soutberg 1991; Hussey 1991). In rural regions of southern Australia, roadside vegetation contributes substantially to natural habitat in the landscape, and is important for the conservation of some plant species (Table 6–2). In the Kellerberrin area of Western Australia, for example, 380km (63%) of the 602km of roads in the district have strips of native vegetation from 2–30m in width on either side of the road (Arnold *et al.* 1991), together comprising about 10% of remnant native vegetation in the district. In other districts in Western Australia, strips of native vegetation up to 200m wide were deliberately retained adjacent to roads to preserve areas for wildflower conservation (Hussey 1991). One road, from Wubin to Mullewa, has a continuous strip of native vegetation from 5–30m in width extending for 222km and connecting small vegetated reserves at 15km intervals (Keals and Majer 1991). In contrast, in many countries in Europe, North America and Asia, roadside vegetation is mainly of grasses and herbs, managed to maintain a low grassy or shrub cover (Niering and Goodwin 1974; Way 1977; Laursen 1981; Parr and Way 1988).

Birds are usually the most conspicuous species of wildlife on roadsides and consequently there are numerous reports from around the world of birds using roadside vegetation as a habitat: from India (Dhindsa *et al.* 1988), United States (Oetting and Cassell 1971; Clark and Karr 1979; Ferris 1979; Warner 1992; Camp and Best 1993); the United Kingdom (Way 1977); Denmark (Laursen 1981); Netherlands (Reijnen and Foppen 1994), Czechoslovakia (Havlin 1987); and Australia (Newbey and Newbey 1987; Middleton 1980; Arnold and Weeldenburg 1990; Leach and Recher 1993).

Detailed studies of the use of roadside vegetation by birds in the Wheatbelt region of Western Australia have shown that more than 80% of land birds in local districts use native vegetation on roadsides as a habitat (Arnold and Weeldenburg 1990; Cale 1990; Saunders and de Rebeira 1991; Lynch *et al.* 1995). The roadside avifauna includes a wide range of species, but numbers tend to be dominated by common species. In the Kellerberrin district, all of the 'very common' species, 96% of 'common' species, 96% of 'uncommon' species and 54% of 'rare' species were recorded using roadside vegetation (Cale 1990). The composition of the avifauna varies in relation to the vegetation type (woodland or shrubland) and the structure of the understorey. Wide (40–50m), densely vegetated roadside strips support an avifauna that is comparable to that in large remnants. Some species are resident year-round in the roadside vegetation, while others move to and from the roadside as a short-term or seasonal habitat. Red-capped Robins are seldom observed on roadsides during the breeding season, but their numbers increase during the non-breeding season consistent with the use of roadsides as a dispersal pathway by young birds (Arnold and Weeldenburg 1990; Cale 1990). The

Box 6–4   Roadside habitat for butterflies in the United Kingdom

Twenty-seven species of butterflies, representing 47% of the butterfly fauna currently found in the United Kingdom, and two burnet moths (Zygaenidae) were recorded during searches on short transects beside 12 main roads in Dorset and Hampshire in the UK (Munguira and Thomas 1992). There was an average of nine species per site, but at one site 23 species (40% of the fauna) were recorded. Most of the butterflies were common species of grasslands, although several rare species were also present.

The range of breeding habitats at each site was found to be the best predictor of species richness. Other variables such as roadside width, nectar sources, or adjacent land use could not add to the model. Most of the species detected live in 'closed' populations and were partly or wholly supported by the roadside vegetation (Munguira and Thomas 1992). Road traffic was estimated to kill up to 7% of populations, but this source of mortality is insignificant compared with that from natural factors. Busy roads were no barrier to the movements of species with open mobile populations, but slightly impeded those with closed populations. However, roads could not be considered a barrier to gene flow in any of the species studied.

The density and richness of butterflies on these roadsides, representing a range of widths, traffic, topography and vegetation structure, was considered high by British standards and indicates that roadsides are a valuable habitat for these species. Active management could enhance the habitat even further in many situations, by a number of actions to provide a greater range of breeding habitats and larval food plants (Munguira and Thomas 1992).

abundance of nectar-feeding birds peaks when there is the greatest availability of flowers in roadside trees and shrubs.

In south-western Victoria, Australia, a network of forested roadside strips from 5–40m in width was found to be used as habitat by 18 species of non-flying mammals (78% of the local fauna) and at least seven species (70%) of bats (Bennett 1988, 1990c). The remnant forest strips on the roadsides (Fig. 6–4) link many of the forest patches remaining amongst farmland (see Box 2–1). Small native mammals such as the Long-nosed Potoroo, Bush Rat and Swamp Rat, are resident and breed within suitable roadside vegetation. They do not occur in grassy open farmland, but use the roadside vegetation to move between forest fragments. Arboreal species also live within roadside forests, while bats use both the road and roadside as a foraging resource. Other studies in Victoria have also shown that forested roadside vegetation is an important habitat for arboreal marsupials that depend on tree cover (Suckling 1984; Downes *et al.* 1997) (Box 6–5).

There is limited knowledge of the invertebrate fauna of roadside vegetation (Port and Thompson 1980; Baur and Baur 1992; Munguira and Thomas 1992; Vermeulen 1994). In one study in Western Australia, ants were censused on 16 roadside sites and compared with those in habitat fragments and adjacent farmland (Keals and Majer 1991). Almost all of the 93

Box 6–5   Forested roadsides as linkages for native mammals in Victoria, Australia

In the Strathbogie Ranges of north-eastern Victoria, Australia, a replicated experimental design was used to examine the value of remnant strips of forest along roadsides as habitat for native mammals (Downes *et al.* 1997). Transects were surveyed for mammals in four types of situations, each replicated six times: remnant patches of forest 20–80ha in size; 'near' roadside strips located 300m from a forest patch to which the strip was connected; 'distant' roadside strips located 1500m from a forest patch; and 'pasture' in the cleared agricultural land surrounding forest patches.

All fourteen species of native mammals recorded during the study were present in remnant forested strips (15–32m wide) along roadsides, and one species, the Common Brushtail Possum, was detected in roadside vegetation but not in forests. The mean species richness per site did not differ significantly between forests and near roadsides, but distant roadsides had a lower species richness than either of the former. The main difference was due to fewer terrestrial mammals in distant roadsides. Each type of site had a similar richness of arboreal mammals (except farmland, where there were none), but there was a greater abundance of these species in forested roadside habitats than in forest patches (Downes *et al.* 1997). The few native mammals that were detected in open farmland were large herbivores that venture out from forest margins, such as the Eastern Grey Kangaroo, Black Wallaby and Common Wombat.

These results demonstrate that forested strips along roadsides are a valuable habitat for a wide range of native mammals in this area. In contrast to cleared farmland in which few species occur, most native mammals are resident in roadside vegetation and occur over distances of at least 1.5km from forest patches. By providing a continuous strip of habitat that is occupied by native mammals, these forested roadsides maintain continuity of populations between forest patches, facilitate dispersal movements of individuals, and enhance landscape connectivity in this modified environment. Clearly, populations of native mammals in forest patches linked in this way are more likely to maintain an interchange of individuals and genes than are populations in those forest patches surrounded by farmland.

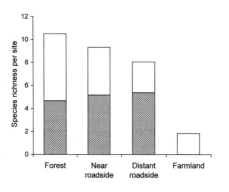

Mean species richness of native arboreal mammals (shaded) and terrestrial mammals (clear) for sites in forest patches, near roadsides, distant roadsides, and pasture in farmland. Data from Downes *et al.* (1997).

Fig. 6–4   Remnant roadside vegetation at Naringal, Victoria, Australia, used as linkages between forest patches in farmland. (Photo: A. Bennett).

species recorded during the study were detected from roadside vegetation, although the richness and composition was related to the quality of the vegetation. The widest strips of natural vegetation (greater than 20m) supported an ant fauna comparable to that in fragments of native vegetation. Narrower strips had a reduced fauna, while cleared roadsides and farm paddocks both had a low diversity of ants per site. If ants are reliable indicators of other invertebrate taxa, this suggests that roadsides with broad strips of suitable habitat have a valuable conservation role for invertebrates.

Box 6–6   Retained forest strips as habitat for wildlife in montane ash forests of south-eastern Australia

Montane ash forests in the Central Highlands of Victoria, Australia, are dominated by monotypic stands of the eucalypt trees, Mountain Ash, Alpine Ash and Shining Gum. These species grow rapidly, have diameters greater than 3 metres at maturity, and may reach canopy heights of 70m or more. These highly productive forests are the resource base for a major hardwood timber industry in central Victoria. They are also an important habitat for forest wildlife and, consequently, there has been considerable debate about the adequacy of measures to conserve wildlife in the ash forests (Loyn 1985b; Lindenmayer *et al.* 1990; Milledge *et al.* 1991; Smith 1991; Land Conservation Council 1994; Lindenmayer 1996). Central to this debate is the conservation of species dependent on characteristics of old-growth forest, especially tree hollows that generally do not develop in these trees until at least 100 years of age (there are no primary excavators such as woodpeckers in Australia). Large forest owls, cockatoos, parrots and other birds require tree hollows for breeding, while a diverse range of arboreal marsupials depend on tree hollows for diurnal shelter and breeding sites. Included in the latter group is the endangered Leadbeater's Possum, a species endemic to this region of south-eastern Australia (Lindenmayer 1996).

The code of forest practice for timber production in Victoria (Department of Conservation, Forests and Lands 1989) specifies areas of forest to be retained from harvesting, such as forests on steep slopes, forest strips adjacent to streams, and areas set aside for flora and fauna conservation including, in some situations, 'wildlife corridors'. To examine the value of retained strips as potential habitat corridors for wildlife, a study was undertaken of the occurrence of native mammals in a range of forest strips within the montane ash forests (Lindenmayer and Nix 1993; Lindenmayer *et al.* 1993, 1994a,b; Lindenmayer 1996). A total of 49 strips was selected, varying in mean width from 37 to 264m, each surrounded on either side by recently felled and regenerating forests aged five years or less. Strips varied in length from 125 to 762m; they included buffers along streams and also forested strips extending across topographic gradients, from gullies to midslopes or ridges.

Surveys for arboreal marsupials were carried out by 'stagwatching', the careful observation of hollow-bearing trees to detect arboreal marsupials emerging at dusk from their daytime shelter in a tree hollow. All of the species of arboreal marsupial in the study area were recorded from forest strips, and most species occurred at frequencies comparable to that expected from predictions based on studies in extensive forest of similar age and structure (see figure below). The marked exception was Leadbeater's Possum. Based on habitat models from continuous forest, Leadbeater's Possum was predicted to occur in at least 16 strips but was detected in only one. Its absence from strips with apparently suitable habitat was attributed to the complex social organisation of the species and its foraging requirements (Lindenmayer *et al.* 1993).

Box 6–6 (cont.)

Although all arboreal marsupials used the forested strips as habitat, the richness and total abundance of these species per linear strip were less than that expected from model predictions. The occurrence of arboreal marsupials in forest strips was strongly associated with the presence and abundance of hollow-bearing trees, a limiting resource for animals in the ash forests. The occupancy of hollow-bearing trees in strips was approximately half that recorded in comparable continuous forest. Of concern was the observation that felling of surrounding forests exposed the retained strips to wind, resulting in the blow down of many hollow-bearing trees. Collapse of these trees is occurring at a faster rate than in continuous forest, and has serious implications for the long term suitability of the strips as habitat for hollow-dependent animals.

These studies and associated work on ground-dwelling mammals (Lindenmayer *et al.* 1993) show that retained unlogged strips do provide habitat and refuge for native mammals in the managed forest mosaic. However, they do not necessarily support a fauna comparable in richness and abundance to that in continuous forest – at least during the early stages of surrounding forest regrowth. Their value and function may change as the surrounding forest regenerates.

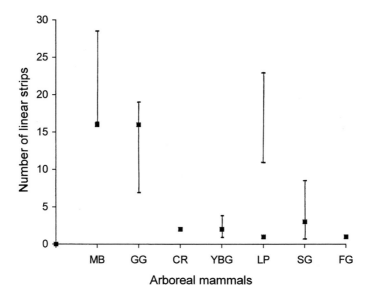

Comparison of the occurrence of arboreal marsupials in retained linear habitats with that predicted from models based on comparable continuous ash forest. Squares indicate the number of linear strips from which each species was actually observed, while vertical lines indicate the 95% confidence interval of the number of strips predicted to be occupied. Predictions were not available for several species. MB Mountain Brushtail Possum, GG Greater Glider, CR Common Ringtail Possum, YBG Yellow-bellied Glider, LP Leadbeater's Possum, SG Sugar Glider, FG Feathertail Glider. Data from Lindenmayer and Nix (1993).

Box 6–6 (cont.)

Tall Mountain Ash forest in the O'Shannassy catchment, Victoria, typical of mature forest occupied by Leadbeater's Possum. (Photo: A. Bennett).

Forest linkages

In response to the potentially detrimental effects of timber harvesting practices on forest wildlife, especially species associated with old-growth habitats, forest ecologists throughout the world have advocated the need for special measures to maintain populations of sensitive species within production forests. The retention of unlogged areas of forest as 'wildlife corridors', 'retained systems of habitat', 'habitat strips', 'leave strips', 'streamside zones' and so on, are included among these measures with the purpose of enhancing the status and connectivity of forest-dependent species in the logged mosaic (Recher *et al.* 1980, 1987; Harris 1984; Laitin 1987; O'Donnell 1991; Taylor 1991; Lindenmayer 1994; Mladenoff *et al.* 1994; Dickson *et al.* 1995).

The nature of the forest landscape means that there are fundamental differences between linkages in managed forests and habitat linkages retained within agricultural landscapes, for example. Unlike cleared farmland, an inhospitable environment that poses formidable constraints on the free movement of many native animals, a forest mosaic of stands of varying ages of regrowth will potentially return to a suitable successional stage for most species. 'Edge effects' between retained stands and felled stands will also decline as regrowth proceeds (Lindenmayer 1994). Young regrowth forests may be suboptimal habitat for numerous species, but it is unlikely that many forest-dependent animals are strongly inhibited from dispersing through the forest mosaic. Consequently, evaluation of the role of linkages in enhancing connectivity in managed forests places greater emphasis on their importance as retained habitats, rather than as pathways for channelling movements (Taylor 1991; Lindenmayer 1994). Retained habitats can enhance forest connectivity in several ways:

- by maintaining continuity of resident populations in linked strips of suitable habitat among sub-optimal regrowth stands;

- by providing a source population for rapid recolonisation of regrowth habitats as the vegetation becomes suitable;

- by providing resources (such as shelter and breeding sites) for species able to forage, but not live, within regrowth habitats;

- by enhancing movements and dispersal of species that *are* inhibited from moving through regrowth forests.

In many situations, these retained areas coincide with buffer strips for the protection of streams and water quality (Dobbyns and Ryan 1983; Recher *et al.* 1987; Darveau *et al.* 1995; Machtans *et al.* 1996). However, in some countries increasing attention is being given to designation of retained habitats in additional topographic locations that complement streamside strips (Taylor 1991; Claridge and Lindenmayer 1994). These may include links between adjacent catchments.

Studies of the ecological values of forest linkages for wildlife have mainly concentrated on their role as a habitat within the logged mosaic. A number have compared retained strips with similar areas of undisturbed forest, or have made comparison between retained strips of varying width or management history (Box 6–6) (Dickson and Huntley 1987; Recher *et al.* 1987; Lindenmayer and Nix 1993; Darveau *et al.* 1995; Huntley *et al.* 1995; Murray and Stauffer 1995; Machtans *et al.* 1996). In general, these studies have shown that forest strips provide habitat for many forest species, but do not necessarily support a species complement identical to that in undisturbed forest. For example, a study of the use of streamside strips by birds in production forests in Quebec, Canada, compared retained strips of 20, 40 and 60m width and control areas of unlogged streamside forest (Darveau *et al.* 1995). In the first year after felling and partial isolation of these streamside strips (continuous forest remained on the other side of the stream), there was an increase of 30–70% in bird density in all strips, compared with pre-harvest levels. The highest density was found in the narrowest strips (20 and 40m strips). In years two and three, bird density subsequently decreased with the fastest decline in the narrow strips. All strips provided habitat for a range of forest birds, but, over time, wider strips were more likely to retain an avifauna of forest-dependent species (Darveau *et al.* 1995). The longer-term suitability of retained strips as habitat for forest birds in this study was also influenced by exposure to wind; since clear-felling, 23% of trees in strips had been killed by windfall compared with 8% in control areas.

Connectivity for wildlife in production forests can also be achieved by managing the entire forest mosaic. With careful planning, the spatial interrelationships of recently felled, regrowth and old-growth forest stands can be maintained through time to provide sufficient areas of suitable habitat and to allow dispersal movements. Forest management prescriptions for conservation of the Spotted Owl in forests of north-western USA are based around managing a forest mosaic that includes patches of unlogged forest spaced at intervals that allow ready dispersal by young owls (Wilcove 1994). In this type of approach, the habitats that enhance connectivity also function as an integral part of the forest habitat mosaic for the entire forest fauna.

Retained areas of forest along streams, that also function as streamside buffer strips, have a key ecological role in maintaining hydrological processes, protecting water quality and protecting and enriching aquatic habitats (see Riparian Vegetation above). In the context of managed forests, these buffer strips have a critical role in filtering and preventing sediments from entering streams (Clinnick 1985; Binford and Buchenau 1993; Barling and Moore 1994). Exposed areas of soil on logging sites and unsealed forest roads are major sources of sediments that are washed downslope with rain. If allowed to enter streams they may have severely detrimental effects on the aquatic ecosystem.

Summary

Most interest in linkages has concerned their potential role in assisting the movements of animals through inhospitable environments. Little consideration has been given to other ecological roles and conservation benefits they may provide. A review of literature and examples for five common types of linkages – landscape links, riparian vegetation, hedgerows and fencerows, roadside vegetation, and forest linkages – shows that they have a wide range of ecological functions in developed landscapes. Of particular importance is their value as a habitat for plants and animals in fragmented landscapes. They may comprise a substantial amount of the remaining habitat available to wildlife, support resident individuals or populations of animals, and play a key role in maintaining the diversity of wildlife and continuity of ecological processes in heavily modified environments.

PART 3

LINKAGES AND
CONSERVATION STRATEGY

7 DESIGN AND MANAGEMENT OF LINKAGES FOR CONSERVATION

Throughout the world, habitat corridors and other linkages are being established for a diverse range of purposes. They may be intended to benefit single species or whole faunal assemblages, or they may be intended to provide benefits to wildlife while also delivering other environmental, recreational and social advantages. Similarly, the operational scale varies greatly, from underpasses and short habitat corridors bridging localized obstacles and gaps, to major landscape links extending many kilometres across elevational gradients or between reserves. The size and shape of these linkages and the issues involved in their design and management vary enormously.

In this context it is neither possible nor desirable to provide specific uniform guidelines for the design and management of habitat links because they will depend on the proposed scale and function of a particular linkage. A more useful approach in this chapter is to discuss biological issues that have a strong influence on the way in which linkages function and on their effectiveness (Table 7–1). These issues should be considered and evaluated for particular situations, in relation to the identified function of the proposed link. The following discussion relates most directly to the management of habitat corridors or stepping stones, but these principles are also of general relevance to the management of broader habitat mosaics to enhance landscape connectivity.

Management for landscape connectivity occurs within a social and political context and, although not always recognized by biologists, local factors and socio-political considerations are often as important as ecological theory and field research in the design and effectiveness of linkages (Newmark 1993). Every link is unique in terms of the social and community issues that are faced. There is a vast difference, for example, between the issues involved in the retention and management of natural corridors in suburban areas of California, USA, and in rural Tanzania or Costa Rica. Consequently, it is also useful to discuss a number of socio-political issues that are potentially important influences on the successful outcome of such projects (Table 7–1).

It is important to recognize that in the real world there is rarely an opportunity to design an 'ideal' system of habitats to maintain landscape connectivity. The all-too-frequent reality is the challenge of how to:

- best manage remnant linkages that have survived in heavily disturbed landscapes;

- maximize landscape connectivity by using habitats retained primarily for other purposes;

- restore connectivity between the vestiges of natural habitats that remain after development.

Table 7–1   Considerations in the design and management of linkages for conservation.

Biological issues	Socio-political issues
Biological purpose of the linkage	Status and tenure of the land
Ecology and behaviour of species	Management responsibility and adequacy of resources
Structural connectivity	Support from local communities
Quality of habitat	Integration with other programmes in sustainable land management
Edge effects	Community education and awareness
Width	Strategic approach to planning
Location	
Monitoring the use of linkages	

Biological issues in design and management

Eight main issues relevant to the design and management of linkages have been identified for discussion: the biological purpose of the linkage, ecology and behaviour of animal species, structural connectivity of the link, quality of habitat, edge effects, width and location of the link, and monitoring of the function of the linkage.

Biological purpose of the linkage

Clear identification of the purpose of a particular link, in terms of how it is intended to provide benefits to the flora and fauna, is an important first step and an essential basis for evaluating design and management requirements. Purposes commonly recognized include to:

- assist movement of wide-ranging or migrating animals through developed landscapes;

- facilitate dispersal of individual animals between otherwise-isolated habitats or populations;

- promote effective continuity and gene flow between populations in two areas by supporting a resident population within the linkage;

- promote the natural continuity of habitats, communities and ecological processes between large areas such as national parks and conservation reserves;

- provide the opportunity for populations to shift in response to change and natural catastrophes;

- provide habitat and continuity for wildlife in conjunction with other environmental and social benefits.

Having clearly identified the purpose(s) of a particular link, the suitability of existing plans or parcels of land can be evaluated, and biological and social issues relevant to design and management can be considered in relation to that purpose (Beier and Loe 1992).

The need to clearly identify a *biological purpose* is paramount given the widespread acceptance of the 'greenway' concept in landscape planning (Smith and Hellmund 1993; Ahern 1995). The primary theoretical justification for proposing greenways as linked systems of open space or natural environment in planning strategies comes from conservation of biodiversity. Yet the actual implementation of such greenways may be influenced more by aesthetic, recreational or cultural considerations than biological values. There is a danger that while the perceived benefits for biodiversity conservation will be the justification for development of greenways, a desire to ensure multipurpose outcomes for humans (such as recreational trails and scenery) will result in the actual benefits for wildlife being compromised or never achieved.

Claims such as 'wildlife corridor' or 'animal movement corridors' should not be included or accepted in planning strategies unless consideration is given to the specific biological purpose of the linkage and how its design, dimensions and management will be directed to meet that goal. The risk of a loose acceptance of what constitutes a 'wildlife corridor' is twofold: it is wasteful of land and resources if the objective has little chance of being achieved, and it devalues the concept and legitimate need for landscape connectivity in conservation.

Ecology and behaviour of species

A basic knowledge of the ecology of the species or assemblage for which connectivity is the goal is an important foundation for managing habitats to achieve this purpose. Knowledge of the spatial scale of a species' movements is of particular value. How large is the home range or territory? How far do animals regularly move? Do they undertake seasonal or nomadic movements? Clearly, the need for a linkage, its optimum dimensions and the way it is used will differ between species whose scale of movements can be measured in metres (such as spiders, frogs or beetles) and larger animals that regularly move hundreds of metres or kilometres.

Information concerning habitat requirements, diet, and other necessary resources will assist in managing habitats within linkages. Other behavioural and ecological attributes, such as the ability to cross gaps, the level of tolerance of disturbed habitats, the role of dispersal in the life-history, the age and sex of dispersing individuals, and dispersal behaviour (random or directed), also determine the most effective type of linkage (continuous corridor, stepping stones, or managed habitat mosaic) and the ability of species to effectively use such links (Harrison 1992).

Social organisation and behavioural spacing mechanisms within populations are also important. Species that live in groups or colonies generally require greater habitat area than do similar solitary-living species and, therefore, may require broader habitat links to meet these demands for living space (Recher *et al.* 1987; Lindenmayer and Nix 1993). Animals also vary behaviourally in their sensitivity to human presence or disturbance. For example, vegetative cover to buffer human presence is necessary for landscape corridors to be effective for several large African mammals, such as Eland and Greater Kudu (Newmark 1993).

Landscape scale links, such as those between conservation reserves, are generally intended to maintain connectivity for entire assemblages rather than individual species. To achieve this goal, particular attention should be given to the requirements of species that are rare and those that have specialized habitat and foraging requirements. Linkages that encompass the requirements of the most 'extinction prone' species will, in most cases, also be effective for the majority of more common species. For linkages to be effective in maintaining continuity of ecological processes, the requirements of the key species involved in such processes must be met. To maintain natural dispersal of seeds of fruiting shrubs and trees, for example, the landscape must be suitable for seed-dispersing animals to move through.

Structural connectivity

Variables influencing structural connectivity of linkages include: the number and length of gaps, the presence of alternative pathways or networks between suitable habitats, and the presence of 'nodes' of favoured habitat in the system (Fig. 7–1) (Forman 1983; Forman and Godron 1986; Noss and Harris 1986; Baudry and Merriam 1988; Bennett 1990a).

Gaps in suitable habitat can severely disrupt animal movements and the continuity of resident populations. What constitutes a gap and how effective it is as a barrier depends upon the type of linkage, the behaviour of animal species, and their habitat specificity and scale of movements. For forest-dependent animals, a gap in a forested corridor might be posed by a broad expanse of cleared grassy vegetation, a recently burned patch of forest, or a discontinuity in the canopy. But these will have different effects on different species. Cleared land that forms an effective barrier to forest-dependent beetles is unlikely to inhibit the movements of most forest birds (Box 7–1). Lengthy gaps in the tree canopy of a forest mosaic may inhibit the movement of an arboreal mammal, but not a terrestrial mammal that moves through the ground vegetation.

The 'barrier effect' of a gap also depends upon the extent of contrast between the habitat favoured by the animal species and that present in the gap. A narrow gap of unsuitable or hostile habitat may more effectively limit animal movements than a broad expanse of low quality habitat. Roads and highways that divide landscape linkages and animal pathways are a particular problem (Fig. 7–2). Not only is there a gap in the natural habitat imposed by two or more lanes of paved roadway, but traffic sounds, lights, chemical emissions and the potential death or injury by vehicles, impose a complex hazard for animals attempting to cross (Harris and Gallagher 1989; Bennett 1991).

There is little empirical information on the effects of gaps on the movement of animals, especially at the landscape scale. Studies of the effects of roads that divide the habitats of small terrestrial mammals indicate that gaps as narrow as 10m can inhibit, but not necessarily prevent, their movement (Kozel and Fleharty 1979; Wilkins 1982; Mader 1984; Merriam *et al.* 1989; Burnett 1992) (and see Box 5–5). Wider roads are even less frequently crossed (Oxley *et al.* 1974). For spiders, beetles and other invertebrates, gaps of the order of 20m can pose an almost total barrier (Mader 1984, 1988; Klein 1989). In Canada, grassy gaps in wooded fencerows had a negative influence on the use of the fencerow network by woodland mammals such as the Eastern Chipmunk (Bennett *et al.* 1994); while a similar negative effect on the occurrence of the Brown Antechinus (a small terrestrial marsupial) in retained forest strips in Australia was attributed to roads and tracks creating gaps in the forest strip (Lindenmayer *et al.* 1994b).

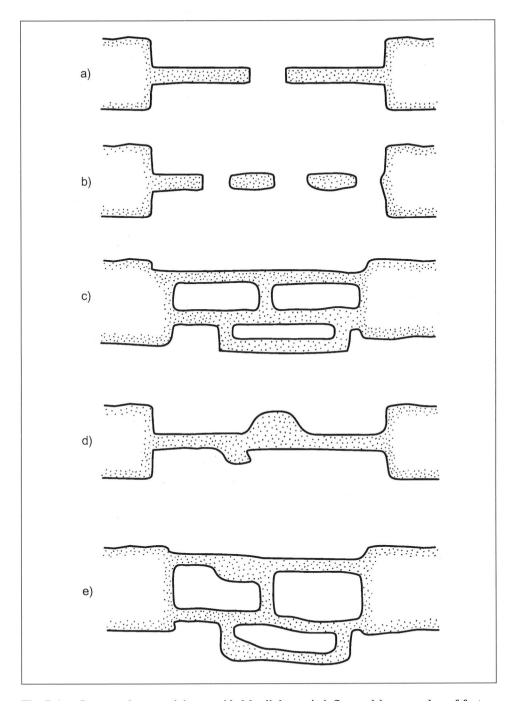

Fig. 7–1 Structural connectivity provided by linkages is influenced by a number of factors including (a, b) the number and length of gaps, (c) the presence of a network or multiple pathways, and (d) the presence of nodes or patches of habitat associated with the link. (e) A linkage that provides continuity, multiple pathways and has associated nodes of habitat is likely to be the most effective way of maintaining connectivity for animal populations. Redrawn from Bennett (1990a).

Box 7–1 Forest patches as stepping stones for Brown Kiwi in New Zealand

For species able to move between stepping stone habitats, key elements of connectivity include the distance between 'steps', the number of alternative steps available, and the land use and quality of habitat in the surrounding matrix. The gaps between steps must be within the range that animals will normally cross.

The Brown Kiwi is a flightless bird endemic to New Zealand. Individuals are sedentary and occupy home ranges of about 20–40ha, usually in forest or regenerating scrub with a dense understory. They forage for soil invertebrates at night and shelter during the day mainly in natural cavities at ground level (Marchant and Higgins 1990). At Paerata Reserve in the North Island of New Zealand, kiwis venture outside the reserve into surrounding farmland in which small forest remnants survive (Potter 1990). Radiotelemetry was used to identify the distribution and track movements of these birds.

Kiwis from the reserve made extensive use of forest fragments in farmland for foraging at night and also for daytime shelter. They crossed gaps between forest patches, often moving quickly across the open ground. Few individuals crossed gaps of more than 120m of pasture, with access to distant remnants occurring by birds using closer remnants as stepping stones (Potter 1990). Most birds were recorded in forest remnants up to 280m from the reserve boundary, and one pair occasionally travelled up to 1200m from the reserve by moving through three intermediate remnants to reach a fourth. All forest remnants isolated from the reserve or from other forest by less than 80m of pasture were used by Brown Kiwis, but only three of nine remnants isolated by more than 80m were used (Potter 1990).

These observations of movement patterns were recorded from resident Brown Kiwis. They suggest that stepping stone patches of forest must be at intervals of approximately 100m or less to ensure functional connectivity of habitat for kiwis living and foraging in this fragmented landscape. Gaps in excess of 300m appear to effectively isolate otherwise-suitable forest remnants from use by these birds. It is not known, though, how far kiwis may move during the dispersal phase of their life-history.

Knowledge of the scale of movements undertaken by Brown Kiwis can be used in a practical way to restore and increase habitats for this species. By protecting or restoring forest patches at appropriate intervals, there is potential to reconnect and expand the area of habitat available to the Brown Kiwi, and thus to extend the conservation potential of reserves in fragmented landscapes.

Birds are generally more mobile than non-flying animals but behavioural avoidance, rather than a physical inability to traverse distances, is probably the reason that many forest-interior birds are inhibited by forest gaps. Approximately 20% of tropical forest birds at diverse sites in southern Brazil and eastern Tanzania are reported to be incapable of crossing gaps wider than several hundred metres (Newmark 1993; Stouffer and Bierregaard 1995a). Clearly, forest corridors that have large gaps will be ineffective for wildlife conservation in these

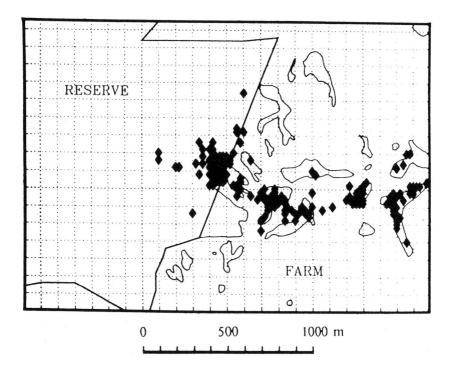

Box 7–1 (cont.)

RESERVE

FARM

0   500   1000 m

Location records for a female Brown Kiwi at Paerata Wildlife Management Reserve illustrating the use of a number of stepping stone remnants outside the reserve boundary. From Potter (1990) with permission, New Zealand Ecological Society.

tropical habitats. Even birds that readily survive in heavily developed landscapes prefer to move through vegetated linkages, where available, rather than cross open country gaps (Johnson and Adkisson 1985; Haas 1995).

The length of a linkage influences its effectiveness in several ways. With increasing distance there is a reduced likelihood of single animals, particularly small ground-dwelling animals, travelling the full length, and an increased reliance on animals resident within the linkage to provide population continuity. Thus, the greater the distance to be connected, the more important it is that the linkage provides habitat and food requirements for key species. Increased length also exposes resident or moving animals to a greater cumulative disturbance from adjacent habitats (such as risk of predation), and there is a greater vulnerability to sudden disturbance or catastrophe, such as fire and illegal clearing, that can cut the link. Several measures to reduce risks associated with length include the provision of duplicate links or a network of connecting habitats to provide alternative pathways (Fig. 7–1), and maximising the width of linkages to provide the largest possible habitat area and minimize external disturbance.

Fig. 7–2   A narrow gap of unsuitable or hostile habitat, such as a busy highway, may more effectively limit animal movements than a broad expanse of low quality habitat. (Photo: A. Bennett).

Incorporation of nodes of favoured habitat as part of a link can increase its effectiveness by providing additional habitat in which animals may take refuge or forage during lengthy movements. Habitat nodes may also maintain larger breeding populations within the linkage, thus introducing more dispersers into the system. Examples of nodes include (Fig. 7–3):

- nature reserves associated with a major landscape link (Noss and Harris 1986).

- floodplain expansions along riparian corridors (Dobbyns and Ryan 1983; Recher *et al.* 1987);

- additional vegetation at T and cross (+) junctions along hedgerow and fencerow networks (Forman and Godron 1986; Lack 1988);

- small forest patches adjacent to roadside corridors.

Intuitively, it is evident that landscape connectivity will be greatest when there is a high level of structural connectivity created by a combination of alternative and network pathways, nodes along linkages, and few gaps or breaks (Fig. 7–1).

Quality of habitat

Animals do not recognize a habitat linkage as such or its functional role as a pathway for movement – animals simply recognize whether the habitat within a linkage is suitable or not (Newmark 1993). Consequently, the availability and reliability of resources such as food,

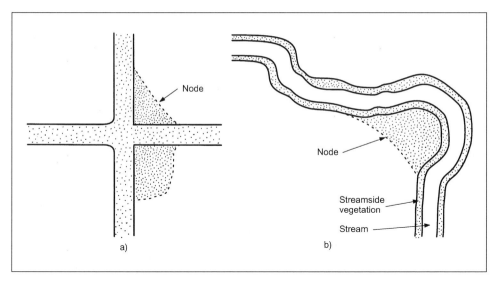

Fig. 7–3   **Nodes of habitat incorporated as part of a linkage provide additional habitat in which animals may live or take refuge during movements. Examples of nodes include: (a) vegetation at junctions of linear habitats such as hedgerows, and (b) vegetation expansion at floodplains or across bends in streams and rivers.**

shelter, refuge from predators and nest sites are critical if animals are to be able to live in linkages and use them as pathways for movement. A variety of studies have shown relationships between the occurrence and abundance of animals in connecting habitats and the availability of certain habitat components (Pollard *et al.* 1974; Yahner 1983a, b; Arnold 1983; Osborne 1984; Recher *et al.* 1987; Lindenmayer *et al.* 1993, 1994b; Bennett *et al.* 1994). The provision of high quality habitat raises several important issues in the design and management of linkages.

First, habitat quality is a critical issue for landscape linkages that form part of an integrated conservation network at the regional scale (Harrison 1992). Landscape links that maintain resident populations and communities must provide year-round resources for feeding, shelter and breeding. Similarly, stepping stone links, such as those that provide short-term 'stopover' points for migratory birds, must provide rich food resources at critical times of the year. Habitat quality is also important at the scale of local networks. Typically, linkages in which animals are resident must provide a greater range and specificity of resources (food, shelter, breeding sites) than those used only for brief movement (Bennett *et al.* 1994; Lindenmayer *et al.* 1994a, b; Lynch *et al.* 1995). Animals undertaking direct movement may simply need adequate cover or refuge for the brief duration of the movement, and may use linkages not otherwise suitable to live in (see Box 4–2).

Second, to provide effective continuity between large reserves that encompass several contrasting habitats (such as ridges and gullies in mountainous forest, dunes and swales in arid environments), landscape links must be sufficiently diverse to provide for species that occur in each habitat. This can be achieved by a broad connecting tract that itself encompasses the range of topography and habitats, or by duplication to provide links of different vegetation types (Bennett 1990a; Claridge and Lindenmayer 1994).

Third, wherever possible, linkages should be based on existing *natural vegetation* rather than on degraded or reconstructed vegetation. A high-quality habitat for wildlife requires the full diversity of natural vegetation, maintained by natural ecological processes. Resources in forests and woodlands, such as leaf litter, tree hollows, large dead trees, hypogeal fungi and diverse invertebrate communities, cannot be created simply by planting trees and shrubs in rows. An urgent task, therefore, is to identify, retain and protect natural links that are still present in the landscape *before they are lost*. Where it is necessary to re-establish vegetated links, priority should be given to restoration that mimics the natural environment. Restoration of existing semi-natural vegetation or revegetation directly adjacent to natural vegetation is likely to enhance the re-establishment of natural processes in new habitats (Hobbs 1993b).

Fourth, wildlife habitats are not static but change with time. Some resources, such as large trees, natural tree hollows and large decaying logs, only develop after long periods of time; whereas other resources may occur only in early successional stages. Animal species show different patterns of occurrence in relation to vegetation age and so the seral stage of the habitat can be a determining influence on its value as a link. In tropical forests in Queensland, Australia, the scarcity of several arboreal mammals in forest remnants was attributed to their inability to use corridors of secondary regrowth forest (Laurance 1990). The Lemuroid Ringtail, although common in primary rainforest, did not occur in secondary forest habitats. Consequently, although potential habitat corridors were present and were used by other species, the nature of the habitat apparently precluded this species from using the links. In the longer term it will be necessary to actively manage vegetation in many conservation networks to ensure that key habitat resources are maintained.

Last, linear habitats are particularly vulnerable to edge effects (see below), and consequently a greater level of management is required to maintain the integrity of vegetation in linkages than for comparable areas within extensive natural environments.

Edge effects

The linear shape of habitat corridors and the relatively small size of stepping stones means that the ratio of edge to area is often high in linkages (Fig. 7–4). Consequently, linkages are particularly vulnerable to what has been termed 'edge effects'. A growing body of research shows that a range of physical and biological effects occur along edges that can affect wildlife either directly or indirectly through changes to habitats (Harris 1988a; Yahner 1988; Bierregard *et al.* 1992; Angelstam 1992; Murcia 1995). In human-dominated landscapes, processes and impacts arising from outside remnant habitats are likely to be as important, or more important, than processes within the habitat in determining conditions for the fauna (Janzen 1986; Saunders *et al.* 1991). The main types of edge effects are summarized below.

Microclimatic changes that occur at the edge of habitats include changes in solar radiation, incident light, humidity, temperature and wind speed (Forman and Godron 1986; Lovejoy *et al.* 1986; Young and Mitchell 1994). Consequently, changes can be expected at newly created edges following exposure from clearing. For example, blow-down and uprooting of trees as a result of increased exposure to wind has been reported from retained forest strips in managed forests in several countries (Esseen 1994; Darveau *et al.* 1995; Lindenmayer *et al.* 1997) (see Box 6–6).

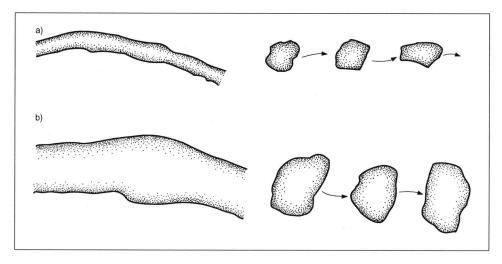

Fig. 7–4 **The linear shape of habitat corridors and relatively small size of stepping stone habitats means that the ratio of edge to area is high. There may be little 'interior' undisturbed habitat in many linkages (a), unless they are wide in relation to edge disturbance processes in that environment (b).**

Changes in the composition and structure of plant communities occur at the edge of a habitat, so that edges are characteristically different from the interior (Ranney *et al.* 1981; Laurance 1991b; Malcolm 1994). These changes arise from the responses of plant species to altered micro-climatic conditions, and from the invasion and establishment of plant species from adjacent habitats. Where remnants and habitat corridors border disturbed and cleared environments there is usually a large array of weedy and pioneer plant species available to colonize, displace native plants and alter the habitat.

Changes to plant communities mean altered habitats for animals – of benefit to some species and a disadvantage to others. For example, dense shrubby vegetation close to forest edges, where increased light penetration allows increased growth of shrubs or small trees, may provide increased foraging and nesting sites for understorey birds (Gates and Gysel 1978). This is not necessarily to their advantage because nests close to edges may experience reduced fledging success due to predation and parasitism (see below). Vegetation changes that affect animals may also be subtle. In coniferous forests of north-western USA, Red-backed Voles are extremely scarce in clear-cut forest but persist in small remnants of old-growth forest (Mills 1995). Trapping studies in the remnants found that the abundance of voles was lowest close to the clearcut edge and highest near the centre of the remnant. Voles are often associated with large logs and other woody debris, but woody debris showed the opposite trend being more abundant near the edges. In this case, the mechanism influencing the 'edge effect' shown by voles appears to be the availability of underground fungi (truffles) which comprise a large part of the voles diet. Truffles were virtually absent from regenerating clearcuts and the edges of remnants, but were present within the old-growth interior (Mills 1995).

Wildlife species that are edge specialists or are typical of disturbed lands can invade linkages and become predators, competitors, or parasites of 'interior' species (Yahner 1988).

- In habitats close to edges the original suite of predators may be supplemented by those from adjacent disturbed land. Experimental and observational studies of predation on birds' nests have shown that a significantly greater level of predation may occur in edge habitats close to disturbed land compared with the forest interior (Gates and Gysel 1978; Wilcove 1985; Andrén and Angelstam 1988; Yahner and Scott 1988).

- Edge species may compete with interior species for food and other resources. For example, the Noisy Miner favours open woodlands in south-eastern Australia and displays a high level of interspecific aggression to other small insectivorous birds. Sites where Noisy Miners are present have fewer bird species than comparable habitats where they are absent (Loyn 1987; Barrett *et al.* 1994). Noisy Miners are common in remnant woodland along roadsides and may greatly affect the use of roadside habitat networks by other birds, by actively displacing them.

- Habitat changes at edges may result in changes to relationships between parasites and hosts (Brittingham and Temple 1983; Taylor and Merriam 1996). In North America, the Brown-headed Cowbird has been found to significantly reduce the breeding success of forest birds close to edges as a result of nest parasitism. In woodlands in Wisconsin, USA, 65% of nests found along the edge of woodlands were parasitized. Close to edges there was an average of 1.1 cowbird eggs per nest while at locations more than 300m from the forest edge the average was 0.23 eggs per nest (Brittingham and Temple 1983).

Edge habitats are prone to a range of disturbance processes, often the result of activities in adjacent developed land. These include the drift of fertilizers and chemicals from farmland, trampling and grazing by domestic stock, fires escaping into forest edges or riparian buffer zones, the placement of access tracks and control burns along edges, and recreational disturbance and littering. In rural environments simple management measures such as fencing to exclude domestic stock (Scougall *et al.* 1993) can greatly reduce the amount of disturbance to streamside vegetation, fencerows, hedgerows, and stepping stone habitat patches that maintain connectivity through the rural landscape.

How far do edge effects extend? How wide is an edge? How wide must landscape links, local habitat corridors or stepping stones be to minimize the impact of edge disturbance and include high quality habitat? These are difficult questions of direct relevance to wildlife conservation. The solutions must be considered in relation to a particular process or parameter (Box 7–2). For example, a study in the USA showed that in terms of vegetation structure the width of a forest edge was less than 13m but, based upon the distribution of birds' nests, the functional width of the edge ranged from 9–64m for three sites studied (Gates and Mosher 1981). In Sweden, higher levels of predation on birds' nests at the forest-farmland edge declined with increasing distance into the forest, but at distances of 100m they were still higher than at 200–500m into the forest (Andrén and Angelstam 1988). Changes to the microclimate in forest patches adjacent to cleared farmland in New Zealand extended from 30m to more than 100m into the forest, depending on the aspect of the edge (Young and Mitchell 1994). Disturbances such as grazing by domestic stock, fires, and fertilizer drift, can also extend many metres inside the apparent forest edge.

The impact of edge disturbance processes is greatest where there is a sharp contrast between two types of habitat, such as forest and farmland. They are less marked at interfaces between two forest types, or different age classes within continuous forest (Rudnicky and

Hunter 1993). Narrow habitat corridors within rural environments, such as streamside strips, hedgerows, and roadside vegetation may effectively be entirely edge habitat. Within extensive forest, in contrast, a strip of mature forest surrounded by earlier successional stages of the same forest type is more likely to have an interior habitat and support animal species dependent on the forest interior environment.

Clearly, careful consideration of the type and intensity of potential edge effects is an important issue in designing and managing linkage networks. It is equally relevant to local linkage networks and to major landscape links in regional and national conservation strategies. Active management to minimize edge effects will be necessary in many situations.

Width of linkages

The width of linkages is a particularly important issue because width influences most aspects of how linkages function. Maximising width is one of the most effective options that land managers can exercise to increase the effectiveness of linkages for wildlife conservation. There are at least three main benefits of increased width of connecting habitats.

First, reduction of edge effects can be most effectively countered by increasing the width or size of the habitat. Wider linkages are more likely to maintain some habitat little disturbed by edge effects. For this reason, it is imperative that linkages between nature reserves or large natural areas that aim to preserve continuity for whole communities of animals are as large as possible. Continuity of populations depends on the quality and integrity of the habitat being maintained so that communities are able to live throughout the length of the linkage.

Second, for a linkage of given length, increased width incorporates a larger area and the potential for a greater diversity of habitats and a greater abundance and diversity of wildlife. This is simply an application of the well known species-area relationship: larger areas tend to support more species than smaller areas. A number of studies have shown positive relationships between species richness of birds and width of linear habitats such as riparian vegetation (Stauffer and Best 1980; Recher *et al.* 1987), roadsides (Arnold *et al.* 1987; Saunders and de Rebeira 1991) and hedgerows (Parish *et al.* 1994). For example, censuses of streamside vegetation in Iowa, USA, showed that the number of species of breeding birds increased from 10–15 species in wooded strips about 15m in width, to 25–30 species in strips greater than 150m wide (Stauffer and Best 1980).

Last, greater width increases the likelihood that a linkage will provide for species with requirements for large amounts of space or specialized feeding and habitat requirements. Thus, the relative composition of faunal assemblages in wide habitat corridors differs from that in narrow strips. Recher *et al.* (1987) used optimal foraging theory to predict that arboreal mammals with small home ranges were more likely to occur in streamside corridors of eucalypt forest among pine plantations in New South Wales, Australia, than were species that occupied larger home ranges. In accordance with these predictions, the Greater Glider was present in all corridors surveyed, but the Yellow-bellied Glider was present only in the widest reserve. The Greater Glider is a solitary folivorous marsupial that occupies a home range of 1–2ha, whereas the Yellow-bellied Glider is social, has specialized feeding requirements, and family groups occupy a large home range of 20–60ha (see also Box 6–6). Similarly, wider streamside habitats (50–95m) retained amongst pine plantations in eastern Texas, USA, were

Box 7–2   Edge disturbance and the width of habitat corridors in tropical forests

Tropical forests are under intense pressure in many countries. Given the inevitability of further clearing, biologists have been encouraged to find ways to 'creatively fragment' a landscape (Laurance and Gascon 1987). Retention of habitat corridors as part of an interconnected network of remnant tropical forest is one relevant principle. But how wide should such linkages be? Recent studies of edge effects provide some guidance for the design of tropical forest corridors.

Changes associated with forest edges have been recorded as part of the Biological Dynamics of Forest Fragments study in the Brazilian Amazon (Lovejoy *et al.* 1986; Bierregaard *et al.* 1992; Malcolm 1994). Compared with the core of a 100ha forest reserve, temperatures and vapour pressure deficit were elevated for up to 40m inwards from the forest edge and soil moisture was lower in the 20m closest to the edge. Deaths and damage to trees was greater close to edges, with the incidence of trees damaged by wind and other trees greatest in the first 60m. Significant changes in seedling recruitment were documented up to 25m from the edge with a non-significant trend over greater distances (Bierregaard *et al.* 1992). There were significant changes in bird communities within 50m of forest edges, and even 50m from the edge common forest-interior species were rare (Lovejoy *et al.* 1986). 'Light-loving' butterflies common to openings and second growth became more prominent following forest fragmentation and it was estimated that these species penetrate 200–300m into the forest (Lovejoy *et al.* 1986).

In north Queensland, Australia, a group of disturbance-adapted plants was surveyed in tropical rainforest fragments and in continuous rainforest at varying distances from the forest edge (Laurance 1991). Elevated levels of forest disturbance were evident for up to 500m from edges, but 'striking' ecological changes were apparent up to about 200m from the edge, including high levels of canopy damage and an increased frequency of occurrence of lianas and rattans.

Studies of the effects of tropical forest fragmentation on forest understorey birds in Tanzania (Newmark 1991) yielded information on distribution in relation to the forest edge. Birds were captured in nets extending inwards from the edge of a large forest. The distance from the edge at which understorey birds were captured provides a measure of their response to altered conditions near the edge. For the species encountered furthest from the edge (Northern Olive Thrush), the median distance was 266m.

These studies from three continents show that ecological changes associated with tropical forest edges have marked effects within at least the first 50m and have implications for ecological processes over distances of at least 200m or more. To retain tropical forest linkages that have a core of relatively undisturbed vegetation for species dependent on the forest interior, they will need to be at least 400–600m in width, and preferably wider in order to buffer and protect the core vegetation.

found to support a greater representation of forest-dependent birds than did narrow strips (15–25m) (Dickson *et al.* 1995).

How wide should a linkage be? This question is frequently asked of ecologists, to which the most common response is 'the wider the better'. The simple answer is that a linkage is wide enough when it effectively maintains connectivity for the species or assemblage of animals for which it is intended. Thus, the optimum width depends upon the purpose and function of the linkage, the behavioural ecology and movements of the key species, and the nature of the surrounding land use. Long-term changes in the integrity of the habitat and the intensity of edge effects on fauna must also be considered. There is no single uniform answer. Systematic study of the ecology of wildlife in existing linkages of varying types and widths is the first step to a solution.

In the absence of empirical information on the requirements of particular species or communities, the most useful measure for determining an optimum width appears to be the distance over which edge disturbances are likely to affect the function of the linkage. To ensure that the link maintains some portion relatively free of disturbance, the width must be *more than twice* that over which edge disturbances influence ecological processes. This measurement must be based on the circumstances of a particular link and the disturbance to which it is subject. Examples of various methods suggested (Janzen 1986; Laurance 1991b ; Newmark 1991; Harrison 1992; Noss 1993) include the distance over which:

- altered microclimatic conditions extend and influence plant composition;

- invasion of alien weed species and edge species penetrate and alter habitats;

- elevated rates of predation occur;

- there is an elevated rate of tree blowdowns;

- elevated levels of nest parasitism extend;

- forest-interior animal species avoid forest edges;

- recreational disturbance extends and affects natural communities.

Harris and Scheck (1991) incorporated many of these considerations in proposing a 'rule of thumb' guide relating the width of a corridor to its function and the time scale over which it must operate:

'for the movement of individual animals where much is known of their behaviour and the corridor is intended to function over weeks or months, the appropriate width can be measured in metres;

for the movement of a species, when much is known of its biology and when the corridor is expected to function over years, the width should be measured in 100's of metres;

when the movement of entire assemblages is considered and/or when little is known of the biology of the species concerned, and/or the corridor is intended to function over decades, the appropriate width must be measured in kilometres.' (Harris and Scheck 1991).

In the light of the suggestions above, determining a suitable width for a linkage may seem a daunting task, particularly in situations where there is little detailed knowledge of the fauna or the local ecosystem, and there are competing demands for land use. In such circumstances, those planning linkages should:

- clearly identify the purpose of the link;

- use all available knowledge about the fauna;

- apply the precepts 'the wider the better' and 'as wide as possible';

- keep in mind that most existing and planned linkages are likely to be much less (rather than more) than the optimum width for long-term ecological function.

Location of linkages

In heavily disturbed landscapes there may be no choice as to where linkages can be located. The challenge is to implement the best management practices to maintain connectivity of existing linkages, or to maximize connectivity based around existing vegetation patterns. In other situations, such as extensive forested regions, options still remain as to where linkages can be most effectively placed to maintain natural connectivity. Location is also an important issue in landscapes where plans are underway to regenerate or establish new linkages.

The primary function of linkages is to maintain connectivity for populations and habitats that were naturally continuous. Habitat corridors should not be established to link populations or habitats separated by some form of natural environmental barrier: for instance, it is inappropriate to establish wooded linkages across a natural grassland plain. Care should also be taken when re-establishing habitat continuity to ensure that it does not facilitate the spread of diseases that may have established in isolated populations. Although these concerns have been raised as criticisms of habitat corridors, they are of limited relevance because they apply primarily to situations where linkages are being deliberately re-established. The protection of *existing tracts of natural vegetation* is simply maintaining natural ecological connections.

Linkages will be most effective when they protect known pathways taken by animals, such as seasonal migratory routes of large mammals, stopover points of migratory waterfowl, daily foraging or movement routes of large animals, or habitats typically used by individuals dispersing between populations (Harrison 1992). Clearly, preliminary observations of actual movements, or information from ecologists or knowledgeable local people will be particularly useful. For example, radiotelemetry observations were invaluable in identifying natural travel paths for Cougars in California (see Box 5–11); often along topographic features such as ridgetops, canyons, and stream systems.

In general, linkages should be located along, rather than across, environmental or topographic contours to ensure continuity of habitats for animals. Exceptions to this principle include some habitat corridors deliberately designed to cross ecological contours. For example, forest corridors may be located to extend across ridges to connect adjacent forested catchments (Claridge and Lindenmayer 1994). Similarly, some landscape links are located along elevational gradients to maintain natural continuity between habitats at lower and higher elevations and to assist the altitudinal migration of birds and other species (Loiselle and Blake 1992).

Whenever possible, linkages should be located away from known sources of human disturbance, or the disturbance should be moved from the designated linkage. Where disturbance is unavoidable, its impact will be reduced if it is located to one side, rather than centrally within a link. Disturbance to natural environments from two key sources – encroaching human settlements and road systems – are a major challenge to the management of landscape linkages. For example, the presence of an army camp and expanding village settlements across the remaining link used by Indian Elephants between sections of Rajaji National Park in India; the encroachment by thousands of people into the Kibale Forest Game corridor in Uganda; and the threat from forest harvesting, grazing and human settlements in remaining linkages between areas occupied by Giant Pandas in China (see Chapter 9 for further details of these examples), illustrate the threat and severity of human disturbance to the function of landscape linkages throughout the world.

The designation of buffer zones or the deliberate establishment of buffer vegetation may help to protect sensitive habitats within linkages (Noss and Harris 1986; Noss 1992). This may take several forms. To protect broad landscape links, a system of land zoning can be used to permit limited use of natural resources or limited recreational use in an outer buffer zone, while excluding such activities from the core of the linkage. The use of buffer zones in this way has been widely advocated to protect tropical reserves (Sayer 1991) and is a key element in the planning strategy for Biosphere Reserves under the Man and the Biosphere Programme of UNESCO (see also Box 8–3). Another form of buffering is to use strips of natural or planted vegetation adjacent to linkages to protect them from environmental change and other disturbance. Such narrow buffers can also serve as a clear marker of the boundary of the linkage, to limit incremental encroachment or clearing. Obviously, if buffer strips are established adjacent to habitat corridors care must be taken to ensure that they are of indigenous vegetation, not of species that will invade and degrade the linkage.

When compatible with maintaining ecological values, linkages for wildlife conservation should be located to complement and enhance other resource conservation strategies. For instance, in addition to maintaining connectivity for wildlife, linkages contribute to the protection of water quality, the reduction of soil erosion, the conservation of rare plant species and communities, the retention of indigenous plant stock and seed sources, and so on (see Chapter 6).

Monitoring the use of linkages

Monitoring programmes to assess whether linkages or networks of linkages are achieving their objectives are frequently a missing element in conservation plans. There is little point setting aside, or acquiring, land and carrying out expensive management activities if it is not known whether the goal is likely to be achieved. Monitoring programmes can be carried out at three levels.

First, there is a need for basic survey and inventory associated with the establishment of landscape linkages or networks, to ensure an informed basis for their location and implementation. For instance, in situations where a regional network of linkages is planned (Examples 5–11 in Chapter 9), it is usually based on qualitative principles rather than on quantitative knowledge of that environment. It will rarely be possible to survey every linkage, but it is important to have representative data from the types of linkages that are incorporated:

for example, the species of animals able to use 200m wide linear reserves in forests (Example 10), revegetated links along streams (Example 7), or hedgerows between woods (Example 5).

Second, there is an urgent need for monitoring programmes that assess the *effectiveness* of linkages, to determine whether they are achieving their goals. Such research programmes are not easy to design or implement, and require long-term commitment to be of greatest value. They may take several forms:

- regular monitoring of the occurrence and status of the fauna *within* linkages (either living there or passing through) to provide information on how the link is being used and the identity of species for which it facilitates connectivity;

- monitoring of individual animals within the linked system (by radiotelemetry for example) to obtain data on the extent, frequency, direction and type of movements made through particular linkages;

- monitoring of the status of populations and communities in habitats connected by links to assess changes in response to enhanced connectivity.

Third, monitoring of the use of linkages by animals is an important way of providing feedback concerning the most suitable design, dimensions and management practices. For example, management of linear 'rides' used by butterflies and birds in British forests has been improved as a result of forest managers and scientists co-operatively testing different management techniques (such as width, shape and orientation of rides) to develop optimum habitat conditions (Ferris-Kaan 1991, 1995). Such knowledge from monitoring programmes, even if only for single examples of linkages, can benefit the future design and management of other links operating in similar situations (Beier and Loe 1992).

Socio-political issues in design and management

Not surprisingly, conservation biologists and wildlife managers tend to focus on biological issues when addressing the reservation of natural areas, the management of threatened species, and similar topics. The same is true when considering the role of linkages for conservation. However, successful conservation requires more than just biological knowledge. The achievement of conservation outcomes requires an understanding of people and their aspirations, an awareness of the political and economic climate, and skills in effective implementation of programmes. Thus, achieving conservation goals requires a sound understanding of both the biological and socio-political dimensions in wildlife conservation and land-use planning (McNeely 1987; Clark *et al.* 1994; Grumbine 1994; Yaffee 1997).

What are the issues that need to be addressed to effectively implement biological plans for linkages and to ensure that they are successful in the long term? The following points are not an exhaustive treatment of social and political issues, but are intended to serve as a starting point for further discussion. The proceedings of a symposium addressing the complementary roles of networks of people and networks of vegetation for nature conservation (Saunders *et al.* 1995) provides many relevant examples. Case studies and examples outlined in Chapter 9 of different types of linkages and linkage networks, also illustrate some of the practical issues that arise in their development and management.

Status and tenure of the land

Habitat corridors, stepping stones and other linkages require land. For them to operate effectively the land must be managed in a way that ensures that conditions are suitable for animals to continue using the link. Thus, land tenure and the ability to effectively manage that land to achieve desired outcomes are critical considerations. The land required to maintain or establish linkages may be in private ownership, public (government) ownership, or it may comprise multiple parcels with a diverse range of owners including private individuals, companies, government agencies or authorities, and community or conservation groups. Ideally, a secure long-term arrangement with the responsible land managers is required to ensure that there is an ongoing commitment to the objectives of the linkage.

Where a number of options are available for the location of linkages, land tenure is an important criterion. In most developed countries there is a greater capacity (through community input and statutory planning processes) to have land owned by governments managed in an environmentally sensitive manner. However, in many cases there may be only a single option for the location of a linkage and a commitment to sympathetic management of the land can be a major challenge to the implementation of an otherwise ecologically sound plan.

Securing commitment to sympathetic land management may be achieved in a number of ways, including: purchase or acquisition of land by governments or conservation consortiums, co-operative management agreements, statutory covenants on land use, planning controls on permitted uses of land, or by informal agreements among local communities. Creativity and innovation are required. In some situations compromise will be required to meet the needs of land managers or indigenous peoples. For example, a broad landscape link between upland and lowland areas of Mt. Kilimanjaro in Tanzania (see Box 8–5) will be administered under district bylaws that allow the Masai people to continue traditional pastoral practices (Newmark 1993). In a different context, networks of remnant vegetation along roadsides in southern Australia are a valuable conservation resource (see Chapter 6), but their management must recognize the legitimate need to maintain a safe travelling environment and to minimize the risk of wildfire. This might require land managers (local governments in most cases) to remove trees close to the road surface and occasionally to reduce the fire hazard of the vegetation.

In areas where there is intense pressure for further development and future changes in land use are likely, obtaining a commitment to the use of land for an ecological linkage is difficult. Negotiations with a number of land managers may be required. The seemingly simple step of ensuring that the location and full extent of the area to be managed as an ecological link is clearly marked on appropriate maps, planning documents and land-use strategies, is critical to the long-term maintenance of the land's status and its effective function as a linkage (Beier 1993).

Management responsibility and adequacy of resources

Improved conservation outcomes are not necessarily assured once land is committed to a linkage. Ongoing management is required to maintain ecological values and to evaluate whether the linkage is achieving its objectives. The level of management required varies depending on the function, location, and surrounding land use. Passive management may be

Box 7–3   The Talamanca-Caribbean corridor, Costa Rica: involving the community in corridor development

Encompassing an area of 31,500 ha (plus an additional 5000 ha of marine areas and corralline reefs), the Talamanca-Carribbean Biological Corridor in southern Costa Rica extends from the high-elevation La Amistad International Park to the Carribbean coast. Included within this major landscape link are several reserves with various levels of environmental protection (part or all of Hitoy-Cevere Biological Reserve; the Talamanca Cabecar, Talamanca Poribri and Kekoldi-Cocles Indigenous Reserves; and the Gandoca/Manzanillo Wildlife Refuge), but 46% of the area is privately owned with no existing formal protection (Talamanca-Carribbean Biological Corridor Commission 1993).

The major objective of the link is to protect biodiversity along an elevational gradient of continuous forest through the involvement of (and to the benefit of) the communities of the region. The entire linkage is located within the La Amistad Biosphere Reserve that extends across the border between Costa Rica and Panama, a region of outstanding biological diversity with a large number of endemic plants, reptiles, amphibians and birds (TCBCC 1993). This region is also an ethnically and culturally diverse area and is home to 65% of Costa Rica's indigenous population.

Potential biological benefits of the linkage include:

- protection of natural ecosystems with high diversity. The corridor includes nine of the 12 'life zones' in Costa Rica and interconnects areas of high endemism within the biosphere reserve;

- opportunities for movement of species that undertake altitudinal migrations, including frugivorous and nectarivorous birds with ecological roles in pollination and seed dispersal;

- maintenance of regional populations of animal species (such as large predators) that require large areas of habitat.

The project is being developed by the Talamanca-Carribbean Biological Corridor Commission, which has wide representation (11 member organisations) to ensure that all community groups participate actively in setting policy and making decisions. The major challenges are to co-ordinate conservation measures across different land tenures and amongst many groups, and to limit activities that degrade the natural environment. Degradation is occurring in many forms: from land encroachment and clearing by squatters, by exploitative logging on private and public lands, by clearing of private land for agriculture and plantations, from mining concessions, through uncontrolled tourism developments, from expansion of banana plantations, and from illegal hunting.

Box 7–3 (cont.)

A series of project activities are being implemented (TCBCC 1993), based on the need to:

- promote the protection and management of biodiversity, especially to stop deforestation and develop systems of sustainable forest use;

- support communal action, such as community participation in the use and responsible management of natural resources;

- contribute to economic and social development of the community.

Evaluation of the success of these activities is included within the life cycle of the project, with proposed indicators including: the extent of forest cover compared with that at the start of project, the number and quality of land aquisition projects, the results from biological monitoring to track reduction in threats, and the level of effort shown by local organisations in carrying out project goals.

---

sufficient to maintain the integrity of linkages in some situations, such as broad undisturbed landscape links between reserves, or retained systems of unlogged habitat within managed forests. In other situations, active management and continual vigilance is required if the ecological function of the linkage is not to be compromised and ultimately destroyed. Maintaining semi-natural corridors for Cougars in the Santa Ana Range, California (see Box 5–11) (Beier 1993), requires conservation biologists to regularly monitor (and be willing to take legal action) the decisions and plans of five county governments, 17 municipal governments, two transport authorities and a major water authority!

Most linkages are intrinsically difficult to manage because their shape (high edge to area ratio) makes them particularly prone to disturbance, and because they frequently span multiple parcels of land that have different land managers and land uses. There are a number of important issues to consider for their effective management.

It is essential that there is a clear understanding of where responsibility for management lies, or how responsibility is to be shared among the parties involved. In the absence of such understanding, loss of ecological function may easily occur without any of the parties taking action to remedy the problem. It is also necessary to have agreement concerning the goals of management among those charged with this responsibility. This may be by formal management plan, or an informal agreement on measures required to maintain the status of the land and the quality of the habitat.

Skills in project management are required to ensure that planning and implementation are carried out effectively. A high level of skill is needed in situations where a number of landholders and competing land management objectives are involved, or where negotiation is required to purchase or acquire land for the linkage. Linked systems of habitat at the regional scale that involve co-ordination amongst private landholders, land developers and multiple public authorities, are a major challenge (Reid and Murphy 1995; see Chapter 9). Important components include clearly defining goals and objectives, identifying the sequence of actions to be undertaken, identifying milestones to monitor progress, and ensuring effective co-ordination and liaison among all concerned.

Adequate resources (human and financial) must be available to achieve the management objectives. Clearly, the resources required depend on the scale of the linkage and the complexity of land-use issues involved. At a local scale, many links and networks can be maintained by the voluntary contributions of landholders or community groups; whereas the management of landscape linkages frequently requires dedicated personnel and large operating budgets. For major projects, management agencies require personnel with a range of complementary skills, including biological expertise, project management skills, land management skills and sociological experience (such as community workers). Development of the Talamanca-Caribbean corridor in Costa Rica (Box 7–3) involves co-ordination among many local community groups, national organisations and international agencies; and the staff of the Commission includes an anthropologist, two lawyers, a geographer, a forest engineer and a biologist (Talamanca-Caribbean Corridor Commission 1993). Financial resources are required at all stages of such major projects, but especially during the development phase (often involving land acquisition) and initial implementation.

A further challenge for management is to anticipate the nature of future land use within or adjacent to a particular linkage that may compromise its function: changes such as new roads or housing developments, demands for access to natural resources, and the introduction of invasive plants and animals.

Support from local communities

Community support and involvement is a key element in community development work and conservation (Sayer 1991; Blyth *et al.* 1995; Saunders *et al.* 1995). The same principle is true for the maintenance and protection of systems of ecological linkages. In most situations, unless key stakeholders, management agencies and community groups are sympathetic, it will be difficult to achieve the planned goals of the linkage. Several points are relevant.

First, land ownership or management authority for a particular linkage may lie partly, or wholly, within the community rather than with governments. Unless these people support, or at least do not oppose, the objectives of the linkage it will have little chance of success. At a local level, for instance, linear networks of fencerows, hedgerows or streamside vegetation providing connectivity within rural environments are largely owned by farmers and other private landholders, and depend for their future on the land-use practices of these people.

The capacity of governments and local authorities to administer and enforce laws to prevent disturbance to linkages, such as that from grazing by domestic stock, poaching of native animals, tree felling or incremental clearing, is limited. Pressure from, and the expectations of, local communities that have an active involvement in land conservation is a more effective form of protection at local levels than judicial authority.

Governments allocate limited funds for nature conservation. Involvement of the community may greatly increase the resources available for land management, as well as tap into a large store of local knowledge and experience (Bradby 1991; Siepen *et al.* 1995). Individuals and community groups can be involved in restoration of habitats, ongoing management of disturbance, and monitoring of wildlife. The harnessing of the skills and enthusiasm of volunteer observers has been a major source of wildlife inventory through schemes such as the Christmas Bird Count in North America (Root 1988) and the Australian Bird Atlas (Blakers *et al.* 1984).

Land uses adjacent to linkages have a profound effect on their viability and the maintenance of their ecological function. Support and sympathetic management by adjoining landholders can greatly reduce disturbance across edges. Adjacent landholders may also protect and enhance linkages by maintaining buffer habitats on their property or by protecting adjoining nodes of habitat.

The support and active involvement of local communities requires additional commitments beyond the immediate biological goals of a particular linkage. Issues that are of primary importance to the local community, such as potential loss of access to natural resources (firewood, native fruits and other forest produce), problems arising from native animals damaging crops or killing stock in farmland, or the threat of weed infestations, must be considered sympathetically to prevent community opposition.

Integration with other programmes in sustainable land management

One of the most effective ways to obtain broad support for biological linkages is to integrate their planning and management with other programmes that deliver benefits in sustainable land management (such as protection of water resources or sustainable use of natural products). The challenge is to find ways to achieve both goals without compromising conservation objectives. Indeed, in many situations it is the protection of soil and water resources, or provision of recreational benefits, that are the primary reason for conservation measures gaining support. The retention of linked systems of natural vegetation along rivers and streams is the most promising opportunity to integrate linkages for wildlife with sustainable land management in developed landscapes. Streams are usually the template for retained systems of habitat in managed forests because they provide a rich habitat for wildlife while also acting as buffers to minimize sedimentation and protect water quality in streams (Harris 1984; Recher *et al.* 1987; Darveau *et al.* 1995; Dickson *et al.* 1995). Similarly, stream systems are the focus of many urban conservation links (Adams and Dove 1989; Little 1990; Smith 1993; Roberts 1994). Protection of urban streamside habitats provides recreational opportunities and improves water quality; and, where the streamside habitats are broad and well-managed, they also maintain wildlife in the developed suburban landscape and provide continuity between urban and outer-urban nature reserves.

Opportunities to maintain landscape connectivity by integrating linkages with other goals in sustainable land management are critical because in most developed landscapes historical patterns of clearing and land use have resulted in the loss of most natural areas. This is true of many European countries, where there is a long cultural history of intensive land use (Agger and Brandt 1988; Gulinck *et al.* 1991). Designing an optimum conservation network is no longer possible in most heavily populated regions, but as ever-intensifying land use makes the landscape more and more inhospitable for most plant and animal species, the effective integration of efforts to improve connectivity with other programmes in sustainable land management needs priority attention.

Table 7–2 Summary of measures that may be taken to enhance the value of linkages for wildlife conservation.

Issue	Measures to enhance the conservation value of linkages
Purpose of the linkage	• Clearly define the purpose of the link as a basis for management actions and goals
Ecology and behaviour of species	• Match the type and dimensions of the linkage with the ecology and movement patterns of the target species • Plan landscape links to provide habitat and resources for entire faunal assemblages, with particular attention to species having specialized requirements
Structural connectivity	• Manage habitats to minimize gaps in linkages • Monitor external disturbances that potentially may damage sections of links • Develop networks of links to provide alternatives in case of unforeseen disaster • Incorporate nodes along linkages to provide additional habitat
Quality of habitat	• Manage habitats to ensure appropriate resources (food, shelter, refuge, breeding sites) are present for all species using the link • Establish new linkages based on existing areas of natural or semi-natural vegetation rather than disturbed land • Recognize the need to manage linkages and their habitat resources over time
Edge effects	• Evaluate likely edge effects and their potential impacts on wildlife • Maximize the width of linkages to minimize edge effects • Seek ways to reduce disturbance close to or within linkages, or move the sources of disturbance • Incorporate buffer zones along edges to limit impacts of external disturbance sources
Width	• Match the width of the linkage to its biological purpose. Measure the width of landscape linkages in kilometres • Assess the area requirements of key species using the link • Maximize the width of linkages wherever possible to increase the total size and diversity of habitats for fauna • Ensure that width is sufficient to counter severe edge disturbances

Table 7.2 (cont.)

Location	• Use knowledge of animal pathways to locate linkages
	• Avoid establishing linkages across natural ecological barriers
	• Locate linkages along environmental contours to maximize continuity of homogeneous habitat (unless the goal is to deliberately link across contours)
	• Locate linkages to complement other resource conservation strategies
Monitoring	• Include monitoring as an integral part of the management of linkages
	• Design monitoring procedures to assess the effectiveness of linkages for fauna
	• Use the results of monitoring to improve ongoing management
Land tenure	• Ensure security of land status and tenure for linkages to avoid future detrimental changes in land use
	• Ensure that the location and extent of the linkage are clearly marked on maps, planning documents and land-use strategies
Management responsibility	• Specify responsibility for management
	• Ensure agreement on management goals among all responsible land managers
	• Ensure adequate financial and human resources, and land management skills are available
	• Anticipate likely changes in land use that could affect the link
Support from local communities	• Involve local communities in decisions, management and monitoring
	• Encourage sympathetic management of adjacent lands
	• Be aware of the wider concerns of local people
Integration with other programmes in sustainable land management	• Investigate ways to integrate ecological linkages with other programmes in natural resource management
	• Identify and communicate the wider ecological and social benefits of linkages
Community education and awareness	• Ensure that communication and sharing of information is an integral part of management
	• Determine the most effective means for providing information to all groups involved
	• Encourage the involvement of local people and community group
Strategic approach to planning	• Plan for connectivity at broad spatial scales (landscape, region) and with a long-term perspective
	• Identify future needs for connectivity before opportunities are foreclosed by changed land use

Community education and awareness

The exchange and provision of information is an essential part of the process of establishing and managing linkages. This includes effective communication between scientists and land managers, with those involved in making decisions about land use (including politicians), and with the community. This may seem self evident, but typically scientists are not skilled in communicating with the wider community and have limited knowledge of how to bring about changes in land use. Community education and awareness involves issues of *what to communicate*, the most appropriate *form* in which to communicate, and *how to involve people* in the process.

The message to be communicated has several parts. First, the purpose and need for the linkage, or network of linkages, must be clearly presented. This includes information about the animal species concerned and their habitat requirements, and how the linkage will assist their conservation. Second, the value of maps (preferably in colour) that clearly show the location and dimensions of the linkage and the habitats to be connected, can not be overestimated. Third, people need to know how the proposal will affect them and their regular activities, or the new opportunities it will provide them.

There can easily be a mismatch in the forms of communication between those involved, especially between scientists, land managers and members of local communities. Scientific communication is usually in written form, but few land managers and political decision makers read scientific journals. Information must be in a form that is readily assimilated by the person for whom it is intended. The most sophisticated conservation plans are of little value if the bulldozer driver does not know where to stop! Visual and spoken communication are important, particularly on-site demonstrations and discussion where possible. Making time to discuss issues with those involved and sharing personal experience of wildlife and their conservation requirements can be very effective. The interest, enthusiasm and commitment of those advocating conservation measures carries much weight and is an essential complement to scientific data and reasoned analysis.

The most effective form of community education and communication of information is to *involve* people in the activities associated with the project. This may be through active participation in decision making and planning, assisting with surveys and monitoring of flora and fauna, or involvement in restoration of habitats. For example, management plans for networks of roadside vegetation in southern Australia have depended largely on volunteer community involvement to assess roadside values (Example 17, Chapter 9); while volunteers from groups such as Earthwatch have contributed to surveys of the birds that occur in roadside networks (Saunders and de Rebeira 1991; Lynch *et al.* 1995).

Strategic approach to planning linkages

Planning, negotiation, reservation and protection of linkages takes time, and it is easy for critical sections of habitat to be lost in the meantime. This is particularly true when linkages are being established in a reactive sense, in an urgent response to development proposals that involve destruction and isolation of natural environments. There is an urgent need for strategic forward planning for conservation in those areas where continued pressure will be exerted on the natural environment. What do we want the landscape to look like in 20, 50, or

100 years time? Can we identify the critical habitats and linkages needed to maintain landscape connectivity in advance of developmental pressures that will destroy them?

It is simpler, more cost-efficient and ecologically far more effective to protect habitats *before* they are lost, than to attempt to restore landscape connectivity afterwards. It is reasonable to expect that planning processes for new conservation reserves should consider both the present and future context of the reserve, and how the future connectivity of natural environments will be achieved. Incorporation of connectivity as an element of conservation strategy is discussed further as the theme of the next chapter.

Summary

Linkages are established for a wide range of purposes and consequently there is no uniform set of guidelines for their design and management. For a particular situation, the most effective type of linkage and its optimum dimensions depend on the animal species or ecological processes concerned and their requirements for landscape connectivity. The most appropriate management for a particular link depends on its geographic and social context. To determine the most suitable design and management for linkages, it is necessary to understand both the biological issues and socio-political issues that may influence effectiveness in the particular situation. Biological issues include: the biological purpose of the link; the ecology and behaviour of the animal species concerned; the structural connectivity and quality of habitats of the proposed link; and its proposed location, width and potential vulnerability to edge effects. Socio-political issues that influence the implementation, future management and function of a particular link include: the status and tenure of the land, management responsibilities and resources, the level of support and involvement by the local community, and the degree of integration with other resource management programmes.

8   CONNECTIVITY AND CONSERVATION STRATEGY

Strategic conservation planning that operates at the scale of landscapes or regions and has a forward time span of decades is a critical priority in developed areas and in those areas where further environmental change is imminent. Effective conservation of natural environments and their wildlife can not be achieved by short-term reactions to an ongoing series of crises in land management and land-use planning – the tyranny of 'case by case' decision making. A strategic approach is especially required for the concept of connectivity to be fully incorporated in conservation planning. Many of the examples of linkages presented earlier in this book are situations where 'corridors' or other connecting habitats have been retained by default, rather than by careful planning. Similarly, many linkages currently being developed around the world are localized responses to the threat of habitat loss or intensive land use. This is not to imply that these attempts are necessarily ill-founded: rather, it emphasizes the need for strategic planning.

The main thesis of this chapter is that a primary goal of conservation planning in developed regions should be the delineation of *linked systems of habitat* within the broader context of an integrated landscape approach to conservation. A network of linked habitats that maintains effective connectivity for populations and ecological processes is unlikely to be achieved by *ad hoc* reservation or restoration of linkages in response to an ongoing series of development proposals. It is essential that forward planning is carried out to maximize opportunities for the most efficient use of land before options are foreclosed by further habitat change or destruction.

The purpose of this chapter is to discuss the role of connectivity in conservation strategies. The first issue to consider concerns the role of linkages as a conservation measure compared with other types of actions to counter the impacts of habitat loss and fragmentation. Other relevant issues include how and when to incorporate linkages in the development of conservation strategies and practical conservation actions. The following discussion responds to these issues by addressing three main questions.

- What is the role of connectivity in conservation planning and strategy?

- How can linkages be incorporated in an integrated approach to landscape management?

- Which linkages warrant the highest priority?

The chapter concludes by presenting a checklist of points for consideration by those planning linkages, or restoring or managing existing connections.

Role of connectivity in conservation strategy

Problems arising from the loss and fragmentation of habitats in developed landscapes were explored in Chapter 2. To counter these problems, there are essentially four general

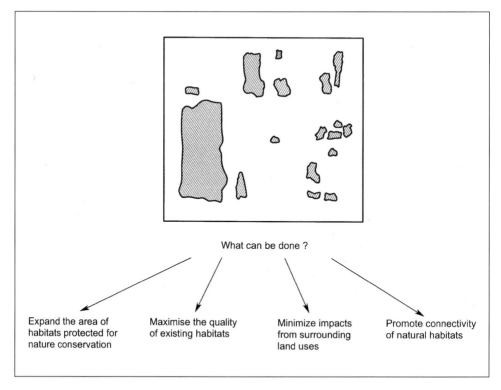

Fig. 8–1   Diagrammatic representation of four types of measures that can be undertaken to counter the effects of habitat fragmentation.

approaches that can be incorporated in land-use planning and land management. Planners and land managers can implement measures to: expand the area of protected habitats, maximize the quality of existing habitats, minimize impacts from surrounding land uses, and promote connectivity of natural habitats to counter the effects of isolation (Fig. 8–1). These four measures can be undertaken at a range of spatial scales – from the development of conservation plans for individual properties, to the planning and implementation of regional and national conservation strategies.

Expand the area of protected natural habitats

The protection and management of natural habitats, whether as conservation reserves or through other means, is the fundamental and essential basis for nature conservation. Measures that prevent further destruction or fragmentation of habitats, that increase the total amount of habitat managed for conservation, or that expand the overall area of habitat available to wildlife, are each ways of responding to problems associated with area-based changes in animal populations and communities. Large tracts of habitat are more likely than smaller areas to support self-sustaining populations of plants and animals, especially for large animals that require extensive areas of land. Increased habitat size also enhances the capacity for an area to retain a greater richness of species, to support entire communities, and to maintain natural ecological processes (Forman 1995).

Throughout the world, this objective is being addressed in a variety of ways:

- by including additional areas of habitat in nature reserves to increase the size of existing reserves or to add to the overall reserve system;

- by implementing statutory provisions or community programmes to protect natural areas and to minimize further clearing and fragmentation of habitats outside the reserve system. This may apply to lands held by private individuals or communities, by companies, or to government-owned land not within the reserve system. The largest tracts of natural environment in each district or region should receive particular attention for protection;

- by undertaking programmes to deliberately regenerate or revegetate land adjacent to existing habitats to expand the size and total extent of natural areas;

- by recommending and requiring that where habitats are cleared, they are subsequently regenerated or that comparable new areas are revegetated to minimize the overall loss of habitat.

Maximize the quality of existing habitats

Within the constraints of the existing size and spatial pattern of habitats in the landscape, the value of each area of habitat is increased when it is managed to enhance resources essential for the native fauna. Management activities can be directed toward, for example:

- minimizing and controlling land uses that degrade the natural environment and reduce its sustainability, such as intensive grazing by domestic stock that leads to altered vegetation structure and lack of plant regeneration;

- managing the harvesting of natural resources such as timber, fruits and wildlife, to ensure their long-term sustainability and to minimize adverse effects of harvesting on wildlife habitats;

- maintaining natural disturbance regimes that promote vegetation succession and temporally-varying habitats and resources.

Management to maintain the quality of habitats is particularly relevant in those areas designated for multiple use, where the goals of nature conservation must be weighed against other land-use objectives. Forests used for timber production, for example, make an invaluable contribution to wildlife conservation, but there is also the ever-present threat that logging activities may remove critical habitat components and result in the loss of animal populations.

Minimize the impacts from surrounding land uses

There is growing evidence that in heavily fragmented landscapes, processes arising outside fragments are a major influence on populations and communities within fragments (Saunders *et al.* 1991; Hobbs 1993a). Invasion by pest species of plants and animals, altered climatic and physical conditions along boundaries, and human incursion and development, all reduce the conservation potential of remnant natural areas. Large natural areas, including nature reserves, are also vulnerable to external disturbance (Janzen 1986).

The effects of external disturbance can be countered by a range of actions including:

• zoning of land uses and the prohibition of certain forms of land use close to important natural areas;

• the use of buffer zones around conservation areas to minimize the impact of external influences on the natural environment;

• management programmes to control the numbers and impacts of pest species of plants (introduced species, invasive weeds) and animals (predators, competitors, parasites).

Promote connectivity of natural habitats to counter the effects of isolation

The promotion of habitat configurations that enhance connectivity within fragmented landscapes directly counters the detrimental effects of isolation. Linkages have a number of major benefits (Table 4–3). They assist the movement of individual animals through otherwise inhospitable environments, including wide-ranging animals, migratory species and dispersing individuals. Dispersal movements between fragments can benefit declining populations by supplementing small populations before they disappear; or they allow opportunities for habitats to be recolonized should local extinction occur. Linkages also assist in the continuity and maintenance of ecological processes, especially those that depend on animal vectors, such as pollination, seed dispersal and predation. Different types of habitat configurations that promote landscape connectivity have been described in Chapter 4, and various forms of land use that function as connecting habitats were reviewed in Chapters 5 and 6.

These four general responses set the context in which connectivity has a role in the conservation of wildlife in fragmented landscapes. Promoting landscape connectivity is but one of a number of general measures that can be taken to enhance nature conservation. Clearly, linkages that restore landscape connectivity are not a universal panacea or unique solution to ecological problems arising from habitat loss and fragmentation. In practice, conservation strategies often employ all four measures, with particular attention given to retaining and expanding the area of protected natural habitats. Indeed, a strategy primarily based around developing linkages which does not also address the need to maximize the area of protected habitat, to manage the quality of habitats and to minimize external disturbances, is deficient.

Promoting landscape connectivity does, however, have a distinctive role; it allows a fundamentally different approach to nature conservation in developed landscapes. The first three measures outlined above are each based on improving the conservation potential of *individual* areas of habitat. However, where there is effective connectivity, there is the opportunity to achieve conservation goals through *linked systems of habitat*. Multiple tracts of habitat that function together as an interacting system are a more effective means of conservation than a similar set of isolated tracts (Fig. 8–2). Thus, the distinctive role of connectivity in a conservation strategy is to 'tie together' habitats into a linked system to restore the natural flow and interchange of plants and animals across the landscape. The concept of linked systems of habitat for nature conservation is developed further in the context of an integrated landscape approach to conservation.

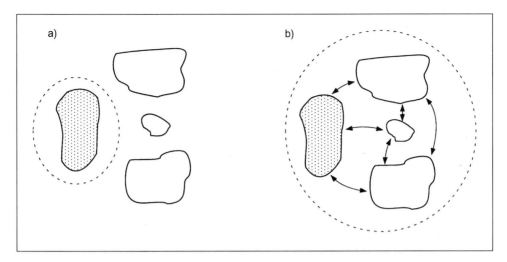

Fig. 8–2   Isolated reserves or habitats (a) may have limited potential for long-term conservation of populations and communities on their own, but this may be greatly enhanced if they function as part of an integrated system (b).

Linkages and an integrated landscape approach to conservation

The traditional approach to nature conservation has been based on selecting and managing areas as reserves of one form or another. These are usually national parks or similar reserve categories in which nature conservation is given high priority; or, in some cases, other types of reserves in which conservation goals must be balanced with other forms of land use. The typical pattern of reserves is that of a set of separate parcels of land, scattered in location across a particular region or country, and representing a range of different ecosystems. A growing view among conservation biologists is that a reserve-based approach, on its own, will not be adequate to ensure the long-term conservation requirements of the native flora and fauna. Substantially increasing the number and extent of reserves is an important step, but even this (if it can be achieved) will not be sufficient in many regions.

There is widespread recognition that in many regions it is necessary to extend the reserve-based approach and find ways to enhance nature conservation through management of the whole landscape. The concept of an integrated landscape approach to conservation has been advocated by workers in a range of different contexts and in relation to different types of developed landscapes. This includes discussion of conservation planning at regional and national scales (Noss 1983, 1992; Noss and Harris 1986; Grumbine 1994; Forman 1995); conservation in landscapes dominated by forest production (Harris 1984; Bissonette *et al.* 1991; Norton and Lindenmayer 1991; Franklin 1992; Mladenoff *et al.* 1994); nature conservation in extensive agricultural landscapes (Hobbs and Saunders 1991; Hobbs *et al.* 1993; McIntyre 1994); and conservation of biodiversity in intensively-managed cultural landscapes (Harms and Opdam 1990; Jongman 1995; Kubeš 1996). An integrated landscape approach to conservation is also important in the context of potential future change in the global climate in response to changing levels of CO_2 and other 'greenhouse' gases (see Box 8–1).

Box 8–1   Climate change and the role of linkages

There is increasing concern that anthropogenic changes to the composition of atmospheric gases may have significant impacts on the global climate. The presence of carbon dioxide (CO_2) in the atmosphere contributes to a natural 'greenhouse' effect, due to the atmosphere absorbing some of the energy radiated from Earth's surface, thus maintaining warmer conditions than if this energy all escaped. However, increased levels of CO_2 and other 'greenhouse gases' (such as methane and chlorofluorocarbons) resulting from the burning of fossil fuels, deforestation and other activities, are predicted to enhance the greenhouse effect and warm the Earth's surface over future decades (Peters and Darling 1985). Such global warming is likely to cause a range of secondary effects, including changes in precipitation, winds, sea levels and ocean currents.

There is much uncertainty about the likely rate and magnitude of greenhouse-induced climate changes, especially at regional levels, but it is clear that there is the potential for significant impact on the status of flora and fauna throughout the world (Peters and Darling 1985; Brereton *et al.* 1995; Hobbs and Hopkins 1991). Analyses of the climatic profiles presently occupied by plant and animal species, compared with future climatic conditions under various scenarios, suggest that the present geographic distributions of many species will be climatically unsuitable within a relatively short time (e.g. Brereton *et al.* 1995). If such changes eventuate, survival of species will depend upon their ability to adapt to new climatic conditions, or their capacity to shift their geographic distribution to track suitable climates. Those groups likely to be most affected include geographically localized taxa, peripheral or disjunct populations, specialized species, poor dispersers, genetically impoverished species, and montane and alpine species (Peters and Darling 1985).

It has been suggested that linkages may have an important conservation role in response to climate change (Harris and Scheck 1991; Hobbs and Hopkins 1991; Noss 1993). First, in some situations linkages may assist plant and animal species to extend their geographic range to track suitable climatic conditions. However, great caution is warranted before concluding that linkages will fulfil this role.

- For most species, especially plants, the rate of range expansion required to respond to projected climate change is much greater than that known to have occurred historically or revealed by paleoecological analyses (Hobbs and Hopkins 1991; Noss 1993).

- Range expansion may be limited by ecological or anthropogenic factors despite the maintenance of seemingly-suitable linkages. For example, climatic conditions may become more suitable in adjacent areas, but differing geological substrates and soil nutrient levels may be unsuitable for the plant species concerned.

- Many species are dependent on complex ecological interrelationships with other plants and animals, and consequently an effective range shift would require migration of assemblages of co-adapted plants and animals.

Box 8–1 (cont.)

• The geographic location and necessary dimensions of linkages for such biotic migrations are not known, but it is likely that vast tracts of continuous natural habitat would be required.

Linkages across elevational gradients are those most likely to facilitate effective range shifts because the geographic displacement needed to track climate change is much less than at uniform elevations.

Second, linkages have a potentially important role in countering climate change by maintaining the continuity of species' populations throughout their *present geographic range*, thus maximizing a species' ability to persist within those parts of its range where climatic conditions may remain suitable. Redistribution within an existing range is more feasible than range shifts to new areas.

Third, linkages also have a role in countering climate change by interconnecting existing reserves and protected areas in order to maximize the resilience of the present conservation network. Those linkages that maintain large contiguous habitats or that maintain continuity of several reserves along an environmental gradient are likely to be most valuable in this regard. Large populations and those that span environmentally diverse areas are likely to have greater demographic and genetic capacity to respond to changing conditions.

In the light of present uncertainty about the nature and magnitude of future climate change and its potential impacts, it appears that maintaining and restoring linkages are prudent measures that have conservation benefits regardless of the exact nature of impending climate change.

Before discussing further the elements of an integrated landscape approach, it is appropriate to outline some of the limitations of a conservation strategy primarily dependent on dedicated conservation reserves.

Reserves do not represent all natural communities

Nature reserves rarely provide a balanced representation of biological communities within a region or country. Areas set aside for nature conservation are often those on the least productive soils, on steep slopes and mountain ranges, or in areas such as wetlands where it is difficult to use the land for agriculture or other economic production (Leader-Williams *et al.* 1990; Pressey 1994; Pressey and Tully 1994). Biological communities on the most fertile and accessible parts of the landscape usually have been greatly transformed and are poorly, or not at all, reserved. This lack of (or limited) representation means that there are many plant and animal species whose populations occur mainly or wholly outside reserves.

To incorporate poorly reserved communities in a regional reserve system may pose great difficulty because of financial costs, because the land is committed to other uses, or because the nature of the habitat (such as numerous small fragments amongst farmland) does not fit within appropriate reserve definitions and regulations.

Most reserves are too small to sustain viable populations and natural ecological processes

Reserves vary greatly in size. Some well known reserves such as Yellowstone National Park, USA, Gir Sanctuary in India, and Serengeti National Park in Tanzania, are relatively large (greater than 100,000ha), but this is not typical of most reserves. Few nature reserves are of sufficient size to support viable populations of all of their indigenous species of wildlife in the long term. Large predators are a particular test case, but species with specialized foraging or habitat requirements may also require large areas to sustain viable populations. Estimates of the area requirements for viable populations of predators such as Grizzly Bears, Wolves, Cougars, or large forest raptors, suggest that even the largest reserves in some countries are unlikely to be sufficient in their own right (Sullivan and Shaffer 1975; Thiollay and Meyburg 1988; Beier 1993). Already there is evidence of the loss of species in major reserves in North America, even though not yet fully isolated (Newmark 1987, 1995). Predictive models, such as those for some African reserves (East 1981; Western and Ssemakula 1981), suggest further species will be lost simply due to insufficient size, regardless of additional pressures such as poaching or habitat degradation. If large reserves cannot meet the challenge of maintaining viable populations of all species, there is little likelihood that the majority of smaller parks, reserves and protected areas will be sufficient.

Further, for reserves to conserve entire faunal assemblages, they must be of sufficient size to allow natural disturbance regimes, such as fire, windthrow and flooding, to continue without eliminating species. A 'minimum dynamic area' is defined as the smallest area with a natural disturbance regime that maintains internal recolonization sources (Pickett and Thompson 1978). Wildfire, for example, may burn a large portion of a reserve, but if the reserve is sufficiently large there will always be unburnt areas to act as sources for recolonization. In contrast, small reserves may be entirely burned and populations eliminated (Fig. 8–3). In addition, some species depend on particular stages of vegetation succession following disturbance, so reserves must be adequate to maintain an array of habitat patches of different successional stages. The area required to meet this goal depends on the context of the reserve and the type and source of natural disturbances (Pickett and Thompson 1978; Baker 1992; Forman 1995). Typically, the minimum dynamic area must be large in relation to the maximum disturbance size.

Other disturbance processes of human origin, such as acid rain, rising saline groundwater, wildlife epidemics and the spread of pest plants and animals, all operate at scales greater than most conservation reserves and potentially can disrupt natural functions over entire reserves.

Movement patterns of animals frequently cross reserve boundaries

The movement patterns of many animals regularly cross the boundaries of nature reserves. If the habitats they use and the resources they obtain outside of a reserve are ultimately lost through lack of suitable management or protection, the effectiveness of the reserve is greatly diminished (Box 8–2).

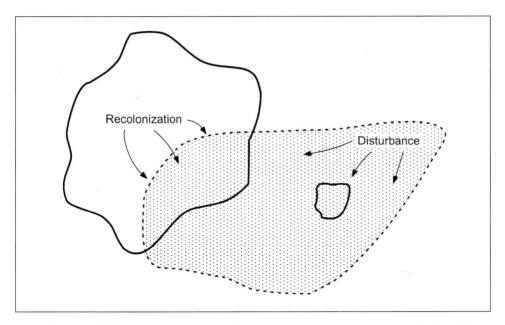

Fig. 8–3   For the long-term conservation of flora and fauna, reserves must be sufficiently large to withstand major disturbances and to maintain internal sources of recolonization. Smaller reserves or patches of habitat may be entirely disturbed.

- Some species regularly use feeding, sheltering or breeding resources that occur in markedly different habitats. Common Bent-wing Bats, for example, occur in caves or abandoned mines in a number of conservation reserves in Victoria, Australia, but do not breed there. Reproduction of this species in Victoria is known from only two sites, neither within conservation reserves, where there are caves with suitable microclimatic conditions (Menkhorst and Lumsden 1995).

- Many species undertake annual migrations between altitudinal zones or geographic locations, from several kilometres to thousands of kilometres apart (Chapter 4). A reserve may protect representative breeding habitat for such species, but non-breeding habitats in other locations may lack any protection.

- Other species undertake irregular seasonal movements to exploit resources that are patchy in space or time. Animals that feed on nectar, fruits, or seeds move in response to the phenologies of the host plants and the variability in fruiting and seed set between years. Nomadic waterbirds in dry regions move in response to rainfall and flooding patterns. In environments with unpredictable climates, such as arid and tropical Australia, these movements may be highly variable and result in massive population movements across reserve boundaries (Woinarski *et al.* 1992).

- For species that occupy short-lived or rapidly changing habitats, such as early seral stages in vegetation succession, whole populations may shift in response to the changing quality of habitats through time (Thomas 1994). Movements to 'track' new areas of suitable habitat may take populations into and out of reserves, depending on the dynamic nature of the habitat.

Box 8–2   Migration pattern of the Resplendent Quetzal in Central America: implications for reserve design and conservation

The Resplendent Quetzal is a large fruit-eating bird of the montane tropical forests of Central America, that has a complex pattern of seasonal migration between low and high elevation forests. To identify forest habitats important for the survival of quetzals, and to assess the adequacy of existing conservation reserves, movements of individual birds were monitored by radio-telemetry throughout their annual cycle in montane forests of Costa Rica (Powell and Bjork 1995).

Quetzals were found to nest at elevations of 1500–1800m on both the Pacific and Atlantic slopes of the montane forests of Costa Rica, largely within reserved areas associated with the Monteverde Park. After breeding, individuals moved to the west down the Pacific slope where they remained outside the reserve system for 3–4 months, feeding in fruiting trees in small forest fragments. Subsequently, they moved across the range to forests on the Atlantic slope, also mostly outside the reserve system, where they foraged for 2–3 months before returning to their breeding area. The reserve complex, although relatively large (greater than 20,000ha) and encompassing their known breeding habitat, was not sufficiently extensive to encompass all altitudinal zones used by the birds during their complex migration (Powell and Bjork 1995).

Following this research, extensions were made to the reserve system on the Atlantic slope to incorporate forests used there by the Resplendent Quetzal. On the Pacific slope, protection of habitats by reservation is difficult because almost all land is in private ownership, mostly small dairy farms, and the forests are heavily fragmented. Given this difficulty, Powell and Bjork (1995) recommended that efforts be made to secure a patchwork of interconnected forest fragments along streams and steeper slopes that together could function as a system of suitable habitat.

The complex migration pattern of the Resplendent Quetzal, a 'flagship' species for conservation in the region, clearly illustrates the need for reserve systems to encompass the full range of habitats required throughout the life cycle. Where this is not possible, such as in the Pacific slope forests at lower elevations, the reserve system must be complemented by ecologically linked habitats to allow animals to maintain access to seasonally-critical habitat resources.

Reserves are not isolated from surrounding land uses

Conservation reserves are frequently portrayed as 'islands of natural habitat within a sea of developed land'. While this analogy has some illustrative value, unfortunately it has a fundamental weakness (Wiens 1995). Unlike true islands surrounded by water – an inhospitable environment to terrestrial plants and animals – reserves are surrounded by modified and varied land uses, stocked with their own flora and fauna. Thus, reserves are not isolated by an ecologically neutral matrix; they are subject to a host of pressures from their surrounding environments because movements of animals, wind and water do not stop at reserve boundaries. Reserve management, however, frequently *does* stop at the reserve boundary, because reserve managers have little or no authority to influence land uses and management practices on adjacent lands. This means that reserve managers have little capacity to counteract ecological processes *outside* the reserve, that may ultimately determine the fate of ecological systems *within* the reserve. Reserves can not remain as pristine, self-sustaining environments when they are surrounded by degrading or unsustainable land uses.

An integrated landscape approach to conservation

The underlying premise of an integrated landscape approach to conservation is that the focus for conservation planning and management must extend beyond the boundaries of nature reserves to encompass the whole landscape. Long term conservation of native flora and fauna and the maintenance of natural ecological processes, can not be assured by depending solely on lands dedicated to nature conservation. We must find creative ways to develop networks of habitat across 'reserved' and 'off-reserve' lands, that together can function as integrated systems of habitat for conservation of biodiversity.

This is not to downplay the value and significance of conservation reserves. Far from it! An integrated approach is not a substitute for national parks and other protected areas in which nature conservation is the primary management priority. Reserved areas, representative of all natural ecosystems and committed to the conservation of native biota and the maintenance of natural ecological processes, are a critical component of strategies. Rather, this approach builds upon and extends from the reserve system to include other parts of the landscape.

An integrated landscape approach is relevant in a range of situations where conservation reserves are few, sparsely distributed or inadequate for effective long-term conservation. For example, in countries with an increasing human population, where land use is dominated by agricultural and urban developments, and there is intense pressure on dwindling natural environments, conservation will largely depend on the capacity to conserve species within cultural and agricultural environments. It is also relevant in sparsely populated regions dominated by cleared agricultural lands or intensive production forestry, with few or no conservation reserves. Here, the challenge is to integrate conservation of biodiversity with sustainable management of land for food and timber resources for the human population.

The concept of an integrated landscape approach to conservation can be applied at a range of scales, from local conservation plans to regional or national conservation strategies (Box 8–3). It is useful to identify a number of common elements in this approach (Table 8–1).

Table 8–1   Common elements in an integrated landscape approach to conservation.

Plan at broad spatial scales

Protect key areas of natural habitat

Maximize conservation values across a variety of land tenures

Maintain and restore connectivity

Integrate conservation with surrounding land uses

Box 8–3   The Wildlands Project: networks of habitat at the continental scale in North America

The Wildlands Project is an ambitious conservation initiative that seeks a transformation of the North American continent over the next century and beyond. It arises from concern over the failure of existing conservation reserves to adequately protect the biodiversity of the continent, the continued decline and endangerment of many species, and the loss of wilderness (Foreman *et al.* 1992). The mission of the project is to 'help protect and restore the ecological richness and native biodiversity of North America through the establishment of a connected system of reserves', and this will require 'the recovery of whole ecosystems and landscapes in every region of North America' (Foreman *et al.* 1992).

The conceptual basis of the wilderness recovery strategy advocated by the Wildlands Project is a continent-wide, interconnected system of 'core reserves' surrounded by 'buffer zones' and linked together to maintain functional connectivity of populations and ecological processes (Noss 1992). Core reserves are envisaged as large areas, strictly protected for nature conservation, that together encompass the range of ecological communities and habitats in each region. Buffer zones are areas surrounding core reserves in which human activities consistent with the maintenance of biodiversity are allowed. Linkages are required at multiple spatial scales to connect the reserves and buffers into a functional system. These links may range from local connections between core areas to regional linkages hundreds of kilometres in length that tie regional reserve systems into a continental network (Noss 1992).

The extent of the area recommended for inclusion in the wilderness recovery network is enormous. It is suggested, for example, that 50% of the land area of the USA should eventually be incorporated in core reserves and inner zones of linkages (Noss 1992). Estimates of the sizes of core reserves are mainly based on the area required to sustain viable populations of large carnivores such as the Grizzly Bear, Gray Wolf, Wolverine and Cougar – species with the greatest area requirements for conservation.

At present the Wildlands Project is largely a vision rather than a firm strategy, although preliminary proposals have been advanced for wilderness networks in regions such as the state of Florida, the Adirondack Mountains, the southern Rocky Mountains, and the southern Appalachians in USA (Medeioros 1992; Newman *et al.* 1992; Noss 1992; Soulé 1995). It is intended that regional strategies be developed by local groups as part of a 'bottom up' approach, and gradually amalgamated into a continental strategy. The time frame for the project is centuries.

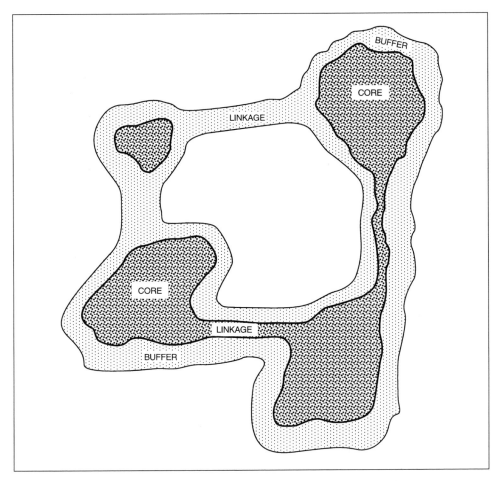

Fig. 8–4   **Diagrammatic representation of the concept of core reserve, buffer zone and linkage, that forms the basic template for the Wildlands strategy. This concept can be applied at varying spatial scales. Adapted from Noss and Harris (1986) and Noss (1992).**

Plan at broad spatial scales

'Planning' implies a forward looking, strategic approach to conservation, rather than a reactive or *ad hoc* response to changing land uses. Planning is an essential part of an integrated landscape approach because the primary objective is to achieve conservation goals within a mosaic of multiple land uses.

The 'landscape scale' aspect of the approach is necessary to ensure that the planning framework is large in relation to the units of land being managed. A broad perspective is necessary so that the planning process takes into account the wider ecological and social processses that shape and modify the natural environment in the particular study area. For example, management of bushland reserves or remnants of native vegetation on farmland in the Wheatbelt region of Western Australia will be severely limited (however well planned) unless there is recognition of the broader regional context in which rising saline groundwater is killing vegetation in low-lying areas and removing agricultural land from production (Hobbs 1993a; Hobbs *et al.* 1993). A broad planning perspective for conservation is also necessary to ensure that a particular system or network of habitat 'ties in' with that in neighbouring areas and that, in turn, it complements conservation strategies at a broader scale.

Planning at broad spatial scales poses a challenge, because the broader the planning scale the greater the range of land managers and types of land tenure that must be co-ordinated to achieve the overall goal. In contrast to planning, management activities generally occur at the level of individual parcels of land. To achieve effective outcomes, therefore, each land manager must understand and play their part in the broader overall plan.

Protect key areas of natural habitat

Protection of representative areas of natural habitat for which a high priority is given to nature conservation, is the essential 'backbone' of an integrated conservation strategy. Such areas act as reservoirs for the conservation of plant and animal populations and for the maintenance of ecological processes within the overall system. Certainly, other habitats within the landscape mosaic must also be part of the linked system, such as areas managed for multiple purposes or for harvesting natural resources; but these can not guarantee the same level of security for the conservation of wildlife and their habitats. Frequently, the key areas of habitat are likely to be national parks or other conservation reserves, but it is the level of habitat protection that is important, rather than the name. Hence, many other types of protected areas can also form the core of an integrated system of habitats.

Key areas of habitat should be as large as possible, preferably the largest, most intact blocks of habitat remaining within the planning zone. These are the areas most likely to support diverse habitats, intact faunal assemblages, and to maintain natural disturbance regimes. The actual size depends on the scale of the system under consideration. At a local or landscape scale, these areas may be habitat blocks of tens or hundreds of hectares in size. At a regional or continental scale, major nature reserves and wilderness areas least disturbed by human development, are important key habitats. The wildlands project in North America, for example (Box 8–3), proposes that major mountain ranges, such as the Rockies, Adirondacks and Appalachians, should form 'core reserves' in a continental-scale habitat network.

Maximize conservation values across a variety of land tenures

The idea of an integrated system of habitat based entirely on areas protected and managed for nature conservation is rarely possible in heavily developed landscapes. In such landscapes, the co-ordination of integrated systems of habitat will necessarily involve a range of land tenures and uses, including for example, conservation reserves, public lands designated for multiple uses, natural and semi-natural habitats on privately managed land, and habitats on lands managed by companies and community groups. Where conservation reserves are scarce or absent, it may only be possible to develop a system of habitats based around 'off-reserve' habitats of varying quality. In managed forests committed to timber production, a system of habitats might include three main components: scattered conservation reserves; sites exempted from logging for various reasons (such as sites inaccessible or uneconomic to harvest, riparian buffer strips, fauna protection zones); and the forest matrix of regenerating stands of different ages.

The planning process can also ensure that different land tenures and uses are employed in a complementary fashion. For example, semi-natural areas or areas available for limited resource extraction, may be retained adjacent to key areas of natural habitat to function as buffers to minimize disturbance from intensively developed areas.

Maintain and restore connectivity

Landscape connectivity is an essential feature of an integrated approach to conservation. It is only when connectivity is sufficient to enable interchange of individuals and genes between different landscape components, that it functions as a 'linked system' rather than a set of isolated habitats. The most appropriate form and dimensions of linkages to maintain landscape connectivity depends on the scale of the planning area and habitats to be linked, surrounding land uses, and the animal species or ecological processes concerned (Chapter 7). A hierarchy of linkages will usually be appropriate. An integrated conservation strategy in a predominantly agricultural region, for example, may include broad landscape links between conservation reserves and other large natural areas, combined with a network of habitat corridors (such as streamside vegetation) connecting smaller areas of habitat throughout the agricultural lands.

It is also important to identify ways in which systems of habitat within a particular planning area can be integrated with those in other areas. Major river systems are particularly valuable in this regard because they connect habitats *within* a region as well as linking *between* regions.

Integrate conservation with surrounding land use

In regions of heavy human impact, the remaining natural areas are inextricably associated with surrounding modified lands. There is a constant interchange of plants and animals, nutrients, and other materials across their shared boundaries. Consequently, active management of the interactions between the conservation system and surrounding land uses is a challenging element of an integrated approach to landscape management. Indeed, recognition of the importance of managing processes within the surrounding land mosaic, not only within protected areas, is a distinguishing feature of this approach. Management intervention is required for two main types of interactions.

- Where processes associated with surrounding land uses threaten to degrade the conservation potential of natural or semi-natural habitats. Fluxes of toxic chemicals or excess nutrients, spread of invasive plants and animals, degradation of water sources, and introduction of exotic predators, are examples of disturbance processes that demand active management. To be effective, such management must deal with the source of the problem, usually outside the conservation network, rather than treat the effects within conservation areas.

- Where processes associated with natural habitats impinge on the viability and use of surrounding lands by local people. For example, creative solutions are required when native animals (such as large predators and herbivores) threaten human safety, or livestock and crops in lands adjacent to natural habitats.

There is also enormous potential to develop complementarity between conservation and productive use functions in the landscape through a common commitment to sustainability of natural resources. This may take many forms in different parts of the world, depending on the local situation. It is based on managing lands committed to production (i.e. not areas protected primarily for nature conservation) in ways that use the land and its natural resources for economic gain, while maintaining the sustainability of the natural resource base. Examples include (see Meffe and Carrol 1994; Saunders *et al.* 1995):

- protection or restoration of native vegetation on agricultural land to increase the sustainability of soil and water resources;

- farming and harvesting of wildlife in a sustainable manner on productive lands;

- development of ecological tourism programmes that involve and support local communities;

- sustainable harvest of forest products.

It is one thing to describe the elements of an integrated landscape approach to conservation, but the reality of developing and implementing such systems in an effective manner is quite another matter. There are many potential constraints, often relating to human attitudes – antipathy to conservation, lack of shared goals by individuals or agencies, unwillingness to change traditional land uses, inequitable division of economic costs and benefits, lack of political will, and so on.

There are a growing number of proposals for an integrated landscape approach to conservation (see examples in Chapter 9), but as yet few demonstrated examples of effective implementation are apparent. The form and effectiveness of linkages within such systems is one of the issues that require further monitoring and investigation. This type of approach to conservation is likely to be most effectively implemented in the following circumstances:

- where there is community-wide recognition of the need to respond to a particular environmental issue;

- where a centralized approach to land-use planning is traditional or generally accepted (see examples 5, 8 in Chapter 9);

- where the land concerned is managed primarily by a single agency (such as forests managed by governments; see examples 10, 11 in Chapter 9).

Which linkages warrant highest priority?

Implementing a conservation strategy requires decisions about priorities for action and for the use of available resources. Not all goals can be achieved immediately. There is always more that needs to be done than there are resources available for implementation. The effectiveness and efficient use of conservation resources is enhanced when activities are based on systematic priorities rather than *ad hoc* decisions. Can this approach be applied to the development of linkages for conservation? How do we determine which are the most important linkages to fund? Clearly, it is not feasible nor desirable to prescribe rigid rules because every situation has a different set of circumstances.

The most useful approach is to identify criteria against which proposals can be gauged to evaluate their relative importance. In the first instance, criteria for evaluating priorities among linkages must be based on biological values. Ultimately, policy decisions by governments or community organisations include other considerations, but it is important that biological values and priorities can be distinguished from non-biological criteria that influence whether or not resources are made available. Other criteria that influence priorities include:

- the financial costs and other resources required;

- the complexity of administrative and management issues involved;

- the time required to implement and achieve results;

- the level of community support and acceptance;

- the cultural costs and benefits;

- the educational and publicity value to be achieved.

The following criteria (Table 8–2) provide a framework for evaluating relative conservation priorities among different proposals. The issue here is how priorities should be determined, not whether a particular proposal will function effectively in a biological sense. For the purpose of this exercise it is assumed that a proposed linkage will function as intended.

Table 8–2   Criteria to evaluate the relative conservation priority of linkages from a biological perspective.

Criterion	Highest priority
1 Spatial scale at which the linkage maintains ecological processes	Linkages that maintain natural ecological processes and the continuity of species distributions at the biogeographic and regional scale
2 Level of replaceability (redundancy) of the linkage and the connected system of habitats	Linkages and systems of habitat that are unique and essentially irreplaceable
3 Degree of threat to species or communities in the habitats to be linked	Linkages that benefit species and communities of threatened conservation status
4 Present condition of the linkage (e.g. composition of the vegetation, width, sources of disturbance)	Linkages where broad continuous tracts of natural undisturbed vegetation are still present
5 Range of species that the linkage will benefit	Linkages that provide continuity for entire assemblages of species
6 Capacity of the linkage to provide other ecological and environmental benefits	Linkages that provide multiple environmental benefits without compromising their value for fauna conservation

Box 8–4   Paseo Pantera – developing an international linkage in Central America

Paseo Pantera, or 'Path of the Panther', is an international project that aims to reconnect, restore and manage the fragments of the formerly continuous natural environment along the length of the Central American isthmus between North America and South America (Marynowski 1992). The project, being implemented by Wildlife Conservation International and the Caribbean Conservation Corporation with the backing of the US Agency for International Development, envisages an interconnected chain of nature reserves extending the length of Central America to restore the former biogeographic link between the two American continents. The project derives its name from the Panther (or Pantera in Spanish), which formerly occurred along the length of the isthmus and throughout the Americas, from Patagonia in the south to the Yukon in the north.

The goals of Paseo Pantera are being pursued in several ways (Marynowski 1992). By working with governments and non-governmental organizations, support is given to better protection and management of existing reserves, to the design and establishment of new reserves, and to the review of regional conservation strategies. A key element of the project is to contribute to sustainable socio-economic development of the region. An eco-tourism component is based on the principle that carefully planned tourism can provide funds for the acquisition and management of protected areas; enhance the economies of local communities, and have a significant role in environmental education for visitors. Paseo Pantera also aims to promote international co-operation amongst countries along the isthmus, particularly in relation to reservation and management of protected areas that span national borders. The seven nation Central American Council for Environment and Development has prepared a regional agreement for the conservation of biodiversity, which recognizes the concept of a 'Central American Biological Corridor' (Marynowski 1992).

Paseo Pantera is an ambitious undertaking. If successful in meeting its goals it will represent a major achievement in international co-operation for conservation, and will have substantial benefits for biodiversity conservation. However, even if a continuous link is not feasible in the short term, greater protection for a chain of reserves and protected areas along the length of Central America is itself a worthwhile outcome.

Spatial scale at which the linkage maintains ecological processes

Linkages that maintain the integrity of ecological processes and continuity of biological communities at the biogeographic or regional scale have a more significant role than those operating at localized levels. Effective linkages at these scales have a key role in the maintenance of biodiversity at the national level, or at an international level where linkages cross borders between several countries (Box 8–4). Examples of such linkages include major river and riparian systems, forested mountain chains, and critical stepping stones such as wetlands and forest blocks for migratory birds. Regional or biogeographic linkages are difficult or impossible to reconstruct, and consequently high priority must be given to their identification, protection and maintenance before their ecological function is lost and major changes occur in patterns of biodiversity.

Linkages at the regional and biogeographic scale also have benefits at finer scales in the spatial hierarchy. A major river system with its associated riparian vegetation, for example, provides valuable habitat and continuity within landscapes and local areas through which it passes. However, for local linkages the benefits do not extend to broader spatial scales in the same way. A local linkage, such as a forested connection between two fragments, makes only a limited contribution to maintaining biodiversity at the regional scale.

The importance of spatial scale in setting priorities for conservation must also be addressed in relation to the level of responsibility of the organisation or government agency concerned. For example, the relative conservation priority for committing resources to a natural riparian corridor between urban parks in a regional city will be assessed differently by different agencies. To a national conservation agency, whose primary focus is the conservation of biota at the national scale, this proposal will rank as of lower priority than potential linkages at the biogeographic scale or across national boundaries. However, to an urban conservation authority this link may be a high priority because it links the two major parks within the authority's charter. Organisations should give higher priority to linkages that will function at the greatest spatial scale within that organisation's operating area.

Level of redundancy of the linkage and associated habitats

Key questions to be addressed in relation to this criterion include:

- are there alternative ways of maintaining connectivity in this situation?

- is the link replaceable? What would happen if it is lost?

- are other linked systems of habitat already achieving the goals of this proposal?

The highest priority for conservation must be given to those situations where there are no feasible alternatives for maintaining connectivity, where the loss of existing linkages would be essentially irreplaceable, or where no other habitat systems conserve this particular community of animals. Lower priority (but not 'no priority') is appropriate in situations where alternatives exist. Where a linkage forms part of an existing network, the network may still function effectively even if one component is not fully developed.

Based on this criterion, several examples of linkages that warrant high priority for conservation are proposed forest links to maintain connectivity of tropical forests in the Eastern Usambara Mountains of Tanzania (Example 2, Chapter 9); and the remaining strip of undeveloped land that facilitates migratory movements of large mammals to and from Mt. Kilimanjaro, also in Tanzania (Box 8–5).

Degree of threat to species or communities in the habitats to be linked

Reserves or fragments known to support threatened species or communities warrant special consideration. Because of scarcity or restricted distribution, such species are more prone to the risk of decline or local extinction in isolated habitats. However, protection of habitat

---

Box 8–5   Preventing isolation of Mt Kilimanjaro National Park and Forest Reserve, Tanzania

A rapidly increasing human population and the spread of agricultural development around the lower slopes of Mt. Kilimanjaro in eastern Tanzania, are progressively isolating the fauna of the Mt Kilimanjaro National Park and Forest Reserve. All but an 8 km strip of land on the north-western side of the mountain is now under cultivation. The consequence is a reduction in the total area available to the wildlife and disruption to the movements of large mammals between the mountain and the grassland/savannah habitats of the surrounding plains (Newmark *et al.* 1991; Newmark 1993). The local extinction of two large mammals in the national park in the last 50 years, the Klipspringer and Mountain Reedbuck, can be attributed in part to the isolation of upland habitats preventing occasional movements of animals from the lowlands where they are more common (Newmark *et al.* 1991).

Protection of the remaining natural corridor between upland grassland/moorland habitats and lowland grassland and savannah habitats is a high priority for the regional conservation of the large mammal fauna (Newmark *et al.* 1991). If effective isolation occurs, further extinctions can be expected amongst moorland species which have small populations. This landscape link also helps maintain connectivity for large mammals between the montane forests of Kilimanjaro and the nearest protected area, Amboseli National Park, about 20km to the north. African Elephant move annually from Kilimanjaro into Amboseli National Park, and Eland, Buffalo and African Wild Dogs have also been observed moving in and out of the montane forest (Newmark *et al.* 1991).

Cultivation and intensive settlement have not occurred in this remaining strip of land because it has been used exclusively by the Maasai people for traditional pastoral activities. At the request of the Maasai, who wish to continue using the land, the corridor has been given protected area status under Monduli District bye-laws (W. Newmark, pers. comm.). Cultivation has been banned but traditional Maasai uses, such as the collection of firewood and grazing of livestock, are currently permitted. The historical and current seasonal use of the corridor by wildlife suggests that these traditional practices are compatible with the conservation goals (Newmark 1993). The greatest challenge to the management and maintenance of this landscape link will be to ensure that further cultivation and settlement do not incrementally erode and sever this remaining connection.

---

linkages to improve connectivity is not always a straightforward conservation solution and careful consideration must be given to several issues.

- Is there reasonable evidence that provision of effective links will counteract the causes of rarity and threatened status? There is little justification, for example, in giving high priority to linking populations of a threatened species when its decline is clearly due to hunting, poaching or other direct causes, and not related to isolation and fragmentation of its habitat.

- Will the proposed linkage be effective in promoting movements or re-establishing population continuity? By virtue of its rarity, it is likely that such a threatened species may have specialized food or habitat requirements, or may be sensitive to the presence of other species.

- Is existing knowledge of the distribution of the species sufficient to determine the most effective location for linkages to other populations or to suitable habitats?

On a positive note, the presence of one or more threatened species (especially high profile mammals) is likely to attract additional funding to that available from existing conservation budgets.

Present condition of the linkage

Tracts of *natural* vegetation have greater conservation potential as linkages than comparable areas of land that require partial or major restoration of their vegetation. Restoration of habitats requires time for vegetation communities to develop, it is resource-intensive and costly, and may not fully restore all components of the habitat to a natural condition. High priority should be given to broad tracts of existing natural vegetation, especially those having minimal disturbance along the edges or within the tract.

In determining priorities among alternatives it is valuable to assess:

- the degree of current vegetation cover and naturalness;

- the representativeness of the current vegetation in relation to other habitats in the linked system;

- the requirements for habitat restoration and the timescale involved for habitats to mature;

- the relative width of vegetation and the number and location of potential sources of disturbance.

Range of species that the linkage will benefit

This criterion assesses the relative priority for conservation based on the range of species that the linkage benefits. In general, linkages that enhance the conservation status of groups of species (such as woodland-dependent birds or arboreal mammals), or entire communities of animals should receive higher priority than those that function for one, or only a few, species. Clearly, this criterion must also be considered in conjunction with that evaluating the conservation status of target species.

Linkages that are effective in providing connectivity for whole assemblages of species have numerous additional benefits. Such connecting habitats are usually broad landscape links, comprise natural vegetation, encompass a range of habitat types and have limited disturbance (see Chapter 9). These tracts generally have great value as habitats in their own right and fulfil other roles in the ecosystem. Linkages that function for entire communities are also more likely to facilitate continuity of ecological processes among systems of habitats.

Capacity of the linkage to provide other ecological and environmental benefits

Linkages that provide a range of environmental benefits, without compromising their role of ensuring connectivity for wildlife, must attract a higher priority than those that have a single purpose. Streamside corridors are particularly important in this regard, although other types of links also have numerous benefits (Chapter 6). Additional benefits to be gained while also assisting wildlife include:

- provision of habitat for plant species and communities;

- reduction in soil erosion due to reduced wind speeds, binding of soils by vegetation, and modification of water flows;

- maintenance of stable hydrological cycles through groundwater transpiration, modification of flows of water across the ground surface, and infiltration of water into the soil;

- maintenance of water quality by buffering inputs of nutrients, particles and chemicals to streams; provision of nutrients into streams to contribute to aquatic food webs.

By contributing to an integrated approach to environmental management, such linkages also have benefits in terms of efficiency in land management and the use of conservation resources. They are also likely to attract support from a wider section of the community and a broader range of land management agencies, and are open to more diverse sources of funding. Community groups and management authorities that do not have a direct interest in wildlife conservation may support such initiatives because of the other environmental benefits that they recognize (e.g. McNeely 1987).

Checklist of issues for planning linkages

The following points summarize a number of the issues discussed previously concerning the design and management of linkages and their inclusion in conservation planning. The list may at first seem daunting, and in most situations answers will not be readily available to many questions. Nevertheless, the purpose of the checklist is to stimulate a deeper consideration of relevant issues by land managers who are developing plans to protect, manage, or restore linkages. These points refer most directly to a proposal for a habitat corridor, but are equally relevant to other habitat configurations intended to achieve connectivity.

What is the purpose of the proposed linkage?

- How would you describe the purpose of the link and its likely benefits?

- What is the size and conservation value of the habitats being linked? Are they actively managed for conservation? Are they secure from future clearing or disturbance?

What is the current status and tenure of the linkage?

- Is there existing natural vegetation, sections of vegetation, or is reconstruction of the vegetation required?

- What is the tenure of the land and the current management objectives? Are the land owners or management authorities likely to be sympathetic?

- Is it a single link between two areas of habitat or part of a network? Are there alternative linkages or a single option?

- What are the proposed dimensions and shape of the linkage? Is the width sufficient to counteract edge disturbances?

Which species is the linkage intended to benefit?

- Is the linkage primarily intended for a single species or for a group of species? Can you list the species that are expected to benefit?

- Do these species presently occur in the habitat areas connected in this way? Are they secure populations? Do they presently occur within, or use the habitat in the linkage?

- Will the species concerned primarily use the linkage as a habitat to live in, or as a pathway for movement? What types of movements is it likely to be used for – daily, seasonal or annual movements?

What are the species' requirements and how do they relate to use of the linkage?

For species that live within the link:

- Are their requirements for food, shelter and breeding presently available within the linkage?

- What are their requirements for space and how does this relate to the proposed width?

- Are they vulnerable to particular kinds of disturbance?

For species that move through the link:

- Are their requirements for refuge and food during movement available?

- Will they find and enter the linkage?

What is required to make the linkage functional?

- What actions are required to establish secure land status for the linkage?

- Has the scope of the work, the cost and the effort required been estimated?

- Does management of the linkage complement other land-use strategies or conservation strategies?

- What management and restoration is required to make the linkage functional?

What management is required for long-term maintenance of the linkage?

- Who is responsible for ongoing management?

- Are there adequate resources (people with relevant skills, finances) for ongoing management?

- Are there any land uses or pressures that will result in disturbance and degradation of the vegetation and habitats?

- Is there a need for management of introduced plants and animals?

How will monitoring be carried out?

- How will the success of the linkage be evaluated? What are the criteria for success?

- Has a monitoring program been planned? Who will carry it out?

- What is the time scale over which monitoring will be carried out and the linkage evaluated?

What lessons have been learned that can help others?

- Were there any unexpected outcomes?

- What were the greatest challenges in carrying out the work and how were they resolved?

Summary

Promoting habitat configurations that enhance connectivity within developed landscapes is one of four general measures that can be taken to counter the effects of habitat fragmentation and isolation on wildlife. The distinctive aspect of this measure is that it provides the opportunity to achieve conservation goals through managing linked systems of habitat, rather than single blocks. Limitations of a reserve-based approach to conservation suggest that such linked systems should extend beyond reserve boundaries and encompass habitats throughout the landscape. An integrated landscape approach to nature conservation requires planning at broad spatial scales, protection of key areas of habitat, co-ordination of conservation values across land tenures, maintenance and restoration of landscape connectivity, and integration of conservation with surrounding land uses. Decisions about the relative priority to give to linkages are facilitated by evaluating criteria concerning the ecological context and proposed function of the link. A checklist is provided as a reminder of the many issues involved in successful planning and management of linkages to maintain landscape connectivity for wildlife.

9   CASE STUDIES OF LINKAGES IN LAND-USE PLANNING AND CONSERVATION

Around the world there are many situations where projects to protect and manage linkages are underway, or where links and networks of linkages have been proposed as part of conservation strategies. A number of such examples have been presented in previous chapters. This chapter presents further case studies to illustrate the way in which the protection and management of linkages to enhance landscape connectivity is moving from the conceptual stage to that of practical implementation in conservation strategies. The following examples have been selected to show the diverse range of situations in which linkages and systems of linkages have been proposed, the purposes for which they have been advocated, and their potential benefits for conservation. They are grouped into five categories:

- landscape linkages between reserves or large natural areas;

- linked systems of habitat at the regional scale;

- linkages in forest conservation and management;

- linkages for the conservation of large mammals;

- local networks of linear habitats.

Those presented have not been deliberately selected as 'successful' examples of linkages. They represent a variety of situations in which linkages are presently operating, are in the process of implementation, or are only at the proposal stage. They are based primarily on published information and so can not portray all of the complexities of management and implementation. However, information available for some examples makes it possible to discuss the types of challenges and issues involved in their development and implementation.

Landscape linkages between reserves or large natural areas

There are an increasing number of situations where linkages are being established between conservation reserves or large natural areas. In effect, most of these links already exist. They seldom involve the re-creation of habitat, but rather an official recognition and designation (and sometimes acquisition) of already-existing habitat as a link. Protecting landscape links between reserves is a logical, valuable and effective way of increasing the conservation value of reserves that may otherwise become ecologically isolated. The goal is a single, integrated conservation area – not two separate reserves with a narrow strip running between. Hence, such landscape links must be expansive and encompass large areas of habitat. Typically, their width is measured in kilometres and they have great value as a habitat in their own right; justification for their protection is not dependent solely on a capacity to enhance connectivity (Chapter 6). The challenge to land-use planners and governments in all countries is to identify and evaluate opportunities to protect such already-present links before they are lost and reserves become truly isolated.

1   National parks and reserves in the Central Highlands, Victoria, Australia

Recommendations for conservation reserves in Victoria, Australia, over the last two decades have generally incorporated the principle of protecting contiguous areas of habitat, or retaining links between reserved areas, wherever possible (e.g. Land Conservation Council 1989, 1994). Such proposals are made by the Environment Conservation Council (ECC), an agency whose primary function is to carry out investigations and make recommendations to government with respect to the balanced use of public land in Victoria. The process of determining land use for a particular study area has three main steps.

- The ECC prepares and publishes a descriptive report for the study area that includes detailed information on physical and biological resources (soils, climate, water resources, vegetation, fauna) and current land uses (recreation, nature conservation, forest production, mineral production etc).

- Following an opportunity for submissions on future land use, from individuals, community groups, government departments and other organisations, the ECC prepares Proposed Recommendations. These also are published and available for public scrutiny, and comment is invited.

- After considering submissions on the proposed recommendations, Final Recommendations are prepared for the use of public land, including various categories of conservation reserves, resource production areas, educational and other land uses. In general, the recommendations are accepted and implemented by government.

Following deliberations on the use of public land in the Melbourne 2 Study Area, recommendations for conservation included several examples of linked reserve systems (ECC 1994).

Ash Ranges National Park

The Ash Ranges National Park is a major conservation reserve encompassing 75,900ha of forest in the Central Highlands of Victoria (Fig. 9–1). It contains some of the best examples in the state of mature wet forests and cool temperate rainforests. The park is based on three main forest blocks, formerly protected as closed water catchments (Maroondah, O'Shannassy, Upper Yarra catchments), that are linked together to form a contiguous area of high conservation value for flora and fauna. A major consideration in the reserve design was the necessity to protect a range of forest types and ages to maintain a large contiguous area of habitat for the endangered Leadbeater's Possum and other species requiring older-aged forests (ECC 1994). The National Park encompasses more than 20% of the known global distribution of Leadbeater's Possum. Forested links between the major blocks are relatively short and never less than 1km wide. Further, they are embedded within and buffered by extensive surrounding forests used for timber production.

Dandenong Ranges National Park

This newly-designated park consolidates smaller reserves in the Dandenong Ranges (on the south-eastern outskirts of the city of Melbourne) into a single national park encompassing

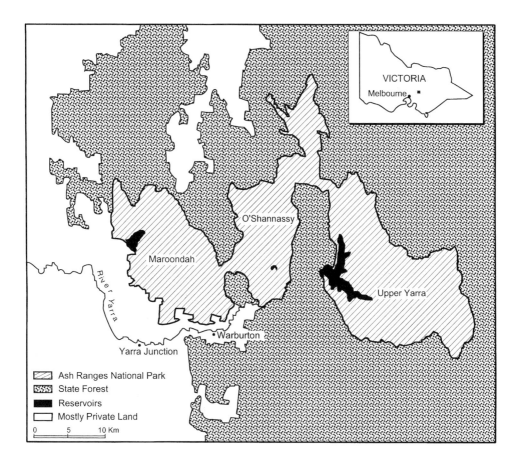

Fig. 9–1   The Ash Ranges National Park in the Central Highlands of Victoria, Australia, encompasses the former Maroondah, O'Shannassy and Upper Yarra water catchments in a single contiguous conservation reserve.

3400ha (LCC 1994). It incorporates four natural areas of high visitor use, linked by a series of smaller blocks of native vegetation on public land. A number of the linking blocks resulted from a land acquisition programme by government for this purpose. They are areas of nature conservation value and also provide opportunities for improving recreational access.

Warrandyte-Kinglake Nature Conservation Link

The main purpose of this link is to maintain continuity of native forest along a topographic gradient between the Yarra Valley (on the north-eastern margins of Melbourne) and Kinglake National Park (LCC 1994). This recommendation proposes that a number of different parcels of public land be managed co-operatively by government agencies, to maintain forest vegetation between two conservation reserves, a water catchment and a major riparian habitat corridor. The conservation link extends for 10km comprising blocks of land of irregular shape that together total more than 1400ha of habitat.

These reserve recommendations have several common features. Each reserve system is based on public land, managed by government. Each involves consolidation of three or more

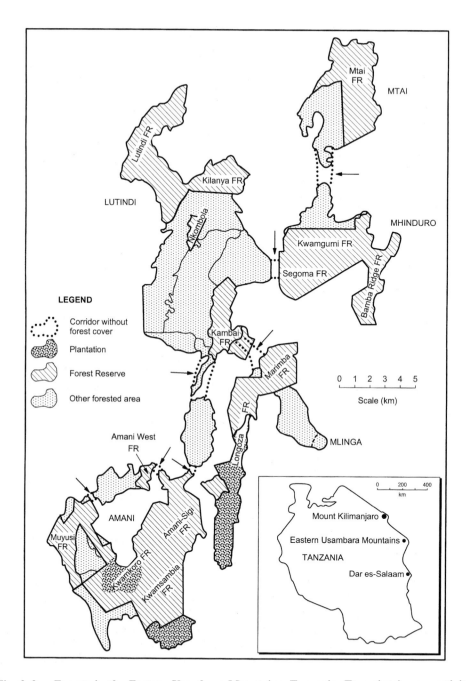

Fig. 9–2   Forests in the Eastern Usambara Mountains, Tanzania. To maintain connectivity among the five main forest areas (Lutindi, Mtai, Mhinduro, Mlinga and Amani) it is necessary to secure forest blocks presently unprotected and to revegetate short gaps between forests. Redrawn from Tye (1993), but subsequent clearing means that further gaps are developing (A. Tye, pers. comm.).

existing reserves or protected areas into a larger contiguous habitat for the flora and fauna. Finally, in each case, the linkages are blocks of land of varying size (cf narrow habitat corridors), that already existed as native vegetation of conservation value.

2   Conservation in the Eastern Usambara Mountains, Tanzania

The Eastern Usambara Mountains in Tanzania are an area of high biological diversity and endemism in eastern Africa. At least 2855 species of indigenous plants are known from the Usambaras, of which approximately 25% are endemic (Newmark 1993). There are also relatively high levels of endemism among various groups of invertebrates, amphibians, reptiles and birds. The most biologically rich habitats are those at higher elevations (800–1200m); lowland forests, although less diverse, also have many rare and endemic species.

Rapid clearing and loss of forest poses a critical and increasing threat to conservation of biodiversity in this region. Much of the remaining tropical forest occurs at higher elevations on the five major mountain blocks (Fig. 9–2), all of which were formerly connected by lowland forests. Severe depletion of lowland forests (less than 15% of forest remains below 600m) is leading to isolation of the montane forests and fragmentation of the overall ecosystem. In total, there is only about 23,000ha of forest above 600m elevation (Newmark 1992). Forest loss also has severe ecological and economic implications because of the importance of the forests as a water catchment (Newmark 1992; Tye 1993).

Part of the forest in each mountain block is protected as a Forest Reserve, but long term conservation of the flora and fauna of the Eastern Usambara Mountains requires protection of all remaining forests as an interconnected system. Many species of birds (one of the best studied groups) occur in low densities, especially globally-threatened species such as the Usambara Eagle Owl, Dappled Mountain Robin, Amani Sunbird, Long-billed Apalis and Tanzanian Mountain Weaver (Newmark 1992). Individual forest reserves, once isolated, will not be adequate to sustain viable populations of all resident species in the long term. Loss of forest-dependent understorey birds has already occurred in forest fragments, with the level of species decline dependent on fragment size and degree of isolation (Newmark 1991). Many forest birds are unable to cross cleared gaps of several hundred metres, and those able to do so disperse across inhospitable environments rarely. As forest clearing proceeds, more and more species will effectively become isolated.

Protection of the Eastern Usambara forests as an interconnected system of tropical forest has been recommended, and international efforts are underway to support the Tanzanian government toward this goal (Newmark 1992; Tye 1993; A. Tye, pers. comm.). Integral to this proposal is the protection and restoration of forested links between the five mountain blocks so that they function as a contiguous habitat for the forest fauna. This involves two stages:

- reservation of remaining unprotected forests that function both as habitat and as strategic links – an urgent priority because forest clearing continues;

- restoration of specific linkages where forest clearing has resulted in gaps between forest blocks. These are short sections, mostly less than one kilometre in length, that require reafforestation.

Empirical data on habitat use by forest-dependent birds has provided guidelines for the dimensions of linkages. Based on a value of twice the median distance of capture from the forest edge for the understorey species (Dappled Mountain Robin) captured furthest from the edge, linkages of at least 600m width are required to maintain connectivity of suitable habitat (Newmark 1993). A recommended width of one kilometre would provide for a buffer zone around a core area of less-disturbed forest.

There are a number of major challenges to implementing recommendations for an interconnected forest system (Tye 1993; A. Tye, pers. comm. 1995):

- the need to gain local support from all levels of the community, and to consult with local people about the most appropriate management of the forest reserves and linkages that is compatible with biological conservation;

- the need to obtain necessary governmental support, both internationally in the form of sufficient funding (for land acquisition and other costs), and nationally to ensure that plans are expedited and implemented;

- the methodological challenge of reafforestation to restore a 'natural' tropical forest in the linking sections that have been cleared;

- the need to develop long-term management strategies for all protected forests.

3   Pinhook Swamp corridor, Florida, USA

The Okefenokee National Wildlife Refuge, spanning 162,000ha across the border of the states of Georgia and Florida in the USA, is the largest wildlife refuge in the eastern United States (Harris and Gallagher 1989). Sixteen kilometres further south, the Osceola National Forest of 65,000ha encompasses wetlands, swamps and pine-dominated uplands (Fig. 9–3). Historically, these areas functioned as an integrated swampland ecosystem. In 1988, the Nature Conservancy and the US Forest Service commenced acquisition of land to protect Pinhook Swamp, a tract of approximately 24,000ha that spans the distance between the two reserved areas (Smith 1993). To date some 12,000ha of land, the core of a linkage roughly 8km wide between the reserves, has been purchased by the Nature Conservancy and resold to the Forest Service as an addition to Osceola National Forest.

On its own, the Osceola National Forest is not large enough to support viable populations of Red-cockaded Woodpeckers, Black Bears, or other endangered species (Harris 1988b). Consolidation of these lands through purchase and management of the Pinhook Swamp link protects a contiguous area of habitat in excess of 250,000ha and provides a greater capacity to sustain large populations of threatened species. In addition, the Pinhook Swamp link has value as habitat for wildlife in its own right, and also serves as the headwaters for the Suwannee and Saint Mary's Rivers (Smith 1993).

The Okefenokee-Pinhook-Osceola system has further potential for incorporation into a wider habitat network in north Florida, linked by riparian corridors along the Suwannee, Santa Fe and other rivers (Noss and Harris 1986; Harris and Scheck 1991; Smith 1993). Extensive land purchase and management to protect important habitats, to maintain water quality, and as a natural flood storage, has already commenced along the Suwannee River.

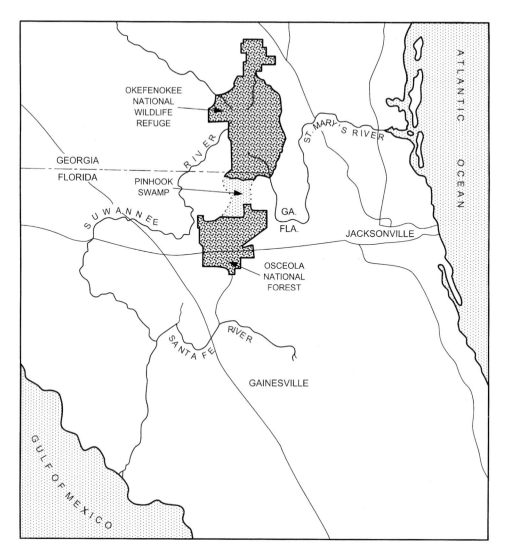

Fig. 9–3 **The acquisition and protection of Pinhook Swamp in Florida maintains a natural link between the Okefenokee National Wildlife Refuge and the Osceola National Forest. Redrawn from Smith (1993) with permission, University of Minnesota Press.**

4 Jungle corridors and reserves in the Mahaweli area, Sri Lanka

The Mahaweli River Development Scheme is a major development programme in Sri Lanka. The building of four new dams in the upper catchments of the Mahaweli River has the objective of greatly expanding the area available for irrigation farming (by more than 100,000ha) and more than doubling the capacity for electricity generation (McNeely 1987). Because such a large development has major environmental impacts, environmental assessment was carried out as part of international support for the project by the US Agency for International Development.

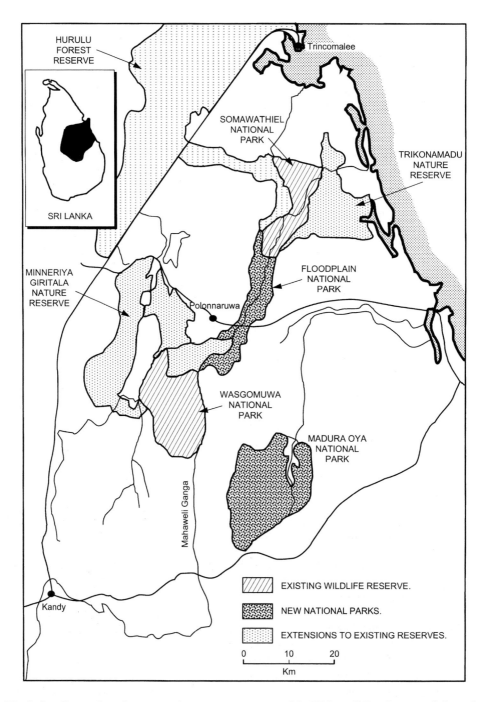

Fig. 9–4   **Expansion of a protected area system as part of the Mahaweli Development Scheme in Sri Lanka includes broad landscape links as extensions of national parks or as jungle corridors between reserves. Redrawn from Harris and Scheck (1991) with permission, Surrey Beatty & Sons, Publishers.**

The Mahaweli basin was identified as a biologically rich region with at least 90 endemic species of plants and animals and substantial populations of large mammals, including Indian Elephants. Intensive agricultural development and human settlement proposed for the area potentially threatened wildlife habitats as well as the hydrological integrity of the catchments. Consequently, the reserve system was expanded and upgraded to protect wildlife habitats and the catchments of the new reservoirs. Plans for the system of protected areas included broad landscape linkages approximately 5km wide as extensions of existing National Parks and reserves or as 'jungle corridors' between reserves (Fig. 9–4). The aim was to develop an integrated reserve system that allowed the continuity of ecological and evolutionary processes, including the migration routes of elephants (McNeely 1987).

This project was designed as an example of how development could proceed in a manner compatible with the effective conservation of natural resources. Indeed, the retention of natural areas to protect watersheds and control sedimentation is an essential part of the development. The establishment of the reserve system encountered difficulties and illustrates the importance of social and political factors in the implementation of ecological concepts and plans (Chapter 7). Difficulties with project administration and with liaison between national and international agencies, shortages of trained personnel, national political tensions and armed conflict, and entrenched views within management agencies, have all contributed to a delay in the implementation and effective operation of the reserve system (McNeely 1987).

Linked systems of habitat at the regional scale

Planning an integrated network of habitat across regions or entire countries extends further the concept of linking nature reserves and other important conservation areas. In this approach, the habitats linked as part of the integrated network include reserves and also off-reserve habitats within developed landscapes. This type of regional approach is well developed in European countries, especially those with a strong tradition of integrated land-use planning, with ecological networks recognized as an important part of the nature conservation strategy (Jongman 1995; Brandt 1996; Kubeš 1996). A diverse group of examples are presented here to illustrate this regional approach. It is notable that each is in the early stages of implementation and that each attempts to integrate ecological objectives with social, recreational, or agricultural objectives.

Several issues require further attention as these types of regional plans are developed and implemented. First, there is an urgent need to incorporate research and monitoring programmes in these conservation strategies to assess the values of proposed linkages and the extent to which they achieve ecological goals. In this way planning can move from a qualitative basis derived from theoretical principles, to a more quantitative understanding of the value of different forms of linkages and how they can be managed to enhance their function and that of the overall network. Second, a cautious attitude is warranted to proposals involving extensive re-establishment of linkages where natural habitats have been cleared. There are questions concerning the capacity to successfully 'create' habitat for wildlife, the relative priority and resources to be allocated to such tasks compared with other conservation goals, and whether existing barriers that inhibit ecological flows across the landscape can be surmounted. Third, continued scrutiny must be given to the relationship between conservation objectives and those for human recreation or productive land use, in designing regional networks. These objectives are not necessarily compatible – provision of a 'green link' of some form does not automatically confer a conservation benefit.

5   Landscape planning in the Netherlands

The Netherlands has a three-tiered planning system, with national, provincial and municipal levels. In 1991, the national government introduced the National Nature Conservation Policy Scheme, in which a conservation strategy was developed that includes a National Ecological Network (Opdam *et al.*1995). The aim of the ecological network is to reduce the impact of the major causes of biodiversity decline, one of which is recognized as habitat fragmentation. There are three main components of the network (Ahern 1995; Opdam *et al.* 1995):

- core nature areas – large areas which are significant landscapes or wildlife habitat;

- nature development areas – farmland areas in which natural environments are to be restored;

- corridor zones – linkages between the core areas and development areas.

The spatial strategy for the National Ecological Network is to protect, buffer and link the core areas and nature development areas for the entire Netherlands, including linkages across national borders with similar areas in Germany and Belgium (Ahern 1995). The provincial level of planning sets out the ecological network in greater detail, and also co-ordinates municipal level plans to ensure consistency with each other and with the national plan.

Ecologists are using predictions and results from metapopulation models of species in fragmented landscapes to provide input into planning processes (Harms and Knaapen 1988; Harms and Opdam 1990; Opdam *et al.* 1995). For example, in the Randstad region of western Netherlands which encompasses the four largest cities (Amsterdam, The Hague, Rotterdam, Utrecht), an urban reafforestation plan involves the development of about 10,000ha of forests and recreation areas over a 15 year period (Harms and Knaapen 1988). A computer spatial model was developed to predict the probability of colonisation and persistence of species in forest patches of varying size located in different parts of the Randstad. The model was based on:

- knowledge of the availability of 'source' forests (deciduous forests larger than 50ha);

- estimates of 'landscape resistance' to animal dispersal, posed by open farmland, roads, urban developments and other ecological barriers;

- statistical relationships for various species between population occurrence and size of habitat patches, derived from field studies (Opdam *et al.* 1984, 1985).

The computer model was used to asess the likelihood that new forests at proposed locations in the Randstad would be accessible to target species, such as woodland dependent birds, and be suitable for their persistence (Harms and Opdam 1990). Different scenarios were tested, such as the likelihood of new forests being suitable given the presence of one or more corridor zones.

A major challenge facing implementation of the National Ecological Network, still in its early stages, involves the extent to which changes in agricultural land will be required

(Jongman 1995). Land must be allocated to nature development areas and to corridor zones, and this requires a reduction in farmland. There is also a need for further ecological data, especially relating to the capacity of fauna to disperse through various landscape patterns.

6   A greenways network for Maryland, USA

The State of Maryland, centred around the vast estuarine Chesapeake Bay in eastern USA, has made a commitment to developing a statewide network of 'greenways' as a community conservation initiative (State of Maryland 1990). A diverse range of linear habitats and natural linkages are envisaged – along stream valleys, coastlines, tidal wetlands, barrier islands, ridgetops, urban and suburban open spaces, and utility rights-of-way – together forming a statewide network. The purpose of the network is broad: to provide habitat and pathways for wildlife, to provide recreational opportunities and open space for people, to buffer waterways and protect the wetlands and water quality of Chesapeake Bay, and to enhance the aesthetics of urban environments. The vision is of a programme that will attract wide involvement and support by the community. Local government and community groups are encouraged to initiate projects within the context of the statewide plan.

Protection of the environmental quality of the biologically productive Chesapeake Bay is an integral part of the plan and in 1984 legislation was passed to establish a resource protection program (Critical Area Program) for the bay. The Chesapeake Bay Critical Area was defined as all waters and lands of the bay and its tidal tributaries and all lands within 305m of the mean high tide (Therres *et al.* 1988). Within this area, encompassing nearly 10% of the state, regulations are designed to protect shorelines, water quality, wetlands and critical habitats of species. These include several provisions directly relating to the establishment of a connected habitat network (Therres *et al.* 1988).

- A minimum 30m buffer zone from mean high tide along shorelines, stream banks, and wetlands is to be protected to minimize the effects of human activities on these habitats, to maintain a transitional zone between aquatic and upland communities, to maintain the natural environment of streams, and to protect riparian wildlife habitat.

- 'Wildlife corridor' systems are to be incorporated into development sites. These linkages must connect the largest undeveloped or most vegetated tracts to similar tracts on adjacent areas of land.

- Protection from new shoreline developments for waterfowl staging points and concentration areas (Chesapeake Bay is famous for its wintering waterfowl populations).

- Riparian forests adjacent to streams, wetlands or the bay shoreline, that are at least 91m in width or at least 40ha in size, are to be protected and conserved (for example as habitat for migratory birds and other forest-dependent species).

The state has already identified a number of major greenways, mostly along river systems. A challenging aspect of this statewide initiative is the extent to which wildlife conservation and recreational goals are compatible and can be integrated in the overall strategy.

7 National Corridors of Green project, Australia

The National Corridors of Green project in Australia involves community groups, landholders, local government and other organisations in activities to manage and restore 'vegetation corridors' (Greening Australia 1994a). The project is part of a national response to the loss and degradation of natural ecosystems and the consequent ecological problems (such as salinization, soil erosion and loss) and loss of productive capacity of agricultural land. While many individuals and local groups are already involved in activities to protect or enhance habitat corridors in rural Australia, the National Corridors of Green project is designed to bring groups together to carry out these works in a strategic manner in areas where environmental restoration is a high priority.

The objective is to promote linear habitats and habitat corridors that have multiple environmental, economic and social benefits, in the context of an integrated regional approach to land management. Revegetation of selected areas is a key part of the project and these habitat corridors may (McCaughey 1995):

- link existing stands of remnant vegetation;
- be located to reduce soil and and water degradation;
- provide for biodiversity conservation and wildlife movements;
- be part of shelterbelts linked across farm boundaries;
- be developed for recreational and tourism activities;
- be a symbolic focus for community and government support.

Fig. 9–5   An example of revegetation along a degraded gully in farmland in southern Victoria, Australia. (Photo: A. Bennett).

The projects are centred on Australia's river systems and their associated catchments. The first major project was the River Murray Corridors of Green which commenced in 1993. In the first year, 17 Community Incentive Contracts were awarded to groups located in eight geographic regions along the 2500km length of the river (Greening Australia 1994b). Each contract involved community groups carrying out a planned revegetation program within 50km of the Murray River.

For example, the Mt Pilot-Ovens Multipurpose Corridor Network is a project undertaken by a group of farmers in north-eastern Victoria. They mapped remnant native vegetation in their district and then identified eroding drainage lines and gaps in streamside vegetation for restoration. Revegetation of these sites will assist in restoring continuity to riparian vegetation, reducing erosion of stream banks and gullies, and add to the sparse network of native vegetation critical to the conservation of wildlife (including threatened species) in these landscapes. The social and community benefits gained by a group of landholders working together to improve the environmental sustainability of their farmland is also recognized as an outcome of these types of projects.

Following this initial trial, the National Corridors of Green Project is being expanded to develop similar projects in eight further regions encompassing all states of Australia. A characteristic of this project is its focus on involvement by local communities in identifying suitable projects to undertake. There are not, as yet, clearly defined regional plans or conservation strategies to guide and co-ordinate local projects in a strategic manner.

8   The 'territorial system of ecological stability' in the Czech Republic

The concept of 'territorial systems of ecological stability' (TSES) was developed in Czechoslovakia in the 1980s as a compromise between social demands for land in intensively developed landscapes and ecological requirements for nature conservation (Kubeš 1996). The goal is to maintain ecological function within the human-dominated environment by linking together the remaining natural elements or 'biocentres' within a designated area. This concept gained official support from national authorities in 1990 and subsequently there has been extensive activity in designing TSES throughout the Czech Republic (Jongman 1995; Kubeš 1996).

The territorial systems are arranged within a hierarchy. *Local* TSES are the basis of the conservation system. They consist of a dense network of local 'corridors' of 10–20m minimum width, connecting local biocentres of 0.5 to 5ha in size. For example, in the Chomutovka river valley a local TSES encompassed an area of about 200ha, and designated local biocentres were based on small oak forests, floodplain forest and meadows, linked by lines of trees and shrubs (Kubeš 1996). The aim is for all natural vegetation types in the planning area to be represented in local biocentres.

Regional biocentres consist of natural or semi-natural habitats of 10–50ha, connected by regional links at least 40m wide, and selected to maintain biodiversity at the next level in the planning hierarchy. At the *supra-regional* level, large biocentres of more than 1000ha are included and the associated supra-regional links may be zones along the valleys of large rivers (Jongman 1995; Kubeš 1996). Locations of regional and supra-regional corridors have already been established for the entire Czech republic (Kubeš 1996).

The conceptual basis for the TSES draws heavily from the 'patch-corridor-matrix' paradigm in landscape ecology (Forman and Godron 1986) and applies it at several spatial scales. Biocentres (and potential biocentres) are selected as important habitats for plants and animals in the landscape, and 'corridors' are intended to link biocentres into a network of habitat. Intensive land use in most areas means that most biocentres are semi-natural or cultural, rather than natural habitats; and, at the local level, few natural habitats may be available upon which to base reconstruction of vegetation (Kubeš 1996). There appears to be little specific knowledge of the conservation values of various types of biocentres, or of how well such a system functions for nature conservation. Further biological data is needed to assess the effectiveness of the TSES for nature conservation, particularly the recommended dimensions of biocentres and corridors (Kubeš 1996).

Linkages in forest conservation and management

In many countries, forests managed for timber production are some of the largest remaining natural areas and consequently have great value for conservation of the flora and fauna. However, there is widespread concern at the detrimental effects on some groups of forest-dependent species of management practices associated with timber production. For species that have difficulty persisting in various stages of younger regrowth, timber harvesting across large areas of forest may result in a marked decline in their distribution and abundance and the relative isolation of populations in the scattered areas of suitable habitat that remain. In some countries, increasing attention is being given to ways in which forests can be managed for economic production of timber and other forest products, while also maintaining the values of the forest as a habitat for wildlife populations. The following examples provide a perspective from several different forest types on ways in which forest ecologists and managers are implementing measures to maintain habitat quality and connectivity for wildlife populations in production forests.

9   Temperate rainforest corridors for forest birds, North Westland, New Zealand

In response to a scheme for the extensive harvesting of beech forests for timber in North Westland, New Zealand, a major 'wildlife corridor' was proposed to maintain the potential for temperate rainforest birds to move between reserves (O'Donnell 1991). This forested link was designed to follow topographic features that could be readily identified, and to have sufficient width to withstand windthrow of trees and other natural disasters. The minimum width is at least 2km (generally greater than 6km) and in total it requires the protection of 10,200ha of forest originally scheduled for logging.

The link may be seen to function at two spatial levels (Fig. 9–6). At the regional scale, it provides a broad forested link between the forests of the Paparoa Range (greater than 150,000ha) and the Southern Alps. The Paparoa Range would otherwise be ecologically isolated by cleared river valleys and logged forests. In this context the aims of the link are to (O'Donnell 1991):

• enhance gene flow and maintain genetic variation in populations in large forest blocks;

• assist movements of obligate forest-dwelling birds over large geographic areas;

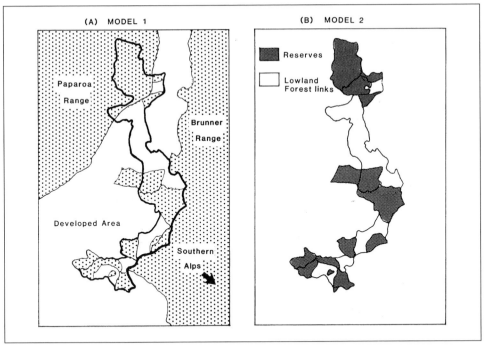

Fig. 9–6   Two models to illustrate the way in which the North Westland forest corridor functions. (a) Regional model: a link between forests of the Paparoa Range and similar forests of the Southern Alps. (b) Reserve model: the forest corridor connects a series of Ecological Reserves via lowland forest links. From O'Donnell (1991) with permission, Surrey Beatty & Sons, Publishers.

- maintain species that require large areas of unmodified habitat.

At a more localized scale, the forest link connects eight Ecological Areas that would otherwise be isolated by logged regenerating forest. Here the linkage may:

- permit seasonal movements of wildlife between high and low altitude reserves;

- maintain species diversity in core areas, especially forest birds that are less mobile or intolerant of habitat modification;

- aid the dispersal of young birds;

- provide additional habitat for rare species and a potential source of colonists for adjoining areas should they be subject to catastrophe.

Six criteria were used to assess forest birds known to occur within the area for which the forest link might be important: distribution status, dependence on forest habitats, degree of mobility across open habitat, habitat specialisation, response to logging, and conservation status (O'Donnell 1991). This analysis identified eight species (26% of forest birds known from the link) that are most likely to benefit from protection of the forest corridor. Three of these in particular, Kaka, Yellow-crowned Parakeet, and Yellowhead are threatened, obligate forest-dwelling species that have very large home ranges (O'Donnell 1991).

Following completion of a five-year research programme on the fauna of the North Westland forest corridor (Overmars *et al.* 1992), a formal recommendation that it be reserved for conservation was accepted by the New Zealand government (C. O'Donnell pers. comm. 1995).

10   Forest management planning in East Gippsland, Victoria, Australia

Major changes have occurred over the last two decades in the management of hardwood eucalypt forests in south-eastern Australia. Increased community concern for protection of flora and fauna and a greater knowledge of the status and habitat requirements of forest-dependent wildlife, have contributed to changes in management practices in order to reduce detrimental impacts of logging on wildlife populations (Loyn *et al.* 1980; Recher *et al.* 1980, 1987; Dobbyns and Ryan 1983; Taylor 1991; Lindenmayer 1994). In Victoria, government policy requires that forest management be economically viable, environmentally sensitive, and sustainable for all forest values.

In East Gippsland, Victoria, publicly-owned forests occur as a large contiguous tract of approximately one million hectares, part of the extensive forests along the Great Dividing Range in south-eastern Australia. The forest management plan for the East Gippsland Forest Management Area (Department of Conservation and Natural Resources 1995) incorporates a number of new measures in a strategy for forest management in this region. State Forests (the forest area available for timber harvesting) within the East Gippsland FMA have been divided into three zones:

- Special Protection Zone – to be managed for conservation and from which timber harvesting is excluded;

- Special Management Zone – to be managed to conserve specific features, allowing timber production under certain conditions;

- General Management Zone – in which timber production has high priority.

The Special Protection Zone (SPZ) encompasses 16% of the East Gippsland FMA and is designed to complement conservation reserves in the region by retaining a linked network of important forest habitats throughout the managed forest (Fig 9–7). The main components of the SPZ are representative areas of vegetation types and old growth forests that are poorly reserved in the reserve system, and forest areas set aside for the conservation of threatened forest-dependent animals. These areas are linked to each other and to conservation reserves by linear reserves, natural features zones along streams and rivers, streamside and rainforest buffers, and other protected zones.

Guidelines for the network of linear reserves (Department of Conservation and Natural Resources 1995) state that they will provide a number of alternative links between conservation reserves and large areas within the SPZ, be an average of 200m wide, span altitudinal and latitudinal gradients, generally comprise old forest of high quality habitat, and complement existing natural features zones and buffers along stream systems. The designated purpose of the linear reserves is to:

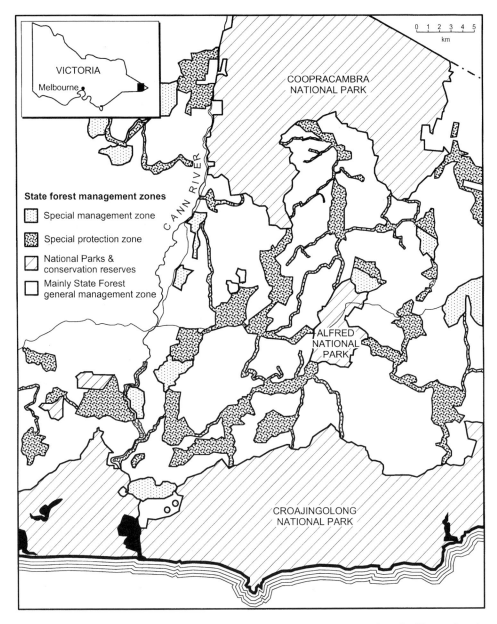

Fig. 9–7   A section of the East Gippsland Forest Management Plan, Victoria, illustrating the linked network of special protection zones within State Forest used for timber production.

- maintain resident populations of most sensitive species of animals and thereby facilitate recolonisation of areas that are harvested or burnt by wildfire;

- provide some of the habitat requirements of wider-ranging species (such as large forest owls);

- help prevent genetic isolation of sensitive forest species;

- guard against possible impacts of climate change.

The Forest Management Plan provides a comprehensive approach to the conservation of flora and fauna in this region, based on retaining throughout the forest a linked network of unlogged habitat that is integrated with the conservation reserve system.

11 Managing systems of open 'rides' in British forests

After centuries of deforestation and loss of the ancient semi-natural woodlands in Britain, reafforestation during the 20th century has greatly increased the extent of woodland cover from 4% in 1920 to about 11% at present (Ferris-Kaan 1995). Much of the increase has been by the establishment of plantations, often of non-indigenous tree species such as conifers. The dense cover and scarcity of open areas amongst many plantations is an important issue because open areas and shrubby edges have been a feature of managed woodlands in Britain for many centuries and the survival of many plants and animals depends on open habitats and early successional stages of vegetation (Ferris-Kaan 1991, 1995; Warren and Fuller 1993). Historically, open areas resulted mainly from the practice of coppicing, in which sections of woodland were cut on a short rotation, often 5–20 year cycles, resulting in a shifting pattern of young regenerating forests of varying successional stages (Ferris-Kaan 1995).

Networks of 'rides', linear strips of grassy vegetation maintained mainly for timber extraction, are one source of open habitats within forests. There is much evidence that such habitats are of great value for plants and animals that require open sunny conditions or favour edge habitats between woodland and grassland (Warren and Fuller 1993; Ferris-Kaan 1991). In conifer plantations, the margins of rides and open glades are often the only place where deciduous trees and shrubs and their associated wildlife occur. Hence, management of rides as habitat for the conservation of plants and animals has assumed great importance, and considerable attention has been given to the design (orientation, width, shape) and management practices (such as timing and frequency of mowing and slashing) needed to maintain habitats of a suitable successional stage (Ferris-Kaan 1991, 1995).

Butterflies are a well-studied group of animals for which conservation and management of woodland rides is particularly important. Butterflies are scarce within heavily-shaded woodlands, favouring a mosaic of open grassland glades, woodland edges and trees, where there are sunlit open spaces and suitable food plants (Porter 1993; Warren and Fuller 1993). The network structure and high level of connectivity of woodland rides provides species such as the Ringlet Butterfly with pathways for movement between fields and grassy glades within woodlands (Sutcliffe and Thomas 1996).

Bernwood Forest in Oxfordshire, a Forest Nature Reserve of national importance for butterfly conservation, is managed for both timber and wildlife. A network of interconnecting rides and glades (Fig. 9–8), together forming 1% of the forest area, is managed to maintain habitat for butterflies and moths (Warren and Fuller 1993; Ferris-Kaan 1995). The network includes major rides greater than 15m width, and minor rides, as well as open glades or 'box junctions' at many intersections. A management strategy specifies particular vegetation conditions to be maintained along rides as habitat for wildlife.

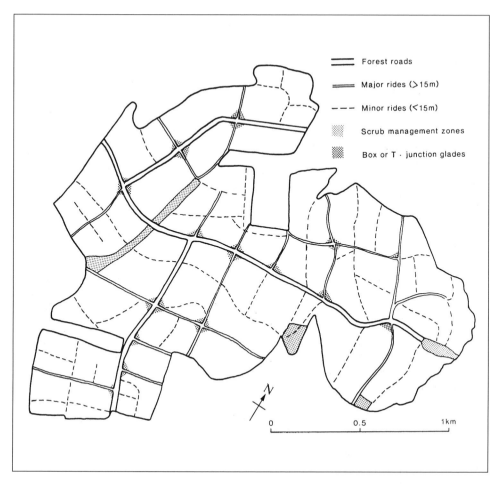

Fig. 9–8 **A network of open 'rides' are managed for wildlife conservation in Bernwood Forest, Oxfordshire, UK. From Ferris–Kaan (1995) with permission, Surrey Beatty & Sons, Publishers.**

Active management to maintain a system of open habitats and edges throughout large forest blocks is surprising to biologists in other countries where such open disturbance strips are generally detrimental to the native fauna (Askins 1994; Rich *et al.* 1994; May and Norton 1996). It is a salient reminder that ecological situations differ between countries – in this case the long history of intensive management of woodlands has led to a quite different context for forest conservation.

Linkages for the conservation of large mammals

Large mammals have been the focus of efforts to identify and protect linkages in many countries. These species have received particular attention for several reasons.

- Large mammals, especially predators, require large areas of land for each individual and much greater tracts for self-sustaining populations. In many regions, maintenance of such populations depends on several reserves or large natural areas in close proximity that together provide sufficient habitat for a population.

- Some species must undertake seasonal migration between different geographic areas for year-round access to food and other resources.

- Large mammals can be used as 'flagship' species – they attract public attention and sympathy, and there is a strong likelihood that linkages designed for these species will also benefit a wide range of other species.

Because they are wide ranging and occupy a variety of habitats, most large mammals do not require specialized habitat, or even continuous habitat, for movement through the landscape. However, experience demonstrates (see examples below) that protection of movement paths is essential if connectivity is to be maintained in the long term. Where links are not protected, their functional role is inevitably lost because the incremental effects of human land use (such as clearing, cultivation and housing developments) eventually become barriers to free movement. Protection along movement paths from direct disturbance by poaching or hunting is also necessary in many situations.

12   Kibale Forest Game Corridor, Uganda

The Kibale Forest Game Corridor was gazetted in 1926 to allow for the movement of large game animals, particularly African Elephant. This linkage, encompassing 34,000ha in area, is a large tract of medium-altitude forest and elephant-grass habitat extending along the western side of Kibale Forest and providing a broad link, approximately 15 kms wide, between the Queen Elizabeth National Park and the Kibale Forest (Fig. 9–9) (Baranga 1991).

Although legally gazetted, failure to manage and protect the Game Corridor led to almost total loss of its function by 1990. Its biological value was severely eroded by human encroachment, settlement and clearing of natural habitats. Encroachment commenced about 1970 and continued without check during a period of political turmoil. The protected habitat in the linkage diminished and it was estimated that by 1990 more than 90% of the link and 10% of the forest reserve had been claimed, with much of these areas under cultivation from a population of about 40,000 people (Baranga 1991). Records of the Uganda National Parks and Game Department indicate that Elephant, Uganda Kob, Waterbuck and Buffalo were using the corridor up to the early 1970s, but this movement ceased (Baranga 1991). Elephant are present in both the Kibale Forest Reserve and the Queen Elizabeth National Park, but their numbers declined from about 3000 in 1973 to 500 by 1989, and they altered their migration patterns.

In March 1992, following concern over the future of the Game Corridor, the Ugandan Government directed encroachers to leave and subsequently evicted 30,000 people from the reserve (C. Dranzoa, pers. comm. 1995). The following year, 1993, both Kibale Forest Game Corridor and the Kibale Forest Reserve were declared a national park, known as the Kibale Forest National Park. There is now an extensive and continuous protected area from the Kibale Forest, which has one of the richest forest faunas in East Africa (Struhsaker 1981; Baranga 1991), to the savannas of Queen Elizabeth National Park. This offers greatly enhanced protection of habitat for a wide range of species and a protected migratory route for large mammals, especially Elephant and Buffalo (C. Dranzoa, pers. comm. 1995).

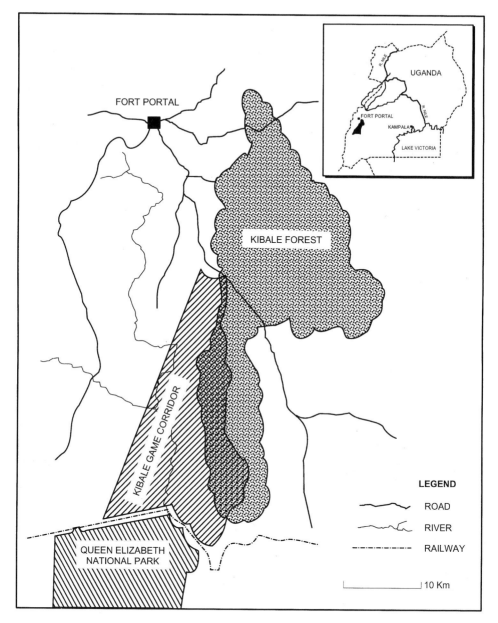

Fig. 9–9   The former Kibale Forest Game Corridor between Kibale Forest and Queen Elizabeth National Park is now incorporated as part of Kibale Forest National Park. Redrawn from Baranga (1991) with permission, Surrey Beatty & Sons, Publishers.

13 Wildlife corridors and buffer zones, Lake Manyara National Park, Tanzania

Lake Manyara National Park is relatively small (11,000ha) and is not considered viable as an 'island' park (Mwalyosi 1991). Historically, there has been regular seasonal migration of large mammals, especially of Wildebeest and Zebra, across the park boundaries. A migration pathway from Tarangire National Park to the northern border of Lake Manyara National Park is one of the major dispersal routes during the wet season for up to 10,000 Wildebeest and 100 – 800 Zebra within the wider Tarangire-Simanjaro ecosystem (Borner 1985; Mwalyosi 1991). However, increasing agricultural settlement, a rapidly increasing human population, and mining activities, are gradually blocking the traditional migration route. Crop destruction by domestic livestock and migrating wild animals as they move through settled areas creates further conflicts between pastoralists, conservation authorities and local farmers.

In anticipation of further increase in the human population and in intensive land use, a proposal was made for a buffer zone around the park to minimize conflict across boundaries between the park and adjacent villages, and for a landscape link between Lake Manyara National Park and Tarangire National Park to maintain connectivity between populations of large mammals in the two reserves (Mwalyosi 1991). Three potential linkages were identified and each was evaluated in relation to topography and natural vegetation, current and potential land use, human population, accessibility for animals, and present use by game animals. The grazing capacity in each link, based on the quality and quantity of fodder for moving animals, was also considered. The most suitable link extends about 60km from the northern end of Lake Manyara along the eastern side of the lake and east to Tarangire National Park (Mwalyosi 1991). This route is currently used intensively by large mammals. Further field work is required to map patterns of animal usage and to identify the most suitable alignment and boundaries. A broad link at least 1km in width was recommended, based on the need for adequate fodder for migrating animals.

Establishment of the link will require changes in land use. It is proposed that only fuelwood collection and livestock grazing would be allowed within the boundary of the link, and that people currently settled there (approximately 1500 people in three villages) should be relocated and compensated (Mwalyosi 1991).

14 Designing protected areas for conservation of the Giant Panda in China

The Giant Panda is well known as one of the most threatened species in the world. It now occurs only within the central Chinese provinces of Gansu, Shaanxi and Sichuan, where it lives in montane forests with dense stands of bamboo, generally at elevations of 2700–3700m. Bamboo shoots and roots are the major food items, although other plants, fish and small rodents are also taken.

In recent decades, the plight of the Giant Panda has deteriorated (Schaller 1993). Mapping of forest cover from satellite imagery has shown that the area of suitable habitat for Giant Pandas in Sichuan Province, the main stronghold, has approximately halved, shrinking from over 20,000km^2 in 1974 to 10,000km^2 in 1989 (McKinnon and De Wulf 1994). The declining conservation status has been further compounded by the mass flowering and subsequent death of large areas of Arrow Bamboo on several occasions. The bamboo flowers at 40–60 year intervals and takes 15–20 years to regenerate to a suitable size for the Giant Panda. Although many starving animals were seen and deaths occurred following the mass flowering, the flowering phenology of bamboo is not the primary cause of concern. Mass flowering and

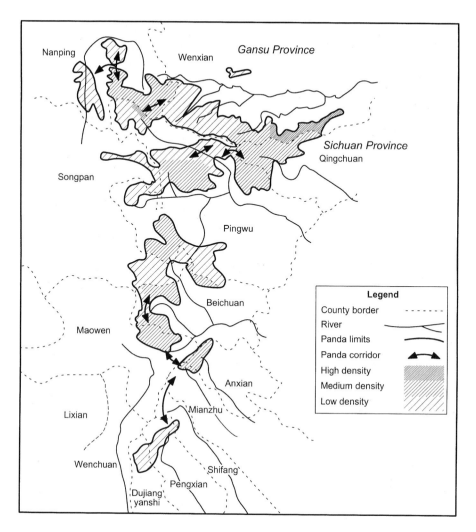

Fig. 9–10 **The distribution of the Giant Panda in the Minshan area of China, with arrows indicating critical corridors needed to maintain continuity of the regional population. Redrawn from McKinnon and de Wulf (1994) with permission, Chapman and Hall Publishers.**

dieback of bamboo is a natural phenomenon and Giant Pandas survived, albeit in low numbers, in every area that was affected (McKinnon and De Wulf 1994).

The main cause of decline is continued loss of habitat, human encroachment on remaining habitats, fragmentation of populations and deaths of animals at the interface with human settlements (from poaching and trapping). When satellite imagery was coupled with results from ground surveys in 1974–1986/88, changes in the distribution of the species could be related to landscape pattern. Giant Pandas had disappeared from several areas that were either small and isolated, at the edge of the species' range, or where habitats had been destroyed (McKinnon and De Wulf 1994). It was also evident that other populations were at risk of becoming fragmented and isolated from nearby populations by continued clearing of forests.

Being a large animal (75–150kg) that occurs at low densities (e.g. an estimated 145 Giant Pandas inhabit the 2000km² Wolong Nature Reserve), it is extremely vulnerable to fragmentation of its forest habitat.

A strategic plan to manage the species and its habitats involves:

- extending and redesigning the existing reserve system to better protect key populations;

- identification and protection of critical habitat links *between* reserves;

- management of habitats and people *within* reserves.

Fifteen habitat links have been identified as critical for maintaining connections between reserves (Fig. 9–10) to allow movements of animals between small populations. These linkages are designed to consolidate the distribution of the Giant Panda in extant reserves. Seven links will require revegetation with suitable habitat (native trees and bamboo species). They are recommended to be at least 1km wide and located to bridge the narrowest gap and flattest terrain between existing blocks (McKinnon and De Wulf 1994). Those links that are presently forested require strict protection from forest harvesting, grazing and human encroachment.

Assessing and mapping of forest habitats using satellite imagery has formed the basis for the species management plan and allowed a critical appraisal of existing reserves and the need for linkages. However, past experience (Schaller 1993) suggests that the political and social dimensions of the conservation and management of Giant Pandas are likely to have the greatest influence on the future status of this species.

15 Linkages for Elephants in India

Two examples from India of loss and disturbance to migration paths of Indian Elephants highlight the need for identification and protection of movement paths if populations of large mammals are not to become isolated.

In southern India, elephants have stopped using the Ariankavu Pass between the Ashambu Hills and the Idduki-Periyar Hills (Johnsingh *et al.* 1991). The Ashambu Hills have about 200 elephants, mostly in the Kalakudu-Mundanthurai Tiger Reserve (900 km²) and several smaller reserves, while the Iddukki-Periyar Hills population is estimated as 800–1000 individuals, largely confined to the Periyar Tiger Reserve (777 km²) and the Grizzled Giant Squirrel Sanctuary (400 km²) (Johnsingh *et al.* 1991). The Ariankuvu Pass is divided by a road and railway line, and human settlements have developed along the road. A survey in 1988 found no evidence of elephants, and local people reported that the area had not been used by elephants for 30–40 years. The isolated population must also contend with poaching for ivory. Large scale poaching in the Periyar population has contributed to a sex ratio of 1 male:23 females (Johnsingh *et al.* 1991).

In northern India, the Rajaji-Corbett National Parks area includes protected reserves and adjacent forest areas that together encompass about 2500 km². This extensive area has a population of about 750 Indian Elephants and 140 Tigers and forms the north-western range limit for both species (Johnsingh *et al.* 1990). Four important links for the movement of large animals between major tracts in this area have been identified. Two of these are bottlenecks in a zone between Laldhang Forest Area and Sonandi Sanctuary, which extend for 6km free from human settlement and cattle camps. The terrain is rugged, there are few places for elephants to move through this region, and few crossings are now believed to occur. However, these links are not an impediment for movement of other large mammals such as Sambar and Tiger.

There are two linkages across the Ganges River between the Chila and Motichur sections of Rajaji National Park. At one site, Binj rau, there is now complete loss of forest cover on the west bank of the river and little evidence from dung counts of its use by elephants. In contrast, the Chila-Motichur link is still used by adult males during summer and is crucial to maintaining any interchange between the two sections of the park. However, this remaining link (approximately 3km long and 1km wide) is threatened by habitat degradation and lack of tree regeneration; by the presence of an army camp, village and plantation; and by the need for animals to cross a bridge over a power channel. Proposals have been developed by the Forest Department to maintain the link by selective acquisition and protection of forest habitat, but the long-term outlook is pessimistic in the face of likely destruction of remaining habitat arising from the pressure of human settlement (A. Johnsingh pers. comm. 1995).

Local networks of linear habitats

Networks of linear vegetation are a characteristic feature of many agricultural landscapes. Frequently, such linear strips are the product of intensive use of the environment by people, and include vegetation associated with hedgerows, fencerows, shelterbelts, ditches, embankments, canals, irrigation channels, railway lines and roads. Although such vegetation is often of human origin, remnant natural vegetation may also occur in local networks, including vegetation along stream systems and native vegetation along roadsides in Australia (see below). In regions of heavy human impact where natural areas are small and scattered, networks of linear habitats are recognized as having an important role in maintaining connectivity in the landscape, and there is growing awareness of the need for ecological values to be recognized in their management (Agger and Brandt 1988; Gulinck *et al.* 1991; Kaule 1995; Burel 1996; Kubeš 1996).

The maintenance of these networks and their ecological function faces a number of difficulties:

- lack of recognition of the ecological values of these features and of their context in the broader landscape;

- lack of co-ordinated management because they may extend across many land parcels and have many land owners;

- incremental clearing and loss resulting in gaps and breaks in the network;

- degradation of habitats due to edge effects and adjacent land uses.

Two examples are presented below of ways in which a co-ordinated approach has been undertaken to manage local networks of such linear habitats.

16   Hedgerow networks and landscape consolidation in France

In parts of rural France, restructuring of farm properties ('remembrement') is being carried out to rationalize the distribution of the land that each farmer owns (Baudry and Burel 1984). Over a number of generations, inheritance customs have resulted in many farms becoming a scatter of fields that may be up to five kilometres apart. Restructuring is done on a municipality basis and at the request of the majority of owners. In those landscapes with extensive hedge networks ('bocages' landscapes), initial attempts at re-distribution involved destruction of hedges; both to increase field sizes and because hedges were no longer needed as property boundaries. This led to numerous environmental problems. Subsequently, much research was carried out to evaluate the microclimatic, biological and agronomic values of hedgerows and the effects of their removal (INRA 1976; Forman and Baudry 1984 ; Burel and Baudry 1990). Since 1978, an impact study has been required before each 'remembrement' proceeds.

Ecological studies of the role of hedgerows in the rural landscape recognized their role as windbreaks, barriers against erosion, habitat for flora and fauna, and pools of genetic diversity amidst an increasingly monocultural landscape (Baudry and Burel 1984). In proposing plans to maintain these functions in the restructured rural landscape (Fig. 9–11), ecologists have suggested that hedges should be:

- primarily located across slopes;

- retained or re-connected in a network;

- have complex structure and high species diversity to provide habitats for birds, insects, small mammals and reptiles.

These recommendations, together with other constraints such as ownership patterns, are used to develop a final land-use plan. The ecological reconmendations are not necessarily adopted in their entirety but they do have an important role in the process of landscape consolidation. Further understanding of the agro-ecological effects of hedgerows and ditches and the provision of such information to local farmers and landowners will assist in the recognition of their values (Baudry and Burel 1984). For example, the retention of hedgerows, and their location and orientation in relation to soil types and topography, is known to influence water flow, drainage and erosion in farmland, and hence the use and productivity of the rural landscape (Burel and Baudry 1990).

17   Conservation of roadside vegetation in southern Australia

Strips of remnant forest, woodland or shrubland along roadsides form extensive networks of linear habitats through many agricultural areas of southern Australia. There is abundant evidence of the value of roadside vegetation as habitat for flora and fauna (Chapter 6), and growing understanding of how it fosters animal movements and maintains connectivity of populations in rural landscapes (Suckling 1984; Bennett 1990b; Saunders and de Rebeira 1991; Lynch *et al.* 1995; Downes *et al.* 1997).

In many regions, protection and management of roadside vegetation to maintain conservation values has been limited or non-existent, and an array of disturbance processes incrementally erode the extent and value of this network of natural vegetation. Clearing of

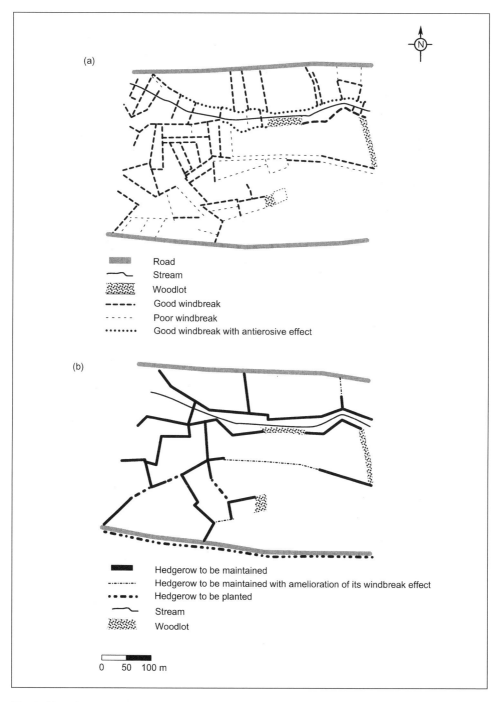

Fig. 9–11   Diagrams of a hedgerow network in Campénéac, France, (a) before "remembrement" and (b) the design that ecologists recommended for retention. Redrawn from Baudry and Burel (1984) with permission, Elsevier Science-NL.

vegetation often occurs during road widening or reconstruction; roadsides are used as easements for powerlines, telephone cables and other services; and fire prevention works such as regular burning or the ploughing of strips of bare earth (and thereby encouraging weeds) are also carried out on roadsides. They are also subject to weed invasion and nutrient enrichment from adjacent farmland, and intermittent grazing by domestic stock.

In the last decade, an increasing awareness of the environmental and community values of roadsides has led to a more sympathetic approach to management by many responsible authorities (usually local governments) and the development of roadside management plans in some areas (Lewis 1991; Loney and Hobbs 1991; Stone 1991; Lamont and Blyth 1995). Involvement of local communities of people in assessing the values of roadsides in their locality has been a key element. By direct involvement the community becomes more aware of the values of the roadside network and gain a sense of stewardship over roadsides in their local area.

Roadside assessment is typically carried out by teams of volunteer observers driving slowly along selected roads and recording attributes of the roadside vegetation, such as width and continuity of the vegetation, diversity of native plants, occurrence of weed species, presence of habitat features for animals and extent of disturbance by utilities (Hussey 1991). Each roadside section is 'scored' for conservation value, and maps are then prepared showing the distribution of roadsides of 'high', 'medium' and 'low' conservation value. The final step involves preparation of a written management plan by the roadside management authority, that specifies conservation measures and appropriate management practices for roadsides of high quality. Implementation of the management plan may involve modification of particular management practices, the use of roadside signs to clearly mark sections of high conservation value, and training courses for those that carry out roadside management in the field.

Summary

Recognition of the role of landscape connectivity in biodiversity conservation within human-dominated landscapes, has moved from the conceptual stage to that of practical implementation of this principle in conservation strategies. Throughout the world, a diverse range of linkages are now being protected, managed or restored to enhance the continuity of animal populations and to maintain ecological processes in fragmented ecosystems. These include specific landscape links between conservation reserves or for the conservation of large mammals; and networks of links in local areas, in managed forests and as part of regional land management strategies. This phase of implementation is in an early stage and there is much to learn. There is an urgent need for research and monitoring programmes to assess the effectiveness of these measures and resolve issues involved in their implementation. Such knowledge should provide the basis for ongoing improvements in the location, design and management of linkages, so that we can more effectively maintain and restore natural landscape connectivity in modified environments.

REFERENCES

Abensberg-Traun, M., 1991. A study of the home range, movements and shelter use in adult and juvenile Echidnas *Tachyglossus aculeatus* (Monotremata: Tachyglossidae), in Western Australian wheatbelt reserves. *Australian Mammalogy* **14**: 13–21.

Adams, L.W. and Dove, L.E., 1989. Wildlife Reserves and Corridors in the Urban Environment. A Guide to Ecological Landscape Planning and Resource Conservation. (National Institute for Urban Wildlife: Columbia).

Adams, L.W. and Geis, A.D., 1983. Effects of roads on small mammals. *Journal of Applied Ecology* **20**: 403–15.

Agger, P. and Brandt, J., 1988. Dynamics of small biotopes in Danish agricultural landscapes. *Landscape Ecology* **1**: 227–40.

Ahern, J., 1995. Greenways as a planning strategy. *Landscape and Urban Planning* **33**: 131–55.

Ambuel, B. and Temple, S.A., 1983. Area dependent changes in bird communities and vegetation of southern Wisconsin forests. *Ecology* **64**: 1057–68.

Andersen, M.C. and Mahato, D., 1995. Demographic models and reserve designs for the California Spotted Owl. *Ecological Applications* **5**: 639–47.

Andrén, H., 1992. Corvid density and nest predation in relation to forest fragmentation: a landscape perspective. *Ecology* **73**: 794–804.

Andrén, H. and Angelstam, P., 1988. Elevated predation rates as an edge effect in habitat islands: experimental evidence. *Ecology* **69**: 544–47.

Andrews, J., 1993. The reality and management of wildlife corridors. *British Wildlife* **5**: 1–7.

Angelstam, P., 1986. Predation in ground-nesting birds nests in relation to predator densities and habitat edge. *Oikos* **47**: 365–73.

Angelstam, P., 1992. Conservation of communities – the importance of edges, surroundings and landscape mosaic structure. pp. 9–70 *in* Ecological Principles of Nature Conservation: Applications in Temperate and Boreal Environments. (Ed. L. Hansson). (Elsevier: London).

Anonymous, 1993. Road plan to save dwindling dormice. *New Scientist* **139** (1883): 6.

Arnold, G.W., 1983. The influence of ditch and hedgerow structure, length of hedgerows, and area of woodland and garden on bird numbers on farmland. *Journal of Applied Ecology* **20**: 731–50.

Arnold, G.W., Algar, D., Hobbs, R.J. and Atkins, L., 1987. A survey of vegetation and its relationship to vertebrate fauna present in winter on road verges in the Kellerberrin

District, W.A. *Department of Conservation and Land Management Western Australia, Technical Report* **18**.

Arnold, G.W., Steven, D.E. and Weeldenburg, J.R., 1993. Influences of remnant size, spacing pattern and connectivity on population boundaries and demography in Euros *Macropus robustus* living in a fragmented landscape. *Biological Conservation* **64**: 219–30.

Arnold, G.W. and Weeldenburg, J.R., 1990. Factors determining the number and species of birds in road verges in the wheatbelt of Western Australia. *Biological Conservation* **53**: 295–315.

Arnold, G.W., Weeldenburg, J.R. and Steven, D.E., 1991. Distribution and abundance of two species of kangaroo in remnants of native vegetation in the central wheatbelt of Western Australia and the role of native vegetation along road verges and fencelines as linkages. pp. 273–80 *in* Nature Conservation 2: The Role of Corridors. (Eds. D.A. Saunders and R.J. Hobbs). (Surrey Beatty & Sons: Chipping Norton, New South Wales).

Asher, S.C. and Thomas, V.G., 1985. Analysis of temporal variation in the diversity of a small mammal community. *Canadian Journal of Zoology* **63**: 1106–10.

Askins, R.A., 1994. Open corridors in a heavily forested landscape: impact on shrubland and forest-interior birds. *Wildlife Society Bulletin* **22**: 339–47.

Askins, R.A., Philbrick, M.J. and Sugeno, D.S., 1987. Relationship between regional abundance of forest and the composition of forest bird communities. *Biological Conservation* **39**: 129–52.

Ayres, J.M. and Clutton-Brock, T.H., 1992. River boundaries and species range size in Amazonian primates. *American Naturalist* **140**: 531–37.

Baker, W.L., 1992. The landscape ecology of large disturbances in the design and management of nature reserves. *Landscape Ecology* **7**: 181–94.

Balát, F., 1985. Birds of narrow belts of vegetation along water channels and ditches in the field landscape of southern Moravia. *Folia Zoologica* **34**: 245–54.

Baranga, J., 1991. Kibale Forest game corridor: man or wildlife? pp. 371–75 *in* Nature Conservation 2: The Role of Corridors. (Eds. D.A. Saunders and R.J. Hobbs). (Surrey Beatty & Sons: Chipping Norton, New South Wales).

Barling, R.D and Moore, I.D., 1994. Role of buffer strips in management of waterway pollution: a review. *Environmental Management* **18**: 543–58.

Barr, C., Benefield, C., Bunce, B., Ridsdale, H. and Whittaker, M., 1986. Landscape Changes in Britain. (Institute of Terrestrial Ecology: Huntingdon).

Barrett, G.W., Ford, H.A. and Recher, H.F., 1994. Conservation of woodland birds in a fragmented rural landscape. *Pacific Conservation Biology* **1**: 245–56.

Baudry, J. and Burel, F., 1984. Landscape project 'remembrement': landscape consolidation in France. *Landscape Planning* **11**: 235–41.

Baudry, J. and Merriam, G., 1988. Connectivity and connectedness: functional vs structural patterns in landscapes. *in* 'Proceedings of the 2nd Seminar of the International Association for Landscape Ecology. (Ed. K.F. Schreiber). (Munster).

Baumgartner, L., 1943. Fox squirrels in Ohio. *Journal of Wildlife Management* **7**: 193–202.

Baur, A. and Baur, B., 1992. Effect of corridor width on animal dispersal: a simulation study. *Global Ecology and Biogeography Letters* **2**: 52–56.

Beier, P., 1993. Determining minimum habitat areas and habitat corridors for cougars. *Conservation Biology* **7**: 94–108.

Beier, P., 1995. Dispersal of juvenile cougars in fragmented habitat. *Journal of Wildlife Management* **59**: 228–37.

Beier, P. and Loe, S., 1992. A checklist for evaluating impacts to wildlife movement corridors. *Wildlife Society Bulletin* **20**: 434–40.

Bennett, A.F., 1987. Conservation of mammals within a fragmented forest environment: the contributions of insular biogeography and autecology. pp. 41–52 *in* Nature Conservation: The Role of Remnants of Native Vegetation. (Eds. D.A. Saunders, G.W. Arnold, A.A. Burbidge, and A.J.M. Hopkins). (Surrey Beatty & Sons: Chipping Norton, New South Wales).

Bennett, A.F., 1988. Roadside vegetation: a habitat for mammals at Naringal, south-western Victoria. *Victorian Naturalist* **105**: 106–13.

Bennett, A.F., 1990a. Habitat Corridors: Their Role in Wildlife Management and Conservation. (Department of Conservation and Environment: Melbourne).

Bennett, A.F., 1990b. Habitat corridors and the conservation of small mammals in a fragmented forest environment. *Landscape Ecol*ogy **4**: 109–22.

Bennett, A.F., 1990c. Land use, forest fragmentation and the mammalian fauna at Naringal, south-western Victoria. *Australian Wildlife Research* **17**: 325–47.

Bennett, A.F., 1991. Roads, roadsides and wildlife conservation: a review. pp. 99–117 *in* Nature Conservation 2: The Role of Corridors. (Eds. D.A. Saunders and R.J. Hobbs). (Surrey Beatty & Sons: Chipping Norton, New South Wales).

Bennett, A.F. and Ford, L.A., 1997. Land use, habitat change and the conservation of birds in fragmented rural environments: a landscape perspective from the Northern Plains, Victoria, Australia. *Pacific Conservation Biology* **3**: 244–61..

Bennett, A.F., Henein, K. and Merriam, G., 1994. Corridor use and the elements of corridor quality: chipmunks and fencerows in a farmland mosaic. *Biological Conservation* **68**: 155–65.

Bentley, J. and Catterall, C. (1997). The use of bushland, corridors, and linear remnants by birds in southeastern Queensland, Australia. *Conservation Biology* **11**: 1173–89.

Best, L.B., 1983. Bird use of fencerows: implications of contemporary fencerow management practices. *Wildlife Society Bulletin* **11**: 343–47.

Bhima, R., 1993. Elephant activity in the Liwonde National Park extension: is there any movement to and from Mangochi Forest Reserve? *Nyala* **16**: 45–54.

Bierregaard, R.O., Lovejoy, T.E., Kapos, V., dos Santos, A.A. and Hutchings, R.W., 1992. The biological dynamics of tropical rainforest fragments. *Bioscience* **42**: 859–66.

Bildstein, K.L., Brett, J.J., Goodrich, L.J. and Viverette, C., 1995. Hawks Aloft Worldwide: a network to protect the world's migrating birds of prey and the habitats essential to their migration. pp. 504–16 *in* Nature Conservation 4. The Role of Networks. (Eds. D.A. Saunders, J.L. Craig and E.M. Mattiske). (Surrey Beatty and Sons: Chipping Norton, New South Wales).

Binford, M. and Buchenau, M.J., 1993. Riparian greenways and water resources. pp. 69–104 *in* Ecology of Greenways. (Eds. D.S. Smith and P.C. Hellmund). (University of Minnesota Press: Minneapolis).

Bird, P.R., Bicknell, D., Bulman, P.A., Burke, S.J.A., Leys, J.F., Parker, J.N., van der Sommen, F.J. and Voller, P., 1992. The role of shelter in Australia for protecting soils, plants and livestock. *Agroforestry Systems* **20**: 59–86.

Bissonette, J.A., Frederickson, R.J. and Tucker, B.J., 1991. American marten: a case for landscape-level management. pp. 115–34 *in* Wildlife and Habitats in Managed Landscapes. (Eds. J.E. Rodiek and E.G. Bolen). (Island Press: Washington DC).

Blake, J.G., 1991. Nested subsets and the distribution of birds in isolated woodlots. *Conservation Biology* **5**: 58–66.

Blake, J.G. and Karr, J.R., 1984. Species composition of bird communities and the conservation benefit of large versus small forests. *Biological Conservation* **30**: 173–88.

Blakers, M., Davies, S.J.J.F. and Reilly, P.N., 1984. The Atlas of Australian Birds. (Melbourne University Press: Melbourne).

Blyth, J.D., Burbidge, A.A. and Brown, A.P., 1995. Achieving co-operation between government agencies and the community for nature conservation, with examples from the recovery of threatened species and ecological communities. pp. 343–67 *in* Nature Conservation 4. The Role of Networks. (Eds. D.A. Saunders, J.L. Craig and E.M. Mattiske). (Surrey Beatty and Sons: Chipping Norton, New South Wales).

Bolger, D.T., Alberts, A.C., Sauvajot, R.M., Potenza, P., McCalvin, C., Tran, D., Mazzoni, S. and Soulé, M.E., 1997. Response of rodents to habitat fragmentation in coastal southern California. *Ecological Applications* **7**: 552–63.

Bolger, D.T., Alberts, A.C. and Soulé, M.E., 1991. Occurrence patterns of bird species in habitat fragments: sampling, extinction and nested species subsets. *American Naturalist* **137**: 155–66.

Bonner, J., 1994. Wildlife's roads to nowhere? *New Scientist* **143** (1939) : 30–34.

Borner, M., 1985. The increasing isolation of Tarangire National Park. *Oryx* **19**: 91–96.

Bradby, K., 1991. A data bank is never enough: the local approach to landcare. pp. 377–85 *in* Nature Conservation 2: The Role of Corridors. (Eds. D.A. Saunders and R.J. Hobbs). (Surrey Beatty & Sons: Chipping Norton, New South Wales).

Brandt, J., 1996. Dispersal corridors in Danish regional planning. *Ekólogia* **15**: 79–85.

Brereton, R., Bennett, S., and Mansergh, I. 1995. Enhanced greenhouse climate change and its potential effect on selected fauna of south-eastern Australia: a trend analysis. *Biological Conservation* **72**: 339–54.

Bridgewater, P.B., 1987. Connectivity: an Australian perspective. pp. 195–200 *in* Nature Conservation: The Role of Remnants of Native Vegetation. (Eds. D.A. Saunders, G.W. Arnold, A.A. Burbidge, and A.J.M. Hopkins). (Surrey Beatty & Sons: Chipping Norton, New South Wales).

Bright, P.W., 1993. Habitat fragmentation – problems and predictions for British mammals. *Mammal Review* **23**: 101–11.

Bright, P.W., Mitchell, P. and Morris, P.A., 1994. Dormouse distribution: survey techniques, insular ecology and selection of sites for conservation. *Journal of Applied Ecology* **31**: 329–39.

Bright, P.W. and Morris, P.A., 1990. Habitat requirements of dormice in relation to woodland management in south-west England. *Biological Conservation* **54**: 307–26.

Bright, P.W. and Morris, P.A., 1991. Ranging and nesting behaviour of the dormouse, *Muscardinus avellanarius* in diverse low growing woodland. *Journal of Zoology, London* **224**: 177–90.

Brittingham, M. and Temple, S., 1983. Have cowbirds caused forest songbirds to decline? *Bioscience* **33**: 31–35.

Brooker, M., 1983. Conservation of wildlife in river corridors. *Nature in Wales* **2**: 11–20

Brown, L.H., 1981. The conservation of forest islands in areas of high human density. *African Journal of Ecology* **19**: 27–32.

Brown, J.H. and Kodric-Brown, A., 1977. Turnover rates in insular biogeography: effect of immigration on extinction. *Ecology* **58**: 445–49.

Burbidge, A., 1985. The Regent Parrot. A report on the breeding distribution and habitat requirements along the Murray River in south-eastern Australia. *Australian National Parks and Wildlife Service, Report Series No.* **4**.

Burel, F., 1989. Landscape structure effects on carabid beetle spatial patterns in western France. *Landscape Ecology* **2**: 215–26.

Burel, F., 1996. Hedgerows and their role in agricultural landscapes. *Critical Reviews in Plant Sciences* **15**: 169–90.

Burel, F. and Baudry, J., 1990. Hedgerow network patterns and processes in France. pp. 99–120 *in* Changing Landscapes: An Ecological Perspective. (Eds. I.S. Zonneveld and R.T.T. Forman). (Springer-Verlag: New York).

Burnett, S.E., 1992. Effects of a rainforest road on movements of small mammals: mechanisms and implications. *Wildlife Research* **19**: 95–104.

Burkey, T.V., 1989. Extinction in nature reserves: the effects of fragmentation and the importance of migration between reserve fragments. *Oikos* **55**: 75–81.

Burkey, T.V. 1995. Extinction rates in archipelagoes: implications for populations in fragmented habitats. *Conservation Biology* **9**: 527–41.

Butcher, G.S., Niering, W.A., Barry, W.T. and Goodwin, R.H., 1981. Equilibrium biogeography and the size of nature reserves: an avian case study. *Oecologia* **49**: 29–37.

Cale, P. 1990. The value of road reserves to the avifauna of the central wheatbelt of Western Australia. *Proceedings of the Ecological Society of Australia* **16**: 359–67.

Camp, M. and Best, L.B., 1993. Bird abundance and species richness in roadsides adjacent to Iowa rowcrop fields. *Wildlife Society Bulletin* **21**: 315–25.

Campbell, B.H., 1981. An aquaduct as a potential barrier to the movements of small mammals. *Southwestern Naturalist* **26**: 84–5.

Cantwell, M.D. and Forman, R.T.T., 1994. Landscape graphs: ecological modeling with graph theory to detect configurations common to diverse landscapes. *Landscape Ecology* **8**: 239–55.

Caughley, G., 1994. Directions in conservation biology. *Journal of Animal Ecology* **63**: 215–44.

Caughley, J. and Gall, B., 1985. Relevance of zoogeographical transition to conservation of fauna: amphibians and reptiles in the southwestern slopes of New South Wales. *Australian Zoologist* **21**: 513–29.

Claridge, A.W. and Lindenmayer, D.B., 1994. The need for a more sophisticated approach toward wildlife corridor design in the multiple-use forests of south-eastern Australia: the case for mammals. *Pacific Conservation Biology* **1**: 301–7.

Clark, T.W., Reading, R.P. and Clarke, A.L. (eds) 1994. Endangered Species Recovery: Finding the Lessons, Improving the Process. (Island Press: Washington DC).

Clinnick, P.F., 1985. Buffer strip management in forest operations: a review. *Australian Forestry* **48**: 34–45.

Coles, T.F., Southey, J.M., Forbes, I. and Clough, T., 1989. River wildlife data bases and their value for sensitive environmental management. *Regulated Rivers* **4**: 179–89.

Connor, E.F. and McCoy, E.D., 1979. The statistics and biology of the species-area relationship. *American Naturalist* **113**: 791–833.

Conyers, T., 1986. Hedgerow and ditch removal in south east Essex, England, 1838–1984. *Biological Conservation* **38**: 233–42.

Crome, F.H.J. and Bentrupperbaumer, J., 1993. Special people, a special animal and a special vision: the first steps to restoring a fragmented tropical landscape. pp. 267–79 *in* Nature Conservation 3. The Reconstruction of Fragmented Ecosystems. (Eds. D.A. Saunders, R.J. Hobbs and P.R. Ehrlich). (Surrey Beatty & Sons: Chipping Norton, New South Wales).

Curatolo, J.A. and Murphy, S.M., 1986. The effects of pipelines, roads, and traffic on the movements of Caribou, *Rangifer tarandus*. *Canadian Field Naturalist* **100**: 218–24.

Curtis, J.T., 1956. The modification of mid-latitude grasslands and forests by man. pp. 721–36 *in* Man's Role in Changing the Face of the Earth. (Ed. W.L. Thomas). (University of Chicago Press: Chicago).

Cutler, A., 1991. Nested faunas and extinction in fragmented habitats. *Conservation Biology* **5**: 496–505.

da Fonseca, G.A.B. and Robinson, J.G., 1990. Forest size and structure: competitive and predatory effects on small mammal communities. *Biological Conservation* **53**: 265–94.

Dambach, C., 1945. Some biologic and economic aspects of field border management. *Transactions of the North American Wildlife Conference* **10**: 169–84.

Danks, A., 1991. The role of corridors in the management of an endangered species. pp. 291–96 *in* Nature Conservation 2: The Role of Corridors. (Eds. D.A. Saunders and R.J. Hobbs). (Surrey Beatty & Sons: Chipping Norton, New South Wales).

Darveau, M., Beauchesnes, P., Bélanger, L., Huot, J. and Larue, P., 1995. Riparian forest strips as habitat for breeding birds in boreal forest. *Journal of Wildlife Management* **59**: 67–78.

Date, E.M., Ford, H.A. and Recher, H.F., 1991. Frugivorous pigeons, stepping stones and weeds in northern New South Wales. pp. 241–45 *in* Nature Conservation 2: The Role of Corridors. (Eds. D.A. Saunders and R.J. Hobbs). (Surrey Beatty & Sons: Chipping Norton, New South Wales).

Davison, V., 1941. Wildlife borders – an innovation in farm management. *Journal of Wildlife Management* **5**: 390–94.

den Boer, P.J., 1981. On the survival of populations in a heterogeneous and variable environment. *Oecologia* **50**: 39–53.

Decamps, H., Joachim, J. and Lauga, J., 1987. The importance for birds of the riparian woodlands within the alluvial corridor of the River Garonne, S.W. France. *Regulated Rivers: Research and Management* **1**: 301–16.

Dennis, P., Thomas, M.B. and Sotherton, N.W., 1994. Structural features of field boundaries which influence the overwintering densities of beneficial arthropod predators. *Journal of Applied Ecology* **31**: 361–70.

Department of Conservation, Forests and Lands, 1989. Code of Practice. Code of Forest Practices for Timber Production. Revision No. 1, May 1989. (Department of Conservation, Forests and Lands, Victoria: Melbourne).

Department of Conservation and Natural Resources, 1995. Forest Management Plan for the East Gippsland Forest Management Area. (Department of Conservation and Natural Resources, Victoria: Melbourne).

Department of the Environment, Sport and Territories, 1995. Native Vegetation Clearance, Habitat Loss and Biodiversity Decline. Biodiversity Series, Paper No. 6. (Biodiversity Unit, Department of the Environment, Sport and Territories: Canberra).

Dhindsa, M.S., Sandhu, J.S., Sandhu, P.S. and Toor, H.S., 1988. Roadside birds in Punjab (India): relation to mortality from vehicles. *Environmental Conservation* **15**: 303–10.

Diamond, A.W., 1981. The continuum of insularity: the relevance of equilibrium theory to the conservation of ecological islands. *African Journal of Ecology* **19**: 209–12.

Diamond, J.M., 1975. The island dilemma: lessons of modern biogeographic studies for the design of natural reserves. *Biological Conservation* **7**: 129–46.

Diamond, J.M., 1984. 'Normal' extinctions of isolated populations. pp. 191–246 *in* 'Extinctions'. (Ed. M.H. Nitecki). (University of Chicago Press: Chicago).

Diamond, J.M., Bishop, K.D. and Van Balen, S., 1987. Bird survival in an isolated Javan woodland: island or mirror? *Conservation Biology* **1**: 132–42.

Dickman, C.R., 1987. Habitat fragmentation and vertebrate species richness in an urban environment. *Journal of Applied Ecology* **24**: 337–51.

Dickman, C.R. and Doncaster, C.P., 1987. The ecology of small mammals in urban habitats. I Populations in a patchy environment. *Journal of Animal Ecology* **56**: 629–40.

Dickson, J.G. and Huntley, J.C., 1987. Riparian zones and wildlife in southern forests: the problem and squirrel relationships. pp. 37–39 *in* Managing Southern Forests for Wildlife and Fish. (U.S.D.A. Southern Forest Experiment Station Gen. Tech. Rep. S0–65).

Dickson, J.E., Williamson, J.H., Conner, R.N. and Ortego, B., 1995. Streamside zones and breeding birds in eastern Texas. *Wildlife Society Bulletin* **23**: 750–55.

Dmowski, K. and Kozakiewicz, M., 1990. Influence of a shrub corridor on movements of passerine birds to a lake littoral zone. *Landscape Ecology* **4**: 99–108.

Dobbyns, R. and Ryan, D., 1983. Birds, glider possums and monkey gums. The wildlife reserve system in the Eden district. *Forest and Timber* **19**: 12–15.

Dowdeswell, W.H., 1987. Hedgerows and Verges. (Allen and Unwin: London).

Downes, S.J., Handasyde, K.A. and Elgar, M.A., 1997. The use of corridors by mammals in fragmented Australian eucalypt forests. *Conservation Biology* **11**: 718–26.

Doyle, A.T., 1990. Use of riparian and upland habitats by small mammals. *Journal of Mammalogy* **71**: 14–23.

Dramstad, W.E., Olson, J.D. and Forman, R.T.T., 1996. Landscape Ecology Principles in Landscape Architecture and Land-Use Planning. (Harvard University Graduate School of Design, Island Press and the American Society of Landscape Architects).

Dunham, K.M., 1994. The effect of drought on the large mammal populations of Zambezi riverine woodlands. *Journal of Zoology, London* **234**: 489–526.

Dunning, J.B., Danielson, J.B. and Pulliam, H.R., 1992. Ecological processes that affect populations in complex landscapes. *Oikos* **65**: 169–75.

Dunning, J.B., Borgella, R., Clements, K. and Meffe, G.K., 1995. Patch isolation, corridor effects, and colonization by a resident sparrow in a managed pine woodland. *Conservation Biology* **9**: 542–50.

East, R., 1981. Species-area curves and populations of large mammals in African savannah reserves. *Biological Conservation* **21**: 111–26.

Eldridge, J., 1971. Some observations on the dispersal of small mammals in hedgerows. *Journal of Zoology* **165**: 530–34.

Emmerich, J.M. and Vohs, P.A., 1982. Comparative use of four woodland habitats by birds. *Journal of Wildlife Management* **46**: 43–49.

Elphick, J., 1995. The Atlas of Bird Migration. (RD Press: Surrey Hills, New South Wales).

Esseen, P-A., 1994. Tree mortality patterns after experimental fragmentation of an old-growth conifer forest. *Biological Conservation* **68**: 19–28.

Faanes, C.A., 1984. Wooded islands in a sea of prairie. *American Birds* **38**: 3–6.

Fahrig, L. and Merriam, G., 1985. Habitat patch connectivity and population survival. *Ecology* **66**: 1762–68.

Fahrig, L. and Merriam, G., 1994. Conservation of fragmented populations. *Conservation Biology* **8**: 50–59.

Fahrig, L. and Paloheimo, J., 1988. Effect of spatial arrangement of habitat patches on local population size. *Ecology* **69**: 468–75.

Feinsinger, P., 1994. Habitat 'shredding'. pp. 258–60 *in* Principles of Conservation Biology (Eds. G.K. Meffe and C.R. Carroll). (Sinauer Associates: Sunderland).

Felfili, J.M., 1997. Dynamics of natural regeneration in the Gama gallery forest in central Brazil. *Forest Ecology and Management* **91**: 235–45.

Ferris, C.R., 1979. Effects of Interstate 95 on breeding birds in northern Maine. *Journal of Wildlife Management* **43**: 421–27.

Ferris-Kaan, R., 1991. Edge Management in Woodlands. *Forestry Commission Occasional Paper* **28**. (Forestry Commission: Edinburgh).

Ferris-Kaan, R., 1995. Management of linear habitats for wildlife in British forests. pp. 67–77 *in* Nature Conservation 4: The Role of Networks. (Eds. D.A. Saunders, J.L. Craig and E.M. Mattiske). (Surrey Beatty & Sons: Chipping Norton, New South Wales).

Fitzgibbon, C.D., 1993. The distribution of grey squirrel dreys in farm woodland: the influence of wood area, isolation and management. *Journal of Applied Ecology* **30**: 736–42.

Ford, H.A., 1987. Bird communities on habitat islands in England. *Bird Study* **34**: 205–18.

Forman, R.T.T., 1983. Corridors in a landscape: their ecological structure and function. *Ekologia (CSSR)* **2**: 375–87.

Forman, R.T.T., 1991. Landscape corridors: from theoretical foundations to public policy. pp. 71–84 *in* Nature Conservation 2: The Role of Corridors. (Eds. D.A. Saunders and R.J. Hobbs). (Surrey Beatty & Sons: Chipping Norton, New South Wales).

Forman, R.T.T., 1995. Land Mosaics. The Ecology of Landscapes and Regions. (Cambridge University Press: Cambridge).

Forman, R.T.T. and Baudry, J., 1984. Hedgerows and hedgerow networks in landscape ecology. *Environmental Management* **8**: 495–510.

Forman, R.T.T. and Godron, M., 1981. Patches and structural components for a landscape ecology. *Bioscience* **31**: 733–40.

Forman, R.T.T. and Godron, M., 1986. Landscape Ecology. (John Wiley and Sons: New York).

Forman, R.T.T. and Hersperger, A.M., 1996. Road ecology and road density in different landscapes, with international planning and mitigation solutions. pp. 1–22 *in* Trends in Addressing Transportation-Related Wildlife Mortality. (Eds. G.L. Evink, P. Garrett, D. Zeigler and J. Berry). (Florida Department of Transportation: Tallahassee, Florida).

Foster, M.L. and Humphrey, S.R., 1995. Use of highway underpasses by Florida panthers and other wildlife. *Wildlife Society Bulletin* **23**: 95–100.

Fowler, N.E. and Howe, R.W., 1987. Birds of remnant riparian forests in northeastern Wisconsin. *Western Birds* **18**: 77–83.

Franklin, J.F., 1989. Toward a new forestry. *American Forests*, **Nov – Dec**: 37–44.

Franklin, J.F., 1992. Scientific basis for new perspectives in forests and streams. pp. 25–72 *in* Watershed Management: Balancing Sustainability and Environmental Change. (Ed. R.J. Naiman). (Springer-Verlag).

Freemark, K.E. and Merriam, H.G., 1986. Importance of area and habitat heterogeneity to bird assemblages in temperate forest fragments. *Biological Conservation* **36**: 115–41.

Fritz, R.S., 1979. Consequences of insular population structure: distribution and extinction of spruce grouse populations. *Oecologia* **42**: 57–65.

Fritz, R. and Merriam, G., 1993. Fencerow habitats for plants moving between farmland forests. *Biological Conservation* **64**: 141–48.

Fritz, R. and Merriam, G., 1994. Fencerow and forest edge vegetation structure in eastern Ontario farmland. *Ecoscience* **1**: 160–72.

Fry, G. and Main, A.R., 1993. Restoring seemingly natural communities on agricultural land. pp. 225–41 *in* Nature Conservation 3. The Reconstruction of Fragmented Ecosystems. (Eds. D.A. Saunders, R.J. Hobbs and P.R. Ehrlich). (Surrey Beatty & Sons: Chipping Norton, New South Wales).

Galli, A.E., Leck, C.F. and Forman, R.T.T., 1976. Avian distribution patterns in forest islands of different sizes in central New Jersey. *Auk* **93**: 356–64.

Gates, J.E. and Gysel, L.W., 1978. Avian nest dispersion and fledging success in field forest ecotones. *Ecology* **59**: 871–83.

Gates, J.E. and Mosher, J.A., 1981. A functional approach to estimating habitat edge width for birds. *American Midland Naturalist* **105**: 189–92.

Getz L.L., Cole, F.R. and Gates, D.L., 1978. Interstate roadsides as dispersal routes for *Microtus pensylvannicus*. *Journal of Mammalogy* **59**: 208–12.

Gilbert, F.S., 1980. The equilibrium theory of island biogeography: fact or fiction. *Journal of Biogeography* **7**: 209–35.

Gilpin, M.E. and Hanski, I., 1991. Metapopulation Dynamics: Empirical and Theoretical Investigations. (Academic Press: London).

Green, R.E., Osborne, P.E. and Sears, E.J., 1994. The distribution of passerine birds in hedgerows during the breeding season in relation to characteristics of the hedgerow and adjacent farmland. *Journal of Applied Ecology* **31**: 677–92.

Greening Australia, 1994a. Towards Corridors of Green. Defining the Role of a National Corridors of Green Program. (Unpublished Background Paper) (Greening Australia: Canberra).

Greening Australia, 1994b. River Murray Corridors of Green. Phase III Program 1994–1995. (Greening Australia: Canberra).

Grumbine, R.E., 1994. What is ecosystem management? *Conservation Biology* **8**: 27–38.

Gulinck, H., Walpot, O., Janssens, P. and Dries, I., 1991. The visualisation of corridors in the landscape using SPOT data. pp. 9–17 *in* Nature Conservation 2: The Role of Corridors. (Eds. D.A. Saunders and R.J. Hobbs). (Surrey Beatty & Sons: Chipping Norton, New South Wales).

Haas, C.A., 1995. Dispersal and use of corridors by birds in wooded patches on an agricultural landscape. *Conservation Biology* **9**: 845–54.

Hadden, S.A. and Westbrooke, M.E., 1996. Habitat relationships of the herpetofauna of remnant buloke woodlands of the Wimmera Plains, Victoria. *Wildlife Research* **23**: 363–72.

Haila, Y., Hanski, I.K. and Raivio, S., 1993a. Turnover of breeding birds in small forest fragments: the 'sampling' colonization hypothesis corroborated. *Ecology* **74**: 714–25.

Haila, Y., Saunders, D.A. and Hobbs, R.J., 1993b. What do we presently understand about ecosystem fragmentation? pp. 45–55 *in* Nature Conservation 3. The Reconstruction of Fragmented Ecosystems. (Eds. D.A. Saunders, R.J. Hobbs and P.R. Ehrlich). (Surrey Beatty & Sons: Chipping Norton, New South Wales).

Hanski, I., 1989. Metapopulation dynamics: does it help to have more of the same? *Trends in Ecology and Evolution* **4**: 113–14.

Hanski, I. and Gilpin, M., 1991. Metapopulation dynamics: brief history and conceptual domain. *Biological Journal of the Linnean Society* **42**: 3–16.

Hansson, L., 1991. Dispersal and connectivity in metapopulations. *Biological Journal of the Linnean Society* **42**: 89–103.

Hansson, L. and Angelstam, P., 1991. Landscape ecology as a theoretical basis for nature conservation. *Landscape Ecology* **5**: 191–201.

Hansson, L., Fahrig, L. and Merriam, G., (Eds), 1995. Mosaic Landscapes and Ecological Processes. (Chapman and Hall: London).

Harms, W.B. and Knaapen, J.P., 1988. Landscape planning and ecological infrastructure: the Randstad study. pp. 163–67 *in* Connectivity in Landscape Ecology. (Ed. K-F. Schreiber). (Munstersche Geographische Arbeiten: Munster).

Harms, W.B. and Opdam, P., 1990. Woods as habitat patches for birds: application in landscape planning in the Netherlands. pp. 73–97 *in* Changing Landscapes: An Ecological Perspective. (Eds. I. Zonneveld and R.T.T. Forman). (Springer-Verlag: New York).

Harris, L.D., 1984. The Fragmented Forest. Island Biogeographic Theory and the Preservation of Biotic Diversity. (Chicago University Press: Chicago.)

Harris, L.D., 1988a. Edge effects and the conservation of biotic diversity. *Conservation Biology* **2**: 330–32.

Harris, L.D., 1988b. Landscape linkages: the dispersal corridor approach to wildlife conservation. *Transactions of the North American Wildlife and Natural Resources Conference* **53**: 595–607.

Harris, L.D., 1988c. The nature of cumulative impacts on biotic diversity of wetland vertebrates. *Environmental Management* **12**: 675–93.

Harris, L.D. and Gallagher, P.B., 1989. New initiatives for wildlife conservation. The need for movement corridors. pp. 11–34 *in* In Defense of Wildlife: Preserving Communities and Corridors. (Ed. G. Mackintosh). (Defenders of Wildlife: Washington).

Harris, L.D. and Scheck, J., 1991. From implications to applications: the dispersal corridor principle applied to the conservation of biological diversity. pp. 189–220 *in* Nature Conservation 2: The Role of Corridors. (Eds. D.A. Saunders and R.J. Hobbs). (Surrey Beatty & Sons: Chipping Norton, New South Wales).

Harris, S. and Woollard, T., 1990. The dispersal of mammals in agricultural habitats in Britain. pp. 159–188 *in* Species Dispersal in Agricultural Habitats. (Eds. R.G.H. Bunce and D.C. Howard). (Belhaven Press: London).

Harrison, R.L., 1992. Toward a theory of inter-refuge corridor design. *Conservation Biology* **6**: 293–95.

Harrison, S., 1991. Local extinction in a metapopulation context: an empirical evaluation. *Biological Journal of the Linnean Society* **42**: 73–88.

Harrison, S., Murphy, D.D. and Ehrlich, P.R., 1988. Distribution of the bay checkerspot butterfly, *Euphydryas editha bayensis:* evidence for a metapopulation model. *American Naturalist* **132**: 360–82.

Havlin, J., 1987. Motorways and birds. *Folia Zoologica* **36**: 137–53.

Helliwell, D.R., 1975. The distribution of woodland plant species in some Shropshire hedgerows. *Biological Conservation* **7**: 61–72.

Henderson, M.T., Merriam, G. and Wegner, J., 1985. Patchy environments and species survival: chipmunks in an agricultural mosaic. *Biological Conservation* **31**: 95–105.

Henein, K. and Merriam, G., 1990. The elements of connectivity where corridor quality is variable. *Landscape Ecology* **4**: 157–170.

Hess, G.R., 1994. Conservation corridors and contagious disease: a cautionary note. *Conservation Biology* **8**: 256–62.

Hibberd, J.K. and Soutberg, T.L., 1991. Roadside reserve condition 1977–89 in the Southern Tablelands of New South Wales. pp. 177–86 *in* Nature Conservation 2: The Role of Corridors. (Eds. D.A. Saunders and R.J. Hobbs). (Surrey Beatty & Sons: Chipping Norton, New South Wales).

Hill, C.J., 1995. Linear strips of rainforest vegetation as potential dispersal corridors for rainforest insects. *Conservation Biology* **9**: 1559–66.

Hobbs, R.J., 1992. The role of corridors in conservation: solution or bandwagon? *Trends in Ecology and Evolution* **7**: 389–91.

Hobbs, R.J., 1993a. Effects of landscape fragmentation on ecosystem processes in the Western Australian wheatbelt. *Biological Conservation* **64**: 193–201.

Hobbs, R.J., 1993b. Can revegetation assist in the conservation of biodiversity in agricultural areas? *Pacific Conservation Biology* **1**: 29–38.

Hobbs, R.J. and Hopkins, A.J.M., 1991. The role of conservation corridors in a changing environment. pp. 281–90 *in* Nature Conservation 2: The Role of Corridors. (Eds. D.A. Saunders and R.J. Hobbs). (Surrey Beatty & Sons: Chipping Norton, New South Wales).

Hobbs, R.J. and Saunders, D.A., 1991. Re-integrating fragmented landscapes – a preliminary framework for the Western Australian wheatbelt. *Journal of Environmental Management* **33**: 161–67.

Hobbs, R.J., Saunders, D.A. and Arnold, G.W., 1993. Integrated landscape ecology: a Western Australian perspective. *Biological Conservation* **64**: 231–38.

Hodson, N.L., 1960. A survey of vertebrate road mortality 1959. *Bird Study* **7**: 224–31.

Hopkins, A.J.M. and Saunders, D.A. 1987. Ecological studies as the basis for management. pp. 15–28 *in* Nature Conservation: The Role of Remnants of Native Vegetation. (Eds. D.A. Saunders, G.W. Arnold, A.A. Burbidge, and A.J.M. Hopkins). (Surrey Beatty & Sons: Chipping Norton, New South Wales).

Houghton, R.A., 1994. The worldwide extent of land-use change. *Bioscience* **44**: 305–13.

Howe, R.W., 1984. Local dynamics of bird assemblages in small forest habitat islands in Australia and North America. *Ecology* **65**: 1585–1601.

Howe, R.W., Howe, T.D. and Ford, H.A., 1981. Bird distributions on small rainforest remnants in New South Wales. *Australian Wildlife Research* **8**: 637–51.

Hudson, W.E., 1991. Landscape Linkages and Biodiversity. (Island Press: Washington, DC).

Huey, L.M., 1941. Mammalian invasion via the highway. *Journal of Mammalogy* **22**: 383–85.

Humphreys, W.F. and Kitchener, D.J., 1982. The effect of habitat utilization on species-area curves: implications for optimal reserve area. *Journal of Biogeography* **9**: 391–96.

Hunt, A., Dickens, H.J. and Whelan, R.J., 1987. Movement of mammals through tunnels under railway lines. *Australian Zoologist* **24**: 89–93.

Hurrell, E. and McIntosh, G., 1984. Mammal Society dormouse survey, January 1975–April 1979. *Mammal Review* **14**: 1–18.

Hussey, B.M.J., 1991. The flora roads survey – volunteer recording of roadside vegetation in Western Australia. pp. 41–48 *in* Nature Conservation 2: The Role of Corridors. (Eds. D.A. Saunders and R.J. Hobbs). (Surrey Beatty & Sons: Chipping Norton, New South Wales).

Inglis, G. and Underwood, A.J., 1992. Comments on some designs proposed for experiments on the biological importance of corridors. *Conservation Biology* **6**: 581–86.

INRA Université de Rennes, 1976. Les Bocages: Histoire, Écologie, Économie. (Editions INRA, Rennes).

IUCN, 1980. The World Conservation Strategy. (IUCN, UNEP, WWF: Gland).

Janzen, D.H., 1986. The eternal external threat. pp. 286–303 *in* Conservation Biology: The Science of Scarcity and Diversity. (Ed. M.E. Soulé). (Sinauer Associates: Sunderland).

Johnsingh, A.J.T., Prasad, S.N. and Goyal, S.P., 1990. Conservation status of the Chila-Motichur corridor for elephant movement in Rajaji-Corbett National Parks area, India. *Biological Conservation* **51**: 125–38.

Johnsingh, A.J.T., Sathyakumar, S. and Sunderraj, S.F.W., 1991. Ariankava Pass, a lost elephant corridor in south India. *Environmental Conservation* **18**: 368.

Johnson, W.C and Adkisson, C.S., 1985. Dispersal of beech nuts by Blue Jays in fragmented landscapes. *American Midland Naturalist* **113**: 319–24.

Jones, K.B., Kepner, L.P. and Martin, T.E., 1985. Species of reptiles occupying habitat islands in western Arizona: a deterministic assemblage. *Oecologia* **66**: 595–601.

Jongman, R.H.G., 1995. Nature conservation planning in Europe: developing ecological networks. *Landscape and Urban Planning* **32**: 169–83.

Karr, J.R., 1982a. Population variability and extinction in a tropical land-bridge island. *Ecology* **63**: 1975–78.

Karr, J.A., 1982b. Avian extinction on Barro Colorado Island, Panama: a re-assessment. *American Naturalist* **119**: 220–39.

Kaule, G., 1995. Protection and rehabilitation of habitat networks in predominantly agricultural landscapes of southwestern Germany: the need for greater integration of research into redefining European Economic Community agricultural policy. pp. 271–81 *in* Nature Conservation 4. The Role of Networks. (Eds. D.A. Saunders, J.L. Craig and E.M. Mattiske). (Surrey Beatty & Sons: Chipping Norton, New South Wales).

Keals, N. and Majer, J.D., 1991. The conservation status of ant communities along the Wubin – Perenjori corridor. pp. 387–93 *in* Nature Conservation 2: The Role of Corridors. (Eds. D.A. Saunders and R.J. Hobbs). (Surrey Beatty & Sons: Chipping Norton, New South Wales).

Keast, A. and Morton, E.S. (Eds), 1980. Migrant Birds in the Neotropics: Ecology, Behaviour, Distribution and Conservation. (Smithsonian Institution Press: Washington DC).

Kindvall, O. and Ahlen, I., 1992. Geometrical factors and metapopulation dynamics of the bush cricket, *Metrioptera bicolor* Philippi (Orthoptera: Tettigoniidae). *Conservation Biology* **6**: 520–29.

Kitchener, D.J., Chapman, A., Dell, J., Muir, B.G. and Palmer, M., 1980a. Lizard assemblage and reserve size and structure in the Western Australian wheatbelt – some implications for conservation. *Biological Conservation* **17**: 25–62.

Kitchener, D.J., Chapman, A., Muir, B.G. and Palmer, M., 1980b. The conservation value for mammals of reserves in the Western Australian wheatbelt. *Biological Conservation* **18**: 179–207.

Kitchener, D.J., Dell, J., Muir, B.G. and Palmer, M., 1982. Birds in Western Australian wheatbelt reserves – implications for conservation. *Biological Conservation* **22**: 127–63.

Kitchener, D.J. and How, R.A., 1982. Lizard species in small mainland habitat isolates and islands of south-western Western Australia. *Australian Wildlife Research* **9**: 357–63.

Klein, B.C., 1989. Effects of forest fragmentation on dung and carrion beetle communities in Central Amazonia. *Ecology* **70**: 1715–25.

Klein, D.R., 1971. Reaction of reindeer to obstructions and disturbances. *Science* **173**: 393–98.

Kozakiewicz, M., Kozakiewicz, A., Lukowski, A. and Gortat, P., 1993. Use of space by bank voles (*Clethrionomys glareolus*) in a Polish farm landscape. *Landscape Ecology* **8**: 19–24.

Kozel, R.M. and Fleharty, E.D., 1979. Movements of rodents across roads. *Southwestern Naturalist* **24**: 239–48.

Kubeš, J., 1996. Biocentres and corridors in a cultural landscape. A critical assessment of the 'territorial system of ecological stability'. *Landscape and Urban Planning* **35**: 231–40.

Laan, R, and Verboom, B., 1990. Effects of pool size and isolation on amphibian communities. *Biological Conservation* **54**: 251–62.

Lack, P.C., 1988. Hedge intersections and breeding bird distributions in farmland. *Bird Study* **35**: 133–36.

Lacy, R.C., 1993. VORTEX – a model for use in population viability analysis. *Wildlife Research* **20**: 45–65.

Laitin, J., 1987. Corridors for wildlife. *American Forests* **Sep–Oct**: 47–49.

Lamberson, R.H., Noon, B.R., Voss, C. and McKelvey, K.S., 1994. Reserve design for territorial species: the effects of patch size and spacing on the viability of the Northern Spotted Owl. *Conservation Biology* **8**: 185–95.

Lamont, D.A. and Blyth, J.D., 1995. Roadside corridors and community networks. pp. 425–35 *in* Nature Conservation 4. The Role of Networks. (Eds. D.A. Saunders, J.L. Craig and E.M. Mattiske). (Surrey Beatty & Sons: Chipping Norton, New South Wales).

Langton, T.E.S., (Ed.) 1989. Amphibians and Roads. (ACO Polymer Products Ltd.: Shefford, Bedfordshire, England).

Land Conservation Council, 1987. Report on the Mallee Area Review. (Land Conservation Council, Victoria: Melbourne).

Land Conservation Council, 1989. Mallee Area Review Final Recommendations. (Land Conservation Council, Victoria: Melbourne).

Land Conservation Council, 1994. Melbourne Area District 2 Review. Final Recommendations. (Land Conservation Council, Victoria: Melbourne).

La Polla, V.N. and Barrett, G.W., 1993. Effects of corridor width and presence on the population dynamics of the meadow vole (*Microtus pennsylvanicus*). *Landscape Ecology* **8**: 25–37.

Laurance, W.F., 1990. Comparative responses of five arboreal marsupials to tropical forest fragmentation. *Journal of Mammalogy* **71**: 641–53.

Laurance, W.F., 1991a. Ecological correlates of extinction proneness in Australian tropical rainforest mammals. *Conservation Biology* **5**: 79–89.

Laurance, W.F., 1991b. Edge effects in tropical forest fragments: application of a model for the design of nature reserves. *Biological Conservation* **59**: 205–19.

Laurance, W.F. and Gascon, C., 1997. How to creatively fragment a landscape. *Conservation Biology* **11**: 577–79.

Laursen, K., 1981. Birds on roadside verges and the effect of mowing on the frequency and distribution. *Biological Conservation* **20**: 59–68.

Leach, G.J. and Recher, H.F., 1993. Use of roadside remnants of softwood scrub vegetation by birds in south-eastern Queensland. *Wildlife Research* **20**: 233–49.

Leader-Williams, N., Harrison, J. and Green, M.J.B., 1990. Designing protected areas to conserve natural resources. *Scientific Progress Oxford* **74**: 189–204.

Leck, C.F., 1979. Avian extinctions in an isolated tropical wet-forest preserve, Ecuador. *Auk* **96**: 343–52.

Lewis, S.A., 1991. The conservation and management of roadside vegetation in South Australia. pp. 313–18 *in* Nature Conservation 2: The Role of Corridors. (Eds. D.A. Saunders and R.J. Hobbs). (Surrey Beatty & Sons: Chipping Norton, New South Wales).

Lewis, T., 1969. The diversity of the insect fauna in a hedgerow and neighbouring fields. *Journal of Applied Ecology* **6**: 453–58.

Limpens, H.J.G.A. and Kapteyn, K., 1989. Bats, their behaviour and linear landscape elements. *Myotis* **29**: 63–71.

Lindenmayer, D.B., 1994. Wildlife corridors and the mitigation of logging impacts on fauna in wood-production forests in south-eastern Australia: a review. *Wildlife Research* **21**: 323–40.

Lindenmayer, D.B., 1996. Wildlife and Woodchips: Leadbeater's Possum as a Test Case for Sustainable Forestry. (University of New South Wales Press: Sydney).

Lindenmayer, D.B., Tanton, M.T. and Norton, T.W. 1990. Leadbeater's Possum – a test case for integrated forestry. *Search* **21**: 156–59.

Lindenmayer, D.B., Cunningham, R.B. and Donelly, C.F., 1993. The conservation of arboreal mammals in the montane ash forests of the Central Highlands of Victoria, south-east Australia. IV The distribution and abundance of arboreal marsupials in retained linear strips (wildlife corridors) in timber production forests. *Biological Conservation* **66**: 207–21.

Lindenmayer, D.B., Cunningham, R.B. and Donnelly, C.F., 1997. Decay and collapse of trees with hollows in eastern Australian forests: impacts on arboreal marsupials. *Ecological Applications* **7**: 625–41.

Lindenmayer, D.B., Cunningham, R.B., Donnelly, C.F., Triggs, B.J. and Belvedere, M., 1994a. The conservation of arboreal marsupials in the montane ash forests of the central highlands of Victoria, south-east Australia. V. Patterns of use and the microhabitat requirements of the mountain brushtail possum *Trichosurus caninus* Ogilby in retained linear strips (wildlife corridors). *Biological Conservation* **68**: 43–51.

Lindenmayer, D.B., Cunningham, R.B, Donnelly, C.F., Triggs, B.J. and Belvedere, M., 1994b. Factors influencing the occurrence of mammals in retained linear strips (wildlife corridors) and contiguous stands of montane ash forests in the central highlands of Victoria. *Forest Ecology and Management* **67**: 113–33.

Lindenmayer, D.B., Burgman, M.A., Akcakaya, H.R. and Lacy, R.C., 1995. A review of the generic computer programs ALEX, RAMAS/space and VORTEX for modelling the viability of wildlife metapopulations. *Ecological Modelling* **82**: 161–74.

Lindenmayer, D.B. and Lacy, R.C., 1995. Using Population Viability Analysis (PVA) to explore the impacts of population subdivision on the Mountain Brushtail Possum, *Trichosurus caninus*, Ogilby (Phalangeridae: Marsupialia) in south-eastern Australia. 1. Demographic stability and population persistence. *Biological Conservation* **73**: 119–29.

Lindenmayer, D.B. and Nix, H.A., 1993. Ecological principles for the design of wildlife corridors. *Conservation Biology* **7**: 627–30.

Lindenmayer, D.B. and Possingham, H.P., 1996. Modelling the inter-relationships between habitat patchiness, dispersal capability and metapopulation persistence of the endangered species, Leadbeater's possum, in south-eastern Australia. *Landscape Ecology* **11**: 79–105.

Little, C.E., 1990. Greenways for America. (The John Hopkins University Press: Baltimore).

Loiselle, B.A. and Blake, J.G., 1992. Population variation in a tropical bird community. *Bioscience* **42**: 838–45.

Loiselle, B.A. and Hoppes, W.G., 1983. Nest predation in insular and mainland lowland rainforest in Panama. *Condor* **85**: 93–95.

Loney, B. and Hobbs, R.J., 1991. Management of vegetation corridors: maintenance, rehabilitation and establishment. pp. 299–311 *in* Nature Conservation 2: The Role of Corridors. (Eds. D.A. Saunders and R.J. Hobbs). (Surrey Beatty & Sons: Chipping Norton, New South Wales).

Lorenz, G.C. and Barrett, G.W., 1990. Influence of simulated landscape corridors on house mouse (*Mus musculus*) dispersal. *American Midland Naturalist* **123**: 348–56.

Lovejoy, T.E., Bierregaard, R.O., Rylands, A.B., Malcolm, J.R., Quintela, C.E., Harper, L.H., Brown, K.S., Powell, A.H., Powell, G.V.N., Schubart, H.O.R. and Hays, M.B., 1986. Edge and other effects of isolation on Amazon forest fragments. pp. 257–85 *in*

Conservation Biology. The Science of Scarcity and Diversity. (Ed. M.E. Soulé). (Sinaeur Associates: Sunderland).

Lovejoy, T.E., Rankin, J.M., Bierregaard, R.O., Brown, K.S., Emmons, L.H. and Van der Voort, M.E., 1984. Ecosystem decay of Amazon forest remnants. pp. 295–325 *in* Extinctions. (Ed. M.H. Nitecki). (University of Chicago Press: Chicago).

Loyn, R.H., 1985a. Birds in fragmented forests in Gippland, Victoria. pp. 323–31 *in* Birds of Eucalypt Forests and Woodlands: Ecology, Conservation, Management. (Eds. A. Keast, H.F. Recher, H. Ford, and D. Saunders). (Surrey Beatty & Sons: Chipping Norton, New South Wales).

Loyn, R.H., 1985b. Bird populations in successional forests of Mountain Ash *Eucalyptus regnans* in central Victoria. *Emu* **85**: 213–30.

Loyn, R.H., 1987. Effects of patch area and habitat on bird abundances, species numbers and tree health in fragmented Victorian forests. pp. 65–77 *in* Nature Conservation: The Role of Remnants of Native Vegetation. (Eds. D.A. Saunders, G.W. Arnold, A.A. Burbidge and A.J.M. Hopkins). (Surrey Beatty & Sons: Chipping Norton, New South Wales).

Loyn, R.H., Macfarlane, M.A., Chesterfield, E.A. and Harris, J.A., 1980. Forest utilisation and the flora and fauna in Boola Boola State Forest. *Forests Commission Victoria, Bulletin* No **28**.

Lumsden, L.F. and Menkhorst, P.W., 1995. Large-footed Myotis *Myotis adversus*. pp. 182–83 *in* Mammals of Victoria: Distribution, Ecology and Conservation. (Ed. P.W. Menkhorst). (Oxford University Press: Melbourne).

Lunney, D. 1991. The future of Australia's forest fauna. pp. 1–24 *in* Conservation of Australia's Forest Fauna. (Ed. D. Lunney). (Royal Zoological Society of New South Wales: Sydney).

Lynch, J.F., 1987. Responses of breeding bird communities to forest fragmentation. pp. 123–40 *in* Nature Conservation: The Role of Remnants of Native Vegetation. (Eds. D.A. Saunders, G.W. Arnold, A.A. Burbidge and A.J.M. Hopkins). (Surrey Beatty & Sons: Chipping Norton, New South Wales).

Lynch, J.F., Carmen, W.J., Saunders, D.A. and Cale, P., 1995. Use of vegetated road verges and habitat patches by four bird species in the central wheatbelt of Western Australia. pp. 34–42 *in* Nature Conservation 4. The Role of Networks. (Eds. D.A. Saunders, J.L. Craig and E.M. Mattiske). (Surrey Beatty & Sons: Chipping Norton, New South Wales).

Lynch, J.F. and Saunders, D.A., 1991. Responses of bird species to habitat fragmentation in the wheatbelt of Western Australia: interiors, edges and corridors. pp. 143–58 *in* Nature Conservation 2: The Role of Corridors. (Eds. D.A. Saunders and R.J. Hobbs). (Surrey Beatty & Sons: Chipping Norton, New South Wales).

Lynch, J.F. and Whigham, D.F., 1984. Effects of forest fragmentation on breeding bird communities in Maryland, USA. *Biological Conservation* **28**: 287–324.

MacArthur, R.H. and Wilson, E.O., 1963. An equilibrium theory of insular zoogeography. *Evolution* **17**: 373–87.

MacArthur, R.H. and Wilson, E.O., 1967. The Theory of Island Biogeography. (Princeton University Press: Princeton).

Machtans, C.S., Villard, M-A. and Hannon, S.J., 1996. Use of riparian buffer strips as movement corridors by forest birds. *Conservation Biology* **10**: 1366–77.

MacNally, R. and Bennett, A.F., 1997. Species-specific predictions of the impact of habitat fragmentation: local extinction of birds in the Box-Ironbark forests of central Victoria, Australia. *Biological Conservation* **82**: 147–55.

Mader, H.J., 1984. Animal habitat isolation by roads and agricultural fields. *Biological Conservation* **29**: 81–96.

Mader, H.J., 1988. Corridors and barriers in agro-ecosystems. pp. 139–46. *in* Proceedings of the VIIIth International Symposium on Problems in Landscape Ecological Research. (Eds. M. Ruzicka, T. Hrnciarova and L. Miklos). (Institute for Experimental Biology and Ecology: Czechoslovakia).

Main, B.Y., 1987. Persistence of invertebrates in small areas: case studies of trapdoor spiders in Western Australia. pp. 29–39 *in* Nature Conservation: The Role of Remnants of Native Vegetation. (Eds. D.A. Saunders, G.W. Arnold, A.A. Burbidge, and A.J.M. Hopkins). (Surrey Beatty & Sons: Chipping Norton, New South Wales).

Malcolm, J.R., 1994. Edge effects in central Amazonian forest fragments. *Ecology* **75**: 2438–45.

Mann, W., Dorn, P. and Brandl, R., 1991. Local distribution of amphibians: the importance of habitat fragmentation. *Global Ecology and Biogeography Letters* **1**: 36–41.

Mansergh, I.M. and Scotts, D.J., 1989. Habitat continuity and social organisation of the mountain pygmy-possum restored by tunnel. *Journal of Wildlife Management* **53**: 701–7.

Mansergh, I.M. and Scotts, D.J., 1990. Aspects of the life history and breeding biology of the Mountain Pygmy-possum, *Burramys parvus* (Marsupialia: Burramyidae) in alpine Victoria. *Australian Mammalogy* **13**: 179–91.

Marchant, S. and Higgins, P.J., 1990. Handbook of Australian, New Zealand and Antarctic Birds. Volume 1. Ratites to Ducks. (Oxford University Press: Melbourne).

Margules, C.R., Milkovits, G.A. and Smith, G.T., 1994. Contrasting effects of habitat fragmentation on the scorpion *Cercophonius squama* and an amphipod. *Ecology* **75**: 2033–42.

Marynowski, S. 1992. Paseo Pantera. The great American biotic interchange. *Wild Earth* (Special Issue) 71–74.

Martin, A.A. and Tyler, M.J., 1978. The introduction into Western Australia of the frog *Limnodynastes tasmaniensis. Australian Zoologist* **19**: 320–44.

Martin, T.E., 1980. Diversity and abundance of spring migratory birds using habitat islands of the Great Plains. *Condor* **82**: 430–39.

Matthiae, P.E. and Stearns, F., 1981. Mammals in forest islands in southeastern Wisconsin. pp. 55–66 *in* Forest Island Dynamics in Man-Dominated Landscapes. (Eds. R.L. Burgess and D.M. Sharpe). (Springer-Verlag: New York).

May, S.A. and Norton, T.W., 1996. Influence of fragmentation and disturbance on the potential impact of feral predators on native fauna in Australian forest ecosystems. *Wildlife Research* **23**: 387–400.

McCaughey, W., 1994. An Australian network of corridors of green. Unpublished manuscript, (Greening Australia Ltd: Canberra).

McCollin, D., 1993. Avian distribution patterns in a fragmented wooded landscape (North Humberside, UK): the role of between-patch and within-patch structure. *Global Ecology and Biogeography Letters* **3**: 48–62.

McDowell, C.R., Low, A.B. and McKenzie, B., 1991. Natural remnants and corridors in Greater Cape Town: their role in threatened plant conservation. pp. 27–39 *in* Nature Conservation 2: The Role of Corridors. (Eds. D.A. Saunders and R.J. Hobbs). (Surrey Beatty & Sons: Chipping Norton, New South Wales).

McIntyre, S., 1994. Integrating agricultural land-use and management for conservation of a native grassland flora in a variegated landscape. *Pacific Conservation Biology* **1**: 236–44.

McIntyre, S. and Barrett, G.W., 1992. Habitat variegation, an alternative to fragmentation. *Conservation Biology* **6**: 146–7.

McKinnon, J. and De Wulf, R., 1994. Designing protected areas for giant pandas in China. pp. 128–42 *in* Mapping the Diversity of Nature. (Ed. R.I. Miller). (Chapman and Hall: London).

McNeely, J.A., 1987. How dams and wildlife can coexist: natural habitats, agriculture and major water resource development projects. *Conservation Biology* **1**: 228–38.

Medeiros, P., 1992. A proposal for an Adirondack primeval. *Wild Earth* (Special Issue) 32–42.

Meffe, G.K. and Carroll, C.R., 1994. Principles of Conservation Biology. (Sinauer Associates, Inc.: Sunderland).

Melquist, W.E. and Hornocker, M.G., 1983. Ecology of river otters in west central Idaho. *Wildlife Monographs* **83**: 5–60.

Menkhorst, P.W. and Lumsden, L.F. 1995. Common Bent-wing Bat *Miniopterus schreibersii*. pp. 180–81 *in* Mammals of Victoria. Distribution, Ecology and Conservation. (Ed. P.W. Menkhorst). (Oxford University Press: Melbourne).

Merriam, G., 1984. Connectivity: a fundamental ecological characteristic of landscape pattern. pp. 5–15 *in* Proceedings of the First International Seminar on Methodology in

Landscape Ecological Research and Planning. (Eds. M. Ruzicka, T. Hrnciarova and L Miklos). (International Association for Landscape Ecology: Roskilde, Denmark).

Merriam, G., 1988. Landscape dynamics in farmland. *Trends in Ecology and Evolution* **3**: 16–20.

Merriam, G., 1990. Ecological processes in the time and space of farmland mosaics. pp. 121–33 *in* Changing Landscapes: An Ecological Perspective. (Eds. I.S. Zonneveld and R.T.T. Forman). (Springer-Verlag: New York).

Merriam, G., 1991. Corridors and connectivity: animal populations in heterogeneous environments. pp. 133–42 *in* Nature Conservation 2: The Role of Corridors. (Eds. D.A. Saunders and R.J. Hobbs). (Surrey Beatty & Sons: Chipping Norton, New South Wales).

Merriam, G., Kozakiewicz, M., Tsuchiya, E. and Hawley, K., 1989. Barriers as boundaries for metapopulations and demes of *Peromyscus leucopus* in farm landscapes. *Landscape Ecology* **2**: 227–35.

Merriam, G. and Lanoue, A., 1990. Corridor use by small mammals: field measurements for three experimental types of *Peromyscus leucopus*. *Landscape Ecol*ogy **4**: 123–31.

Merriam, G. and Saunders, D.A., 1991. Corridors in restoration of fragmented landscapes. pp. 71–87 *in* Nature Conservation 3. The Reconstruction of Fragmented Ecosystems. (Eds. D.A. Saunders, R.J. Hobbs and P.R. Ehrlich). (Surrey Beatty & Sons: Chipping Norton, New South Wales).

Middleton, J. and Merriam, G., 1981. Woodland mice in a farmland mosaic. *Journal of Applied Ecology* **18**: 703–10.

Middleton, J. and Merriam, G., 1983. Distribution of woodland species in farmland woods. *Journal of Applied Ecology* **20**: 625–44.

Middleton, W.G.P., 1980. Roadside vegetation, a habitat for wildlife. *in* Roadsides of Today and Tomorrow. (Roadside Conservation Committee: Victoria).

Milledge, D., Palmer, C. and Nelson, J., 1991. 'Barometers of change': the distribution of large owls and gliders in Mountain Ash forests of the Victorian Central Highlands and their potential as management indicators. pp. 53–65 *in* Conservation of Australia's Forest Fauna. (Ed. D.Lunney) (Royal Zoological Society of New South Wales: Sydney).

Mills, L.S., 1995. Edge effects and isolation: red-backed voles on forest remnants. *Conservation Biology* **9**: 395–403.

Mladenoff, D.J., White, M.A., Crow, T.R. and Pastor, J., 1994. Applying principles of landscape design and management to integrate old-growth forest enhancement and commodity use. *Conservation Biology* **8**: 752–62.

Moore, N.W. and Hooper, M.D., 1975. On the number of bird species in British woods. *Biological Conservation* **8**: 239–50.

Munguira, M.L. and Thomas, J.A., 1992. Use of road verges by butterfly and burnet populations and the effect of roads on adult dispersal and mortality. *Journal of Applied Ecology* **29**: 316–29.

Murcia, C., 1995. Edge effects in fragmented forests: implications for conservation. *Trends in Ecology and Evolution* **10**: 58–62.

Murray, N.L. and Stauffer, D.F., 1995. Nongame bird use of habitat in Central Appalachian riparian forests. *Journal of Wildlife Management* **59**: 78–88.

Mwalyosi, R.B.B., 1991. Ecological evaluation for wildlife corridors and buffer zones for Lake Manyara National Park, Tanzania, and its immediate environment. *Biological Conservation* **57**: 171–86.

Myers, N., 1986. Tropical deforestation and a mega-extinction spasm. pp. 394–409 *in* Conservation Biology: The Science of Scarcity and Diversity. (Ed. M E. Soulé). (Sinauer Associates: Sunderland).

Newbey, B.J and Newbey, K.R., 1987. Bird dynamics of Foster Road Reserve, near Ongerup, Western Australia. pp. 341–43 *in* Nature Conservation: The Role of Remnants of Native Vegetation. (Eds. D.A. Saunders, G.W. Arnold, A.A. Burbidge and A.J.M. Hopkins). (Surrey Beatty & Sons: Chipping Norton, New South Wales).

Newman, B., Irwin, H., Lowe, K., Mostwill, A., Smith, S., Jones, J., 1992. Southern Appalachian wildlands proposal. *Wild Earth* (Special Issue): 46–60.

Newmark, W.D., 1987. Mammalian extinctions in western North American parks: a land-bridge island perspective. *Nature* **325**: 430–32.

Newmark, W.D., 1991. Tropical forest fragmentation and the local extinction of understorey birds in the Eastern Usambara Mountains, Tanzania. *Conservation Biology* **5**: 67–78.

Newmark, W.D., 1992. Recommendations for wildlife corridors and the extension and management of forest resources in the Eastern Usambara Mountains, Tanzania. *East Usambara Catchment Forest Project Technical Paper* No. **4**. (Helsinki, Finland).

Newmark, W.D., 1993. The role and design of wildlife corridors with examples from Tanzania. *Ambio* **22**: 500–504.

Newmark, W.D., 1995. Extinction of mammal populations in western North American national parks. *Conservation Biology* **9**: 512–26.

Newmark, W.D., Foley, C.A.H., Grimshaw, J.M., Chambegga, O.R. and Rutazaa, A.G., 1991. Local extinctions of large mammals within Kilimanjaro National Park and Forest Reserve and implications of increasing isolation and forest conversion. pp. 35–46 *in* The Conservation of Mount Kilimanjaro. (Ed. W.D. Newmark). (IUCN: Gland).

Nicholls, A.O. and Margules, C.R., 1991. The design of studies to demonstrate the biological importance of corridors. pp. 49–61 *in* Nature Conservation 2: The Role of Corridors. (Eds. D.A. Saunders and R.J. Hobbs). (Surrey Beatty & Sons: Chipping Norton, New South Wales).

Niering, W.A. and Goodwin, R.H., 1974. Creation of relatively stable shrublands with herbicides: arresting 'succession' on rights-of-way and pasture land. *Ecology* **55**: 784–95.

Norton, T.W. and Lindenmayer, D.B., 1991. Integrated management of forest wildlife: towards a coherent strategy across state borders and land tenures. pp. 237–44 *in* Conservation of Australia's Forest Fauna. (Ed. D. Lunney). (Royal Zoological Society of New South Wales: Mosman).

Noss, R.F., 1983. A regional landscape approach to maintain diversity. *Bioscience* **33**: 700–706.

Noss, R.F., 1987. Corridors in real landscapes: a reply to Simberloff and Cox. *Conservation Biology* **1**: 159–64.

Noss, R.F., 1991. Landscape connectivity: different functions at different scales. pp. 27–39 *in* Landscape Linkages and Biodiversity. (Ed. W.E. Hudson). (Island Press: Washington DC).

Noss, R.F., 1992. The Wildlands Project: land conservation strategy. *Wild Earth* (Special Issue): 10–25.

Noss, R.F., 1993. Wildlife corridors. pp. 43–68 *in* Ecology of Greenways. (Eds. D.S. Smith and P.C. Hellmund). (University of Minnesota Press: Minneapolis, USA).

Noss, R.F and Harris, L.D., 1986. Nodes, networks and MUMS: preserving diversity at all scales. *Environmental Management* **10**: 299–309.

O'Donnell, C.F.J., 1991. Application of the wildlife corridors concept to temperate rainforest sites, North Westland, New Zealand. pp. 85–98 *in* Nature Conservation 2: The Role of Corridors. (Eds. D.A. Saunders and R.J. Hobbs). (Surrey Beatty & Sons: Chipping Norton, New South Wales).

Oetting, R.B. and Cassel, J.F., 1971. Waterfowl nesting on interstate highway right-of-way in North Dakota. *Journal of Wildlife Management* **35**: 774–81.

Ogilvie, R.T. and Furman, T., 1959. Effect of vegetational cover of fencerows on small mammal populations. *Ecology* **40**: 140–41.

Ogle, C.C., 1987. The incidence and conservation of animal and plant species in remnants of native vegetation within New Zealand. pp. 79–87 *in* Nature Conservation: The Role of Remnants of Native Vegetation. (Eds. D.A. Saunders, G.W. Arnold, A.A. Burbidge, and A.J.M. Hopkins). (Surrey Beatty & Sons: Chipping Norton, New South Wales).

Opdam, P., 1990. Dispersal in fragmented populations: the key to survival. pp. 3–17 *in* Species Dispersal in Agricultural Habitats. (Eds. R.G.H. Bunce and D.C. Howard). (Belhaven Press: London).

Opdam, P., 1991. Metapopulation theory and habitat fragmentation: a review of holarctic breeding bird studies. *Landscape Ecology* **5**: 93–106.

Opdam, P., Foppen, R., Reiknen, R. and Schotman, A., 1995. The landscape ecological approach in bird conservation: integrating the metapopulation concept into spatial planning. *Ibis* **137**: S139–S146.

Opdam, P., Rijsdijk, G. and Hustings, F., 1985. Bird communities in small woods in an agricultural landscape: effects of area and isolation. *Biological Conservation* **34**: 333–52.

Opdam, P., van Dorp, D. and ter Braak, C.J.F., 1984. The effect of isolation on the number of woodland birds in small woods in the Netherlands. *Journal of Biogeography* **11**: 473–78.

Osborne, P., 1984. Bird numbers and habitat characteristics in farmland hedgerows. *Journal of Applied Ecology* **21**: 63–82.

Overmars, F.B., Norton, D.A., Miskelly, C.M., O'Donnell, C.F.J. and Buckman, I.W., 1992. North Westland Wildlife Corridors Research Programme: Report to the Minister for Conservation. *West Coast Conservancy Technical Report Series* No. **1**. (Department of Conservation: Hokitika, New Zealand).

Oxley, D.J., Fenton, M.B. and Carmody, G.R., 1974. The effects of roads on populations of small mammals. *Journal of Applied Ecology* **11**: 51–59.

Pahl, L.I., Winter, J.W. and Heinsohn, G., 1988. Variation in responses of arboreal marsupials to fragmentation of tropical rainforest in north eastern Australia. *Biological Conservation* **46**: 71–82.

Parish, T., Lakhani, K.H. and Sparks, T.H., 1994. Modelling the relationship between bird population variables and hedgerows, and other field margin attributes. I. Species richness of winter, summer and breeding birds. *Journal of Applied Ecology* **31**: 764–75.

Parish, T., Lakhani, K.H. and Sparks, T.H., 1995. Modelling the relationship between bird population variables and hedgerows, and other field margin attributes. II. Abundance of individual species and groups of similar species. *Journal of Applied Ecology* **32**: 362–71.

Parr, T.W. and Way, J.M., 1988. Management of roadside vegetation: the long–term effects of cutting. *Journal of Applied Ecology* **25**: 1073–87.

Patterson, B.D., 1987. The principle of nested subsets and its implications for biological conservation. *Conservation Biology* **1**: 323–34.

Peek, J.M., 1986. A Review of Wildlife Management. (Prentice-Hall: New Jersey).

Peters, R.L. and Darling, J.D.S., 1985. The greenhouse effect and nature reserves. *Bioscience* **35**: 707–17.

Petrides, G., 1942. Relation of hedgerows in winter to wildlife in central New York. *Journal of Wildlife Management* **6**: 261–80.

Petterson, B., 1985. Extinction of an isolated population of the middle spotted woodpecker *Dendrocopos medius* (L) in Sweden and its relation to general theories on extinction. *Biological Conservation* **32**: 335–53.

Pickett, S.T.A. and Thompson J.N., 1978. Patch dynamics and the design of nature reserves. *Biological Conservation* **13**: 27–37.

Picton, H.D., 1979. The application of insular biogeographic theory to the conservation of large mammals in the Northern Rocky Mountains. *Biological Conservation* **15**: 73–79.

Pollard, E., Hooper, M.D. and Moore, N.W., 1974. Hedges. (Collins: London).

Pollard, E. and Relton, J., 1970. Hedges. V. A study of small mammals in hedges and cultivated fields. *Journal of Applied Ecology* **7**: 549–57.

Port, G.R. and Thompson, J.R., 1980. Outbreaks of insect herbivores on plants along motorways in the United Kingdom. *Journal of Applied Ecology* **17**: 949–56.

Porter, K., 1993. Wide rides for butterflies. *Enact* **1**: 17–19.

Potter, M.A., 1990. Movement of North Island Brown Kiwi (*Apteryx australis mantelli*) between forest remnants. *New Zealand Journal of Ecology* **14**: 17–24.

Powell, G.V.N. and Bjork, R., 1995. Implications of intratropical migration in reserve design: a case study using *Pharomachrus moccino*. *Conservation Biology* **9**: 354–62.

Pressey, R.L., 1994. *Ad Hoc* reservations: forward or backward steps in developing representative reserve systems. *Conservation Biology* **8**: 662–68.

Pressey, R.L. and Tully, S.L., 1994. The cost of *ad hoc* reservation: a case study in western New South Wales. *Australian Journal of Ecology* **19**: 375–84.

Presst, I., 1971. An ecological study of the viper in southern Britain. *Journal of Zoology, London* **164**: 373–418.

Prevett, P.T., 1991. Movement paths of koalas in the urban-rural fringes of Ballarat, Victoria: implications for management. pp. 259–72 *in* Nature Conservation 2: The Role of Corridors. (Eds. D.A. Saunders and R.J. Hobbs). (Surrey Beatty & Sons: Chipping Norton, New South Wales).

Pringle, C., Chacón, I., Grayum, M., Greene, H., Hartshorn, G., Schatz, G., Stiles, G., Gómez, C. and Rodríguez, M., 1984. Natural history observations and ecological evaluation of the La Selva Protection Zone, Costa Rica. *Brenesia* **22**: 189–206.

Prober, S.M. and Thiéle, K.R., 1993. The ecology and genetics of remnant grassy White Box woodlands in relation to their conservation. *Victorian Naturalist* **110**: 30–36.

Pulliam, H.R., 1988. Sources, sinks and population regulation. *American Naturalist* **132**: 652–61.

Pulliam, H.R. and Danielson, B.J., 1991. Sources, sinks and habitat selection: a landscape perspective on population dynamics. *American Naturalist* **137**: 50–66.

Rands, M.R.W., 1986. Effect of hedgerow characteristics on partridge breeding densities. *Journal of Applied Ecology* **23**: 479–87.

Ranney, J.W., Bruner, M.C. and Levenson, J.B., 1981. The importance of edge in the structure and dynamics of forest islands. pp. 67–96 *in* Forest Island Dynamics in Man-Dominated Landscapes. (Eds. R.L. Burgess and D.M. Sharpe). (Springer-Verlag: New York).

Recher, H.F., Rohan-Jones, W. and Smith, P., 1980. Effects of the Eden woodchip industry on terrestrial vertebrates with recommendations for management. *Forests Commission New South Wales, Research Note No.* **42**.

Recher, H.F. and Serventy, D.L., 1991. Long term changes in the relative abundance of birds in Kings Park, Perth, Western Australia. *Conservation Biology* **5**: 90–102.

Recher, H.F., Shields, J., Kavanagh, R. and Webb, G., 1987. Retaining remnant mature forest for nature conservation at Eden, New South Wales: a review of theory and practice. pp. 177–94 *in* Nature Conservation: The Role of Remnants of Native Vegetation. (Eds. D.A. Saunders, G.W. Arnold, A.A. Burbidge and A.J.M. Hopkins). (Surrey Beatty & Sons: Chipping Norton, New South Wales).

Redford, K.H., 1985. Emas National Park and the plight of the Brazilian cerrados. *Oryx* **19**: 210–14.

Redford, K. and de Fonseca, G., 1986. The role of gallery forests in the zoogeography of the Cerrado's non-volant mammal fauna. *Biotropica* **18**: 126–35.

Redpath, S.M., 1995. Habitat fragmentation and the individual: tawny owls *Strix aluco* in woodland patches. *Journal of Animal Ecology* **64**: 652–61.

Reed, D.F., 1981. Mule deer behaviour at a highway underpass exit. *Journal of Wildlife Management* **45**: 542–43.

Reed, D.F., Woodard, T.N. and Pojar, T.M., 1975. Behavioural response of Mule Deer to a highway underpass. *Journal of Wildlife Management* **39**: 361–67.

Reid, T.S. and Murphy, D.D., 1995. Providing a regional context for local conservation action. *Bioscience Supplement*: S84–S90.

Reijnen, R. and Foppen, R., 1994. The effects of car traffic on breeding bird populations in woodland. I. Evidence of reduced habitat quality for willow warblers (*Phylloscopus trochilus*) breeding close to a highway. *Journal of Applied Ecology* **31**: 85–94.

Rich, A.C., Dobkin, D.S. and Niles, L.J., 1994. Defining forest fragmentation by corridor width: the influence of narrow forest-dividing corridors on forest nesting birds in southern New Jersey. *Conservation Biology* **8**: 1109–1121.

Roberts, D.C., 1994. The design of an urban open-space network for the city of Durban (South Africa). *Environmental Conservation* **21**: 11–17.

Root, T., 1988. Atlas of Wintering North American Birds. (University of Chicago Press: Chicago).

Rowley, I. and Chapman, G., 1991. The breeding biology, food, social organisation, demography and conservation of the Major Mitchell or Pink Cockatoo, *Cacatua leadbeateri*, on the margin of the Western Australian Wheatbelt. *Australian Journal of Zoology* **39**: 211–61.

Rudnicky, T.C. and Hunter, M.L., 1993. Avian nest predation in clearcuts, forests, and edges in a forest-dominated landscape. *Journal of Wildlife Management* **57**: 358–64.

Ruefenacht, B. and Knight, R.L., 1995. Influences of corridor continuity and width on survival and movement of deermice. *Biological Conservation* **71**: 269–74.

Rushton, S.P., Hill, D. and Carter, S.P., 1994. The abundance of river corridor birds in relation to their habitats: a modelling approach. *Journal of Applied Ecology* **31**: 313–28.

Russell, R.W., Carpenter, F.L., Hixon, M.A. and Paton, D.C., 1994. The impact of variation in stopover habitat quality on migrant rufous hummingbirds. *Conservation Biology* **8**: 483–90.

Sarré, S., Smith, G.T. and Myers, J.A., 1995. Persistence of two species of gecko (*Oedura reticulata* and *Gehyra variegata*) in remnant habitat. *Biological Conservation* **71**: 25–33.

Saunders, D.A., 1980. Food and movements of the short-billed form of the white-tailed black cockatoo. *Australian Wildlife Research* **7**: 257–69.

Saunders, D.A., 1989. Changes in the avifauna of a region, district and remnant as a result of fragmentation of native vegetation: the wheatbelt of Western Australia. A case study. *Biological Conservation* **50**: 99–135.

Saunders, D.A., 1990. Problems of survival in an extensively cultivated landscape: the case of Carnaby's Cockatoo *Calyptorhynchus funereus latirostris*. *Biological Conservation* **54**: 277–90.

Saunders, D.A., Arnold, G.W., Burbidge, A.A. and Hopkins, A.J.M. (Eds.), 1987. Nature Conservation: The Role of Remnants of Native Vegetation. (Surrey Beatty & Sons: Chipping Norton, New South Wales).

Saunders, D.A., Craig, J.L., and Mattiske, E.M. (Eds), 1995. Nature Conservation 4: The Role of Networks. (Surrey Beatty & Sons: Chipping Norton, New South Wales).

Saunders, D.A. and de Rebeira, P., 1991. Values of corridors to avian populations in a fragmented landscape. pp. 221–40 *in* Nature Conservation 2: The Role of Corridors. (Eds. D.A. Saunders and R.J. Hobbs). (Surrey Beatty & Sons: Chipping Norton, New South Wales).

Saunders, D.A. and Hobbs, R. (Eds.), 1991. Nature Conservation 2: The Role of Corridors. (Surrey Beatty & Sons: Chipping Norton, New South Wales).

Saunders, D.A., Hobbs, R.J. and Arnold, G.W., 1993. The Kellerberrin project on fragmented landscapes: a review of current information. *Biological Conservation* **64**: 185–92.

Saunders, D.A., Hobbs, R.J. and Margules, C.R., 1991. Biological consequences of ecosystem fragmentation: a review. *Conservation Biology* **5**: 18–32.

Saunders, D.A. and Ingram, J.A., 1987. Factors affecting survival of breeding populations of Carnaby's Cockatoo in remnants of native vegetation. pp. 249–58 *in* Nature Conservation: The Role of Remnants of Native Vegetation. (Eds. D.A. Saunders, G.W. Arnold, A.A. Burbidge and A.J.M. Hopkins). (Surrey Beatty & Sons: Chipping Norton, New South Wales).

Sayer, J., 1991. Rainforest Buffer Zones. Guidelines for Protected Area Managers. (International Union for the Conservation of Nature: Gland).

Schaller, G.B., 1993. The Last Panda. (University of Chicago Press: Chicago).

Schmiegelow, F.K.A. and Hannon, S.J., 1993. Adaptive management, adaptive science and the effects of forest fragmentation on boreal birds in northern Alberta. *Transactions of the North American Wildlife and Natural Resources Conference* **58**: 584–98.

Schroeder, R.L., Cable, T.T. and Haire, S.L., 1992. Wildlife species richness in shelterbelts: test of a habitat model. *Wildlife Society Bulletin* **20**: 264–73.

Scougall, S.A., Majer, J.D. and Hobbs, R.J., 1993. Edge effects in grazed and ungrazed Western Australian wheatbelt remnants in relation to ecosystem reconstruction. pp. 163–78 *in* Nature Conservation 3. The Reconstruction of Fragmented Ecosystems. (Eds. D.A. Saunders, R.J. Hobbs and P.R. Ehrlich). (Surrey Beatty & Sons: Chipping Norton, New South Wales).

Seabrook, W.A. and Dettman, E.B., 1996. Roads as activity corridors for cane toads in Australia. *Journal of Wildlife Management* **60**: 363–68.

Serena, M., 1994. Use of time and space by Platypus (*Ornithorhynchus anatinus*: Monotremata) along a Victorian stream. *Journal of Zoology, London* **232**: 117–31.

Shafer, C.L., 1990. Nature Reserves. Island Theory and Conservation Practice. (Smithsonian Institution Press: Washington).

Shafer, C.L., 1995. Values and shortcomings of small reserves. *Bioscience* **45**: 80–88.

Shaffer, M.L., 1981. Minimum population sizes for species conservation. *Bioscience* **31**: 131–34.

Shalaway, S.D., 1985. Fencerow management for nesting birds in Michigan. *Wildlife Society Bulletin* **13**: 302–6.

Shreeve, T.G. and Mason, C.F., 1980. The number of butterfly species in woodlands. *Oecologia* **45**: 414–18.

Siepen, G., Gynther, I. and Horler, E., 1995. Nature Search 2001: community nature conservation in action. pp. 436–42 *in* Nature Conservation 4. The Role of Networks. (Eds. D.A. Saunders, J.L. Craig and E.M. Mattiske). (Surrey Beatty & Sons: Chipping Norton, New South Wales).

Simberloff, D.S., 1974. Equilibrium theory of island biogeography; and ecology. *Annual Review of Ecology and Systematics* **5**:161–82.

Simberloff, D.S., 1988. The contribution of population and community biology to conservation science. *Annual Review of Ecology and Systematics* **19**:473–511.

Simberloff, D., 1993. Effects of fragmentation on some Florida ecosystems, and how to redress them. pp. 179–87 *in* Nature Conservation 3. The Reconstruction of Fragmented Ecosystems. (Eds. D.A. Saunders, R.J. Hobbs and P.R. Ehrlich). (Surrey Beatty & Sons: Chipping Norton, New South Wales).

Simberloff, D.S. and Cox, J., 1987. Consequences and costs of conservation corridors. *Conservation Biology* **1**: 63–71.

Simberloff, D.S., Farr, J.A., Cox, J. and Mehlman, D.W., 1992. Movement corridors: conservation bargains or poor investments? *Conservation Biology* **6**: 493–504.

Singer, F., 1975. Behaviour of mountain goats in relation to US Highway 2, Glacier National Park, Montana. *Journal of Wildlife Management* **42**: 591–97.

Sinclair, A.R.E., 1983. The function of distance movements in vertebrates. pp. 240–58 *in* The Ecology of Animal Movements. (Eds. P.J. Greenwood and I.R. Swingland). (Clarendon Press).

Singer, F.I., Langhte, W.L. and Samuelson, E.C., 1985. Design and construction of highway underpass used by mountain goats. *Transportation Research Record* **1016**: 6–10.

Smith, A.T., 1974. The distribution and dispersal of pikas: consequences of insular population structure. *Ecology* **55**: 1112–19.

Smith, A., 1991. Forest policy: fostering environmental conflict in the Australian timber industry. pp. 301–14 *in* Conservation of Australia's Forest Fauna. (Ed. D.Lunney). (Royal Zoological Society of New South Wales: Sydney).

Smith, D.S., 1993. Greenway case studies. pp. 161–208 *in* Ecology of Greenways. (Eds. D.S. Smith and P.C. Hellmund). (University of Minnesota Press: Minneapolis).

Smith, D.S. and Hellmund, P.C. (Eds), 1993. Ecology of Greenways. (University of Minnesota Press: Minneapolis).

Soulé, M.E. (Ed.), 1986. Conservation Biology. The Science of Scarcity and Diversity. (Sinauer Associates: Sunderland, Massachusetts).

Soulé, M.E., 1991. Theory and strategy. pp. 91–104 *in* Landscape Linkages and Biodiversity. (Ed. W.E. Hudson). (Island Press: Washington DC).

Soulé, M.E., 1995. An unflinching vision: networks of people defending networks of lands. pp. 1–8 *in* Nature Conservation 4. The Role of Networks. (Eds. D.A. Saunders, J.L. Craig and E.M. Mattiske). (Surrey Beatty & Sons: Chipping Norton, New South Wales).

Soulé, M.E., Bolger, D.T., Alberts, A.C., Wright, J., Sorice, M. and Hills, S., 1988. Reconstructed dynamics of rapid extinctions of chaparral requiring birds in urban habitat islands. *Conservation Biology* **2**: 75–92.

Soulé, M.E. and Gilpin, M., 1991. The theory of wildlife corridor capability. pp. 3–8 *in* Nature Conservation 2: The Role of Corridors. (Surrey Beatty & Sons: Chipping Norton, New South Wales).

State of Maryland, 1990. Greenways ... a bold idea for today, a promise for tomorrow. (State of Maryland, Department of Natural Resources).

Stauffer, D.F. and Best, L.B., 1980. Habitat selection by birds of riparian communities: evaluating effects of habitat alterations. *Journal of Wildlife Management* **41**: 1–15.

Steer, G., 1987. Tunnel of love. *Australian Geographic* **5**: 21–22.

Stolzenburg, W., 1991. The fragment connection. *Nature Conservancy* **41**: 18–25.

Stone, G., 1991. Roadside management plans in the Roads Corporation, Victoria. pp. 319–25 *in* Nature Conservation 2: The Role of Corridors. (Surrey Beatty & Sons: Chipping Norton, New South Wales).

Stouffer, P.C. and Bierregaard, R.O., 1995a. Use of Amazonian forest fragments by understorey insectivorous birds. *Ecology* **76**: 2429–45.

Stouffer, P.C. and Bierregaard, R.O., 1995b. Effects of forest fragmentation on understorey hummingbirds in Amazonian Brazil. *Conservation Biology* **9**: 1085–94.

Strong, A.M. and Bancroft, G.T., 1994. Post-fledging dispersal of white-crowned pigeons: implications for conservation of deciduous seasonal forests in the Florida Keys. *Conservation Biology* **8**: 770–79.

Strong, T.R. and Bock, C.E., 1990. Bird species distribution patterns in riparian habitats in southeastern Arizona. *The Condor* **92**: 866–85.

Struhsaker, T.T., 1981. Forest and primate conservation in East Africa. *African Journal of Ecology* **19**: 99–114.

Stuart, S.N., 1981. A comparison of avifaunas of seven East African forest islands. *African Journal of Ecology* **19**: 133–51.

Suckling, G.C., 1982. Value of preserved habitat for mammal conservation in plantations. *Australian Forestry* **45**: 19–27.

Suckling, G.C., 1984. Population ecology of the sugar glider *Petaurus breviceps* in a system of fragmented habitats. *Australian Wildlife Research* **11**: 49–75.

Sullivan, A. and Shaffer, M.L., 1975. Biogeography of the megazoo. *Science* **189**: 13–17.

Sutcliffe, O.L. and Thomas, C.D., 1996. Open corridors appear to facilitate dispersal by ringlet butterflies (*Aphantopus hyperantus*) between woodland clearings. *Conservation Biology* **10**: 1359–65.

Szacki, J., 1987. Ecological corridor as a factor determining the structure and organization of a Bank Vole population. *Acta Theriologica* **32**: 31–44.

Szacki, J. and Liro, A., 1991. Movements of small mammals in the heterogeneous landscape. *Landscape Ecology* **5**: 219–24.

Szaro, R.C., 1991. Wildlife communities of southwestern riparian ecosystems. pp. 173–201 *in* Wildlife and Habitats in Managed Landscapes. (Eds. J.E. Rodiek and E.G. Bolen). (Island Press: Washington DC).

Talamanca-Carribbean Biological Corridor Commission, 1993. The Talamanca-Caribbean Biological Corridor Project. (Talamanca-Caribbean Biological Corridor Commission: Talamanca-Limon, Costa Rica).

Taylor, P.D., Fahrig, L., Henein, K. and Merriam, G., 1993. Connectivity is a vital element of landscape structure. *Oikos* **68**: 571–73.

Taylor, P.D. and Merriam, G., 1996. Habitat fragmentation and parasitism of a forest damselfly. *Landscape Ecology* **11**: 181–89.

Taylor, R., 1991. The role of retained strips for fauna conservation in production forests in Tasmania. pp. 265–70 *in* Conservation of Australia's Forest Fauna. (Ed. D. Lunney). (Royal Zoological Society of New South Wales: Sydney).

Tellería, J.L. and Santos, T., 1995. Effects of forest fragmentation on a guild of wintering passerines: the role of habitat selection. *Biological Conservation* **71**: 61–67.

Terborgh, J., 1989. Where Have All the Birds Gone? (Princeton University Press: Princeton).

Terborgh, J. and Winter, B., 1980. Some causes of extinction. pp. 119–133 *in* Conservation Biology: An Evolutionary-Ecological Perspective. (Eds. M.E. Soule and B.A. Wilcox). (Sinauer Associates: Sunderland, Massachusetts).

Therres, G.D., McKegg, J.S. and Miller, R.L., 1988. Maryland's Chesapeake Bay Critical Area Program: implications for wildlife. *Transactions of the North American Wildlife and Natural Resources Conference* **53**: 391–400.

Thiollay, J.M., 1989. Area requirements for the conservation of rain forest raptor and game birds in French Guiana. *Conservation Biology* **3**: 128–37.

Thiollay, J-M. and Meyburg, B.U., 1988. Forest fragmentation and the conservation of raptors: a survey on the island of Java. *Biological Conservation* **44**: 229–50.

Thomas, C.D., 1991. Ecological corridors: an assessment. *Science and Research Series No.* **34** (Department of Conservation: Wellington, New Zealand).

Thomas, C.D., 1994. Extinction, colonization and metapopulations: environmental tracking by rare species. *Conservation Biology* **8**: 373–78.

Thomas, C.D. and Jones, T.M., 1993. Partial recovery of a skipper butterfly (*Hesperia comma*) from population refuges: lessons for conservation in a fragmented landscape. *Journal of Animal Ecology* **62**: 472–81.

Thomas, J.A., Thomas, C.D., Simcox, D.J. and Clarke, R.T., 1986. Ecology and declining status of the silver-spotted skipper butterfly (*Hesperia comma*) in Britain. *Journal of Applied Ecology* **23**: 365–80.

Thomas, M.B., Wratten, S.D. and Sotherton, N.W., 1991. Creation of 'island' habitats in farmland to manipulate populations of beneficial arthropods: predator densities and emigration. *Journal of Applied Ecology* **28**: 906–17.

Timm, R.M., Wilson, D.E., Clauson, B.L., LaVal, R.K. and Vaughan, C.S., 1989. Mammals of the La Selva-Braullio Carillo complex, Costa Rica. (United States Department of the Interior, Fish and Wildlife Service: Washington DC.).

Tscharntke, T., 1992. Fragmentation of *Phragmites* habitats, minimum viable population size, habitat suitability, and local extinction of moths, midges, flies, aphids and birds. *Conservation Biology* **6**: 530–36.

Turner, M.G., 1989. Landscape ecology: the effect of pattern on process. *Annual Review of Ecology and Systematics* **20**: 171–97.

Tye, A., 1993. Establishment of Forest Corridors and Other Protected Forest Areas in East Usambara. Unpublished Report to East Usambara Conservation and Development Project.

van Apeldoorn, R.C., Oostenbrink, W.T., van Winden, A. and van der Zee, F.F., 1992. Effects of habitat fragmentation on the bank vole, *Clethrionomys glareolus*, in agricultural landscapes. *Oikos* **65**: 265–74.

van Dorp, D. and Opdam, P.F.M., 1987. Effects of patch size, isolation and regional abundance on forest bird communities. *Landscape Ecology* **1**: 59–73.

van Gelder, J.J., 1973. A quantitative approach to the mortality resulting from traffic in a population of *Bufo bufo* L. *Oecologia* **13**: 93–95.

van Leeuwen, B.H., 1982. Protection of migrating Common Toad (*Bufo bufo*) against car traffic in the Netherlands. *Environmental Conservation* **9**: 34.

Verboom, B. and Huitema, H., 1997. The importance of linear landscape elements for the pipistrelle *Pipistrellus pipistrellus* and the serotine bat *Eptesicus serotinus*. *Landscape Ecology* **12**: 117–25.

Verboom, B. and van Apeldoorn, R., 1990. Effects of habitat fragmentation on the red squirrel, *Sciurus vulgaris* L. *Landscape Ecology* **4**: 171–76.

Verboom, J., Lankester, K. and Metz, J.A.J., 1991. Linking local and regional dynamics in stochastic metapopulation models. *Biological Journal of the Linnean Society* **42**: 39–55.

Vermeulen, H.J.W., 1994. Corridor function of a road verge for dispersal of stenotopic heathland ground beetles Carabidae. *Biological Conservation* **69**: 339–49.

Villard, M-A., Freemark, K. and Merriam, G., 1992. Metapopulation theory and Neotropical migrant birds in temperate forests: an empirical investigation. pp. 474–82 *in* Ecology and

Conservation of Neotropical Migrant Landbirds. (Eds. J.M. Hagan III and D.W. Johnston). (Smithsonian Institution Press: Washington DC).

Villard, M-A., Merriam, G. and Maurer, B.A., 1995. Dynamics in subdivided populations of Neotropical migratory birds in a fragmented temperate forest. *Ecology* **76**: 27–40.

Walling, E., 1985. Country Roads. The Australian Roadside. (1985 edition, Pioneer Design Studios: Lilydale, Victoria). (First published 1952, Oxford University Press).

Ward, A.L., 1982. Mule deer behaviour in relation to fencing and underpasses on Interstate 80 in Wyoming. *Transportation Research Record* **859**: 8–13.

Ward, J.V. and Stanford, J.A., 1995. Ecological connectivity in alluvial river ecosystems and its disruption by flow regulation. *Regulated Rivers: Research and Management* **11**: 105–19.

Warkentin, I.G., Greenberg, R. and Ortiz, J.S., 1995. Songbird use of gallery woodlands in recently cleared and older settled landscapes of the Selva Lacandona, Chiapas, Mexico. *Conservation Biology* **9**: 1095–1106.

Warner, R.E., 1992. Nest ecology of grassland passerines on road rights-of-way in central Illinois. *Biological Conservation* **59**: 1–7.

Warren, M.S. and Fuller, R.J., 1993. Woodland Rides and Glades: Their Management for Wildlife. (Joint Nature Conservation Committee: Peterborough, UK).

Watson, J.R., 1991. The identification of river foreshore corridors for nature conservation in the South-Coast region of Western Australia. pp. 63–68 *in* Nature Conservation 2: The Role of Corridors. (Eds. D.A. Saunders and R.J. Hobbs). (Surrey Beatty & Sons: Chipping Norton, New South Wales).

Wauters, L., Casale, P. and Dhondt, A., 1994. Space use and dispersal of red squirrels in fragmented habitats. *Oikos* **69**: 140–46.

Way, J.M., 1977. Roadside verges and conservation in Britain: a review. *Biological Conservation* **12**: 65–74.

Webb, N.R. and Haskins, L.E., 1980. An ecological survey of heathlands in the Poole Basin, Dorset, England, in 1978. *Biological Conservation* **17**: 281–96.

Webster, R. and Ahern, L., 1992. Management for Conservation of the Superb Parrot *Polytelis swainsonii* in New South Wales and Victoria. (Department of Conservation and Natural Resources, Victoria: Melbourne).

Wegner, J.F. and Merriam, G., 1979. Movements by birds and small mammals between a wood and adjoining farmland habitat. *Journal of Applied Ecology* **16**: 349–57.

Wegner, J.F. and Merriam, G., 1990. Use of spatial elements in a farmland mosaic by a woodland rodent. *Biological Conservation* **54**: 263–76.

Whitcomb, R.F., Robbins, C.S., Lynch, J.F., Whitcomb, B.I., Klimkiewicz, M.K. and Bystrak, D., 1981. Effects of forest fragmentation on avifauna of the eastern deciduous forest. pp. 125–206 *in* Forest Island Dynamics in Man-Dominated Landscapes. (Eds. R.L. Burgess and D.M. Sharpe). (Springer Verlag: New York).

Wiens, J.A., 1976. Population responses to patchy environments. *Annual Review of Ecology and Systematics* **7**: 81–120.

Wiens, J.A., 1989. Spatial scaling in ecology. *Functional Ecology* **3**: 383–97.

Wiens, J.A., 1994. Habitat fragmentation: island v landscape perspectives on bird conservation. *Ibis* **137**: S97–S104.

Wiens, J.A., 1995. Landscape mosaics and ecological theory. pp. 1–26 *in* Mosaic Landscapes and Ecological Processes. (Eds. L. Hansson, L. Fahrig and G. Merriam). (Chapman and Hall: London).

Wiens, J.A., Crawford, C.S. and Gosz, J.R., 1985. Boundary dynamics: a conceptual framework for studying landscape ecosystems. *Oikos* **45**: 421–27.

Wiggett, D.R. and Boag, D.A., 1989. Intercolony natal dispersal in the Columbian ground squirrel. *Canadian Journal of Zoology* **67**: 42–50.

Wilcove, D.S., 1985. Nest predation in forest tracts and the decline of migratory songbirds. *Ecology* **66**: 1211–14.

Wilcove, D.S., 1994. Turning conservation goals into tangible results: the case of the Spotted Owl and old-growth forests. pp. 313–29 *in* Large Scale Ecology and Conservation Biology. (Eds. P.J. Edwards, R.M. May and N.R. Webb). (Blackwell Scientific Publications: Oxford).

Wilcox, B.A., 1980. Insular ecology and conservation. pp. 95–117 *in* Conservation Biology: An Evolutionary – Ecological Perspective. (Eds. M.E. Soulé and B.A. Wilcox). (Sinauer Associates: Massachusetts).

Wilkins, K.T., 1982. Highways as barriers to rodent dispersal. *Southwestern Naturalist* **27**: 459–60.

Williams, M. and Goodwin, D., 1988. Conservation of biological diversity on the Fleurieu Perinsula. *South Australian Naturalist* **63**: 24–39.

Willis, E.O., 1974. Populations and local extinctions of birds on Barro Colorado Island, Panama. *Ecological Monographs* **44**: 153–69.

Willson, M.F., de Santo, T.L., Sabag, C. and Armesto, J.J., 1994. Avian communities of fragmented south-temperate rainforests in Chile. *Conservation Biology* **8**: 508–20.

Wilson, A-M. and Lindenmayer, D.B., 1995. Wildlife Corridors and the Conservation of Biodiversity. A Review. (Centre for Resource and Environmental Studies, Australian National University; and Australian Nature Conservation Agency: Canberra).

Wilson, E.O. and Willis, E.O., 1975. Applied biogeography. pp. 522–34 *in* Ecology and Evolution of Communities. (Eds. M.L. Cody and J.M. Diamond). (Belknap Press: Cambridge, Massachusetts).

Woinarski, J.C.Z., Whitehead, P.J., Bowman, D.M.J.S. and Russell-Smith, J., 1992. Conservation of mobile species in a variable environment: the problem of reserve design in the Northern Territory, Australia. *Global Ecology and Biogeography Letters* **2**: 1–10.

Yaffee, S.L., 1997. Why environmental policy nightmares recur. *Conservation Biology* **11**: 328–37.

Yahner, R.H., 1983a. Seasonal dynamics, habitat relationships and management of avifauna in farmstead shelterbelts. *Journal of Wildlife Management* **47**: 85–104.

Yahner, R.H., 1983b. Population dynamics of small mammals in farmstead shelterbelts. *Journal of Mammalogy* **64**: 380–86.

Yahner, R.H., 1988. Changes in wildlife communities near edges. *Conservation Biology* **2**: 333–39.

Yahner, R.H. and Scott, P.P., 1988. Effects of forest fragmentation on depredation of artificial nests. *Journal of Wildlife Management* **52**: 158–61.

Yanes, M., Velasco, J.M. and Suárez, F., 1995. Permeability of roads and railways to vertebrates: the importance of culverts. *Biological Conservation* **71**: 217–22.

Young, A. and Mitchell, N., 1994. Microclimate and vegetation edge effects in a fragmented podocarp broadleaf forest in New Zealand. *Biological Conservation* **67**: 63–72.

APPENDIX 1   COMMON AND SCIENTIFIC NAMES OF SPECIES CITED IN THE TEXT

Species are grouped into categories representing the geographic area from which they are referred to in the text.

Mammals

Geographic area	Common name	Scientific name
Africa	African Elephant	*Loxodonta africana*
	African Wild Dog	*Lycaon pictus*
	Buffalo	*Syncerus caffer*
	Bushbuck	*Tragelaphus scriptus*
	Eland	*Taurotragus oryx*
	Greater Kudu	*Tragelaphus strepsiceros*
	Hartebeest	*Alcelaphus buselaphus*
	Impala	*Aepyceros melampus*
	Klipspringer	*Oreotragus oreotragus*
	Leopard	*Panthera pardus*
	Lion	*Panthera leo*
	Mountain Reedbuck	*Redunca fulvorufula*
	Oryx	*Oryx gazella*
	Sable Antelope	*Hippotragus niger*
	Uganda Kob	*Kobus kob*
	Wart Hog	*Phacochoerus aethiopicus*
	Waterbuck	*Kobus ellipsiprymnus*
	Wildebeest	*Connochaetes taurinus*
	Zebra	*Equus burchelli*
Asia	Giant Panda	*Ailuropoda melanoleuca*
	Indian Elephant	*Elephas maximus*
	Sambar	*Cervus unicolor*
	Tiger	*Panthera tigris*

Australasia	Brown Antechinus	*Antechinus stuartii*
	Bush Rat	*Rattus fuscipes*
	Common Bent-wing Bat	*Miniopterus schreibersii*
	Common Brushtail Possum	*Trichosurus vulpecula*
	Common Ringtail Possum	*Pseudocheirus peregrinus*
	Coppery Brushtail Possum	*Trichosurus vulpecula*
	Euro	*Macropus robustus*
	Feathertail Glider	*Acrobates pygmaeus*
	Greater Glider	*Petauroides volans*
	Green Ringtail Possum	*Pseudocheirus archeri*
	Herbert River Ringtail Possum	*Pseudocheirus herbertensis*
	Koala	*Phascolarctos cinereus*
	Large-footed Myotis	*Myotis adversus*
	Leadbeater's Possum	*Gymnobelideus leadbeateri*
	Lemuroid Ringtail	*Hemibelideus lemuroides*
	Long-nosed Potoroo	*Potorous tridactylus*
	Lumholtz's Tree Kangaroo	*Dendrolagus lumholtzi*
	Mountain Brushtail Possum	*Trichosurus caninus*
	Mountain Pygmy-possum	*Burramys parvus*
	Platypus	*Ornithorhynchus anatinus*
	Short-beaked Echidna	*Tachyglossus aculeatus*
	Sugar Glider	*Petaurus breviceps*
	Swamp Rat	*Rattus lutreolus*
	Western Grey Kangaroo	*Macropus fuliginosus*
	Yellow-bellied Glider	*Petaurus australis*
Europe	Badger	*Meles meles*
	Bank Vole	*Clethrionomys glareolus*
	Dormouse	*Muscardinus avellanarius*
	Field Vole	*Microtus agrestis*
	Grey Squirrel	*Sciurus carolinensis*
	Mink	*Mustela vison*
	Pipistrelle	*Pipistrellus pipistrellus*
	Red Squirrel	*Sciurus vulgaris*
	Serotine Bat	*Eptesicus serotinus*
	Wood Mouse	*Apodemus sylvaticus*

North America	Black Bear	*Ursus americanus*
	Bobcat	*Lynx rufus*
	Caribou	*Rangifer tarandus*
	Cat	*Felis catus*
	Columbian Ground Squirrel	*Spermophilus columbianus*
	Cougar	*Felis concolor*
	Eastern Chipmunk	*Tamias striatus*
	Elk	*Cervus elaphus*
	Florida Panther	*Felis concolor coryi*
	Fox Squirrel	*Sciurus niger*
	Gray Fox	*Urocyon cineroargentus*
	Grey Squirrel	*Sciurus carolinensis*
	Grizzly Bear	*Ursus arctos*
	Meadow Vole	*Microtus pennsylvanicus*
	Mountain Goat	*Oreamnos americanus*
	Mule Deer	*Odocoileus hemionus*
	Pika	*Ochotona princeps*
	Pocket Gopher	*Thomomys sp.*
	Raccoon	*Procyon lotor*
	Red Fox	*Vulpes vulpes*
	Red-backed Vole	*Clethrionomys californicus*
	River Otter	*Lutra canadensis*
	Striped Skunk	*Mephitis mephitis*
	White-footed Mouse	*Peromyscus leucopus*
	White-tailed Deer	*Odocoileus virginianus*
	Wolf	*Canis lupus*
	Woodchuck	*Marmota monax*
South/Central America	Brocket Deer	*Mazama americana*
	Coati	*Nasua nasua*
	Collared Peccary	*Tajassu tajuca*
	Howler Monkey	*Alouatta caraya*
	Jaguar	*Felis onca*
	Kinkajou	*Potos flavus*
	Maned Wolf	*Chrysocyon brachyurus*
	Nine-banded Armadillo	*Dasypus novemcinctus*
	Woolly Opossum	*Caluromys philander*

Birds

Geographic area	Common name	Scientific name
Africa	Amani Sunbird	*Anthreptes pallidigaster*
	Dappled Mountain Robin	*Modulatrix orostruthus*
	Long-billed Apalis	*Apalis moreaui*
	Tanzanian Mountain Weaver	*Ploceus nicolli*
	Usambara Eagle Owl	*Bubo vosseleri*
Asia	Brush Cuckoo	*Cacomantus variolosus*
	Hell Blue Flycatcher	*Cyornis banyumas*
	Pied Fantail	*Rhipidura javanica*
Australasia	Blue-faced Honeyeater	*Entomyzon cyanotis*
	Brown Kiwi	*Apteryx australis*
	Common Mynah	*Acridotheres tristis*
	Kaka	*Nestor meridionalis*
	Noisy Miner	*Manorina melanocephala*
	Noisy Scrubbird	*Atrichornus clamosus*
	Pink Cockatoo	*Cacatua leadbeateri*
	Red-capped Robin	*Petroica goodenorii*
	Regent Parrot	*Polytelis anthopeplus*
	Rufous Whistler	*Pachycephalus rufiventris*
	Southern Cassowary	*Casuarius casuarius*
	Superb Parrot	*Polytelis swainsonii*
	Western Yellow Robin	*Eopsaltria griseogularis*
	White-naped Honeyeater	*Melithreptus lunatus*
	White-tailed Black Cockatoo	*Calyptorhynchus funereus latirostris*
	Yellow Rosella	*Platycercus elegans flaveolus*
	Yellow-crowned Parakeet	*Cyanoramphus auriceps*
	Yellowhead	*Mohoua ochrocephala*
Europe	Black-billed Magpie	*Pica pica*
	Blackbird	*Turdus merula*
	Common Raven	*Corvus corax*
	European Jay	*Garrulus glandarius*

	Great-spotted Woodpecker	*Dendrocopos major*
	Hooded Crow	*Corvus corone*
	Jackdaw	*Corvus monedula*
	Marsh Tit	*Parus palustris*
	Middle Spotted Woodpecker	*Dendrocopos medius*
	Song Thrush	*Turdus philomelis*
	Tawny Owl	*Strix aluco*
	Wood Pigeon	*Columba palumbas*
North America	American Robin	*Turdus migratorius*
	Bachman's Sparrow	*Aimophila aestrialis*
	Black and White Warbler	*Miniotilta varia*
	Blue Jay	*Cyanocitta cristata*
	Brown Thrasher	*Toxostoma rufum*
	Brown-headed Cowbird	*Molothrus ater*
	Common Grackle	*Quiscalus quiscula*
	Gray Catbird	*Dumatella carolinensis*
	Hooded Warbler	*Wilsonia citrina*
	House Wren	*Troglodytes aeden*
	Indigo Bunting	*Passerina cyanea*
	Kirtland's Warbler	*Dendroica kirtlandi*
	Loggerhead Shrike	*Lanius ludovicianus*
	Ovenbird	*Seirus aurocapillus*
	Red-cockaded Woodpecker	*Picoides borealis*
	Rufous Hummingbird	*Selasphorus rufus*
	Scarlet Tanager	*Piranga olivacea*
	Spotted Owl	*Strix occidentalis*
	Spruce Grouse	*Canachites canadensis*
	Starling	*Sturnis vulgaris*
	White-breasted Nuthatch	*Sitta carolinensis*
	White-crowned Pigeon	*Columba leucocephala*
	Wild Turkey	*Meleagris gallopavo*
	Wood Thrush	*Hylocichla mustelina*
	Worm-eating Warbler	*Helmitheros vermivorus*
South/Central America	Bare-throated Umbrella Bird	*Cephalopterus glabricollis*
	Emerald Toucanet	*Aulocorhynchus prasinus*
	Green Hermit	*Phaethornis guy*

	Resplendent Quetzal	*Pharomachrus macinno*
	Silver-throated Tanager	*Tangara icterocephala*
	Three-wattled Bellbird	*Procnias tricarunculata*

Reptiles and Amphibians

Geographic area	Common name	Scientific name
Australasia	Cane Toad	*Bufo marinus*
	Peron's Tree Frog	*Litoria peroni*
	Spotted Grass Frog	*Limnodynastes tasmaniensis*
	Tree Goanna	*Varanus varius*
Europe	Common Frog	*Rana temporaris*
	Common Toad	*Bufo bufo*
	Viper	*Viperus berus*

Invertebrates

Geographic area	Common name	Scientific name
Europe	Copper Butterfly	*Hoides virgaureae*
	Ringlet Butterfly	*Aphantopus hyperantus*
	Silver-spotted Skipper	*Hesperia comma*
South/Central America	Bay Checkerspot Butterfly	*Euphdryas editha bayensis*
	Army Ants	*Eciton burchelli*

Plants

Geographic area	Common name	Scientific name
Asia	Arrow Bamboo	*Pseudosasa japonica*
Australasia	Alpine Ash	*Eucalyptus delegatensis*
	Mountain Ash	*Eucalyptus regnans*
	Shining Gum	*Eucalyptus nitens*
North America	Cottonwood	*Populus fremonti*

INDEX